Corner Tower by the Dane John Mound at Canterbury

MEDIEVAL WALLED TOWNS

Mike Salter

FOLLY PUBLICATIONS.

ACKNOWLEDGMENTS

The photographs and old prints are mostly from the author's collections. He drew the town maps, and also the gatehouse and tower plans which are mostly based on his own surveys during forty years of fieldwork and research. Jenny Harper provided the picture of the Richmond postern and Sam Tiler provided pictures of Bridgnorth, Bristol, Cowbridge, Dublin, Gloucester and Kilkenny. The following have helped the author to assemble and process material for this book, eg with transport or accommodation during field trips, computer services, or useful bits of information: Paul Adkins, Phil Hellin, Dave Isaacson, Jeremy Morfey, Ian Rennie, Peter Ryder, Helen Thomas. Thanks are also due to Bernard Mutton for providing numerous extracts from archeological journals, and to Val Cronin for helping with processing material for the town maps and proof reading.

AUTHOR'S NOTES

All the plans in this book are to a common scale of 1:200, the same scale that is used for churches, castle keeps and gatehouses, etc, in the author's other books. The town maps are all to a common scale of 1:10,000 except that of Norwich which has had to reduced to 1:12,500 to fit onto a page. The town maps are sketch maps and features on them may not always be true to scale. In many cases the exact route taken by lost sections of town walls (shown as dashed lines on the maps) is uncertain. Nor is it certain that all the sections of wall shown on the maps were actually all of stone or brick as opposed to earth and timber. Maps are not given for a number of places where there is considerable uncertainty as to the route, nature or even the existence of any defences. Also marked on the maps are castles, parish churches and monastic houses of which there are medieval remains still standing, roofed or otherwise. Details and illustrations of these can be found in many of the author's other titles.

For the purposes of this book the term medieval means the period before the introduction in the mid 16th century of regularly planned artillery fortifications with large arrow-shaped corner bastions as at Haddington and Berwick-upon-Tweed. Brief details of sieges of medieval towns during the 17th century Civil Wars are given, this being often the only time when town walls in places less exposed to attacks by foreign raiders or Welsh rebels were actually put to the test. Details of outworks of that period such as those surviving at Carmarthen and Newark are kept to a minimum. Details of usage of features of town walls in the 17th and 18th centuries are sometimes given where of particular interest or relevant to their loss or present condition.

ABOUT THE AUTHOR

Mike Salter is 59 and has been a professional author and publisher since 1988. He is particularly interested in the planning and layout of medieval buildings and has a huge collection of plans of castles, abbeys and old churches measured during tours (mostly by bicycle and motorcycle) throughout all parts of the British Isles since 1968. Born and bred in Wolverhampton, Mike now lives in an old cottage beside the Malvern Hills. Since walking Land's End to John O'Groats in 2004 he has done many other long distance backpacking trails, averaging 1,000 miles a year. Most of the English and Welsh walled towns lie on routes he has walked over these years. His other interests include railways, board games, morris dancing, folk dancing, and percussion instruments.

First published March 2013. Copyright Mike Salter 2013.
Folly Publications, 151 West Malvern Rd, Malvern, Worcs WR14 4AY
Printed by Aspect Design, 89 Newtown Rd, Malvern, Worcs WR14 2PD

Conwy Town Walls

CONTENTS

INTRODUCTION

Settlements large enough to be regarded as towns existed in Britain during the Iron Age, and some of them were enclosed by earth ramparts surmounted either by hedges or palisades with a ditch on the outside. Often they were located on hills and in Wales and Scotland the ramparts might sometimes take the form of thick but comparatively low dry-stone walls. When the Romans arrived their playing-card shaped campaign forts were also of earth and timber but once they were settled here they began to construct a series of more permanent forts using mortar and stones which were cut or dressed to make regular straight and curved faces and properly shaped doorways and windows. Eventually the Romans enclosed several existing civilian settlements with such walls. Irregularities in local topography and the pre-existing shape of some towns led to some of these larger enclosures being slightly less regular in layout than the purely military forts from which eventually grew the towns of Chester, Gloucester, Leicester, Lincoln and York. All these towns had medieval enclosures rather larger than their Roman ones. At Gloucester and Lincoln the original shape was later distorted by ecclesiastical pre-cincts straddling the line of a Roman wall. Roman walled towns at Caerwent, Colchester, Exeter, Rochester and Winchester were approximately rectangular. Canterbury was an oval, whilst Bath, Chichester and the now-deserted site at Silchester were irregular polygons, and London, by far the largest Roman town in Britain, had quite an irregular layout with a re-entrant angle. In each of these cases the size of the area enclosed by walls in Roman times proved large enough during the medieval period.

Chester City Wall just north of East Gate, with footings of Roman corner tower

Roman bastion at Caerwent

The Roman Duncan's Gate at Colchester

Originally towers along the walls in Roman forts were thinly-walled square structures about 6m across externally projecting internally, as can be seen from footings remaining at Chester and York and in the Hadrian's Wall forts such as Housesteads. External bastions added later in the Roman period survive on the city walls at Chichester and York, and also at Caerwent in South Wales, which was only partially occupied as a small village in the medieval period and later. A Roman gateway arch survives intact at Lincoln where the gates were flanked by U-shaped towers. There are also ruins of two Roman town gateways at Colchester and a fragmentary blocked-up gateway remains at Caerwent. Otherwise Roman town gateways are only known to us from footings revealed by excavation, as at Canterbury and Gloucester. Usually they had two carriageways and a pair of internally projecting square towers.

The Roman fort at Portchester in Hampshire

Of the series of forts built in the later stages of the Roman occupation of southern Britain against Saxon invaders only Portchester seems to have remained occupied as a settlement of importance during the Saxon period. The Roman walls there contain a ruined royal castle (top-middle of picture, page 5) and a still-roofed priory church of the 12th century but no medieval town ever flourished there. The Saxon Shore forts had externally projecting solid bastions as original features. Most of the very regularly spaced series of U-shaped examples at Portchester still survive in quite good condition.

The Romans departed from southern Britain in the early 5th century and the next mention of towns being fortified there is in the Anglo-Saxon Chronicle in late 9th century, when Alfred's kingdom of Wessex was being defended against Danish invaders. Once thought to be of c911-19, when the English were on the offensive against the Danes, but actually perhaps as early as c878-80, is a document known as the Burghal Hidage listing 31 fortified places and stating that "for the maintenance and defence of an acre's breadth of wall sixteen hides are required". A hide was a measurement of land, suggesting there was a system for working out how much land was thought to be required to support the maintenance and manning of the defences of each burgh or town.

Towns founded by the rulers of Wessex, which also included an early 10th century group further north in the Midlands (Bridgnorth, Buckingham, Chirbury, Tamworth, Towcester, Warwick and Worcester) and another group between Chester and Manchester, seem to have mostly had earth and timber defences originally. Timber barriers required frequent repair and replacement which by a law laid down in the reign of Athelstan (924-39) had to take place during the three days before Ascension Day. This law was still in force when the Danish king Cnut was ruling all of England in 1016-35.

Standing remains of secular or military structures of mortared stone dating between the Roman and Norman periods are rare in England. Sections of repairwork to walls at Exeter may be 10th century. A tower at York once regarded as 7th century is now reinterpreted as being Late Roman work. Ramparts at Towcester are said to have been stone faced and excavations have found traces of stone walls added probably in the 890s to earthworks of c878-9 at Christchurch, Cricklade, Lydford, Wareham and Wallingford. It has been suggested that stone-faced ramparts at all these places were systematically and thoroughly dismantled in 1017 on the orders of King Cnut.

Quite a number of the towns mentioned during the 9th and 10th centuries declined before the Norman conquest and were not subsequently fortified. Of Saxon-held towns not of Roman origin only Bridgnorth, Lewes, Oxford, Stafford, Warwick and Worcester later had circuits of medieval stone walls. Earthwork defences at Christchurch, Malmesbury and Langport may have remained in use during the 12th century but not later in the medieval period, although Langport does have a late medieval gatehouse.

Saxon ramparts at Wareham in Dorset

By the early 10th century the Danes held former Roman towns at Colchester, Leicester, Lincoln and York. There is little evidence that they built stone walls but Danish forces founded fortified towns at Northampton, Nottingham and Stamford, all eventually stone walled during the 13th century, and also Bedford, Derby, Hertford, Huntingdon and Tempsford, where no town fortifications were maintained after the 11th century. Even at York additional areas enclosed by the Danes beyond the Roman walls had earth ramparts, and the original Roman wall was also buried within an new earth rampart.

Records of the construction or maintenance of town walls in England during the 11th and 12th centuries are sparse. There is little in the way of either standing remains or archaeological evidence of constructing or rebuilding of stone town walls during that period. There is also a problem with places being mentioned in monastic and royal records in terms that could equally well refer to either the castle or the town as a whole. Roman walls at Bath were ordered to be heightened by King Stephen. Nothing remains standing of a 12th century city wall at Old Sarum, but Carlisle, Durham, Hereford and Malmesbury each have some walling probably of that period and a gateway arch of c1200 remains at Southampton. Ditched village enclosures often adjoin castles, as at Bolsover in Derbyshire, Pleshey in Essex, and Kilpeck in Herefordshire. Hereford itself was fortified by the Saxons against the Welsh in the mid 11th century. At Bury St Edmunds a document of c1121-38 refers to provision for maintaining the then already existing town ditch.

By the time of the civil wars of the 1140s in King Stephen's reign many English fortified towns were dominated by newly built royal castles with keeps or curtain walls of stone, as at Canterbury, Colchester, Exeter, Lincoln, London and Norwich. Records of sieges in 12th century England tend to refer to castles rather than walled towns specifically. Probably 9th and 10th century arrangements for the maintenance of town defences were still quietly working during the 12th century without the need for royal grants. It was only during the reigns of Richard I and King John that the earlier defence maintenance systems started to break down as the towns of England gradually became more autonomous, but with the obligation to provide and maintain their own defences. Richard I's charter of 1189 allowing the citizens of Hereford to impose tolls on goods brought into the city to pay for labour on the defences rather than relying on services provided by landowners is the earliest surviving record of these changes occurring.

Exeter put up a stout resistance to King William for nearly three weeks in 1069 so the Roman walls there must have then still have been defensible, indeed long sections of them still stand today up to 6m high. Substantial parts of the Roman walls at Chichester, Colchester and London also still stand up to 4.5m high. Only footings remain of Roman walls at Canterbury and Rochester used as a base for thinner 13th and 14th century walls, but Canterbury was strong enough in 1010 to defy a Danish army for ten days.

The survival of Roman or Saxon defences in a usable state around English towns in the 1070s is implied by the policy of William I in moving bishops' sees to them. New cathedrals were begun within Roman walls at Canterbury, Chichester, Exeter, Lincoln, London, Rochester, Winchester and York, and others in towns with defences of Saxon origin at Hereford, Norwich and Worcester. Carlisle and Durham were fortified against the Scots in conjunction with building new cathedral-priories. At Old Sarum a Norman cathedral was built within the very formidable Iron-Age defences. Ely was once a natural island fortress. By 1400 most cathedrals had high embattled walls around spacious precincts that were mini-towns in themselves, including the bishops' palaces and houses for clergy and other staff. Ecclesiastical precinct gateways were often more magnificently adorned than any town gateway ever was. Places with large walled cathedral precincts but no town walls of stone were Lichfield, Salisbury, St Andrews, St David's and Wells. Cathedrals were not associated with walled towns in Wales and Scotland.

Water Gate next to the Dominican friary at Shrewsbury

Walled towns commonly contained religious houses other than cathedral-priories. A Benedictine abbey took up a corner of the walled area at Chester. Another at York had its own fortified precinct just outside of the Roman walls. Precincts of an abbey at Gloucester and the cathedral at Lincoln pushed out beyond the line of former Roman walls. Precincts of cathedrals and monasteries with their own embattled walls and gates could take up a quarter or more of the space within a walled town. Monastic hospitals often lay just outside town gates, where they might collect alms from wealthy passers-by.

In England and Wales the establishment of friaries in the 13th and 14th centuries coincides with the main period for the construction of stone town walls. There were no friaries at Durham or Rochester where in each case a castle and cathedral took up much of the modest area within walls of pre-13th century origin. All other walled cathedral cities of England had at least two houses of friars by the late 13th century, as did many of the walled towns. Finding enough space for friaries within the walls often proved difficult so the friars often ended up with precincts just outside town walls, as with all four friaries at Stamford and the three at Shrewsbury. At Chester three friaries, an abbey and a nunnery within the walls took up much of the space available, as did colleges at Oxford.

The Trinitarians tended to run properly endowed hospitals but other friars were mendicants who often had to rely on alms collected locally each day to survive. Most of their houses were located within urban areas, except that the Carmelites sometimes lived further out in the countryside. The number of friaries a town could support is a good measure of its prosperity and importance in the medieval period. There were six of them at Lincoln and Oxford and five at each of Berwick-upon-Tweed, London and Newcastle-upon-Tyne. There were four friaries at each of Aberdeen, Boston, Bristol, Cambridge, Chester, Northampton, Norwich and Stamford, whilst there were three each at Canterbury, Edinburgh, Great Yarmouth, King's Lynn, Plymouth, Salisbury and Shrewsbury.

Some medieval towns ended up with numerous small parishes within the walls each with a small church crammed in amongst other buildings. Such a pattern was usually a lagacy of the Saxon period when most churches were quite small. Norwich still has over thirty medieval churches, out of about fifty that once existed, each with a medieval congregation estimated at two hundred. London once had even more, many of the original buildings being lost to the great fire of 1666 and bombing of the 1940s. York still has nineteen medieval churches, Exeter ten out of seventeen existing in the 1570s, Oxford eight and Worcester seven. Towns founded later on tended to have larger parishes and spacious churches set within proper open graveyards. The late 13th century towns at Rye and Winchelsea each have one large parish church, as do 13th century towns in Ireland and Wales and the older Scottish royal burghs of Edinburgh, Perth and Stirling. Town churches were sometimes subservient to an older mother church some way outside the walls, as at Caernarfon, Kingston-upon-Hull and Southampton.

In England the series of frequent references to maintaining town walls or building them anew begins during the crises of the end of King John's reign and the minority of his son Henry III when both the Welsh and the French were a threat. By this time 20% of the population may have lived in towns. Between 1212 and 1220 there were royal grants of materials (mostly timber) for works at Bridgnorth, Colchester, Hereford, Shrewsbury, Stafford, Stamford, Winchester and York, plus a £100 cash gift to London. Other royal allowances towards work on town walls is recorded in the same decade at Bath and Exeter and in the 1220s at Canterbury, Northampton, Oxford and Worcester.

In 1220 occurs the first record of the English Crown granting murage, under which a town was allowed to tax certain commodities being brought into it to raise funds for the construction and maintenance of its walls, ditches and gates. Initial grants were usually for a year, but before long grants lasting for three to five years became common. Later on grants were often made for seven years until the 1350s, after which ten year grants became the norm. The twenty year grant to Oswestry in 1283 was exceptional and reflected the town's pivotal role as a supply base for the scheme of new royal castles and walled towns then under construction in North Wales. By the 1270s it was necessary to address abuses of the scheme, such as at Scarborough, where the tax had been collected beyond the specified period and less than a third of it actually spent on any walls. At Newcastle and Southampton some of the murage funds were spent on building quays rather than defensive walls, although it appears that that was the royal intention. At Bristol some of the funds actually paid for supervision of work at the castle.

When the citizens of Carmarthen were granted murage in 1233 they were exempted from having to pay a similar tax at Bristol. Many others eventually obtained exemptions, including ecclesiastics and the occupants of religious houses and their servants. Some towns made agreements not to charge each other's citizens, such as that between Lincoln and York in 1260. It was sometimes claimed that the tax caused a loss of trade, as in London in 1319, Portsmouth in 1344 and Coventry in 1370. In the latter case it was mooted that the merchants of the town be assessed for tax instead. In later years a property value tax was sometimes made on the inhabitants of a town to raise funds for the defences. Totnes in 1355 affords a rare instance of townsfolk surrendering a royal grant back to the crown because no works on the walls were expected to progress.

Many of the 14th century grants of murage followed serious raids by the Scots or the French. Vulnerable towns along the south coast were ordered to strengthen their defences after a treaty with France expired in June 1377. The previous year the inhabitants of Southampton asked for a royal pardon of part of the fee-farm on the town, claiming that the place was only half-inhabited because of the heavy financial burdens upon it. This was finally granted at the end of 1377, and again in 1400. There was a similar arrangement at Great Yarmouth in 1457. The citizens of Winchester received a royal grant of £20 annually for five years from alnage duty. By the 15th century ports commonly had a grant from customs duties towards maintenance of defences. In the early 15th century Newcastle was frequently pardoned the payment of subsidies granted in Parliament.

Maintenance of defences by the authorities was clearly often an uphill struggle. Commonly, for a variety of reasons, murage taxes or other grants failed to bring in sufficient funds even for basic maintenance, let alone any new construction. Records of defences being described as ruinous are common and from Domesday Book onwards there are mentions of houses encroaching on the ditches and walls of a town or the lanes giving access to them. Ditches soon silted up or became full of rubbish and pilfering of materials was common. Commonly the authorities found themselves having to allow extra posterns to be made to allow access to quays, gardens or cemeteries, and holes were made through walls for other purposes, such as friary water supplies or land drainage.

Walled towns were not only administrative centres but they also aided government control of ports and river crossings. This helped to check not only the progress of hostile forces but also to control the movements of goods. Walls, and gates in particular, were useful as toll barriers, often retaining such uses long after the wars of the 1640s. They were also useful to help control smugglers, beggars, outlaws and diseased persons. Clearly embattled walls were about controlling people as much as defending them.

For all these reasons the English crown encouraged the building of town walls during the 13th and 14th centuries, especially in Ireland and Wales, amongst Marcher lordships on the Anglo-Welsh borders, and at ports along the south and east coasts vulnerable to French raids. Cowbridge was probably walled specifically to allow taking tolls at the gates for the lord of Glamorgan's benefit rather than because it needed defending against the Welsh. In the 1320s the townsfolk of Beaumaris and Kingston-upon-Hull claimed that making their towns more secure would attract further trade to them, but it is not easy to say why "safe" places like Coventry bothered to build expensive walls.

The town walls at Aberystwyth, Caernarfon, Conwy and Denbigh were unusual in that they were built very quickly at great expense as part of a royal policy of control of North Wales. Caernarfon and Conwy were remarkable for having walls even along shore-lines, something not often done in England, where the estuary sides of Great Yarmouth, King's Lynn, Kingston-upon-Hull, London and Newcastle did not have continuous walls. A circuit of stone walls at Shrewsbury seems to have been completed within the two or three decades up to 1242. Elsewhere it often took fifty years or more to complete a circuit of town walls, as at Newcastle and Norwich, where the circuits are thought to have been completed respectively in 1318 and 1343. At Coventry it took 180 years to complete the circuit. One marvels at the faith shown by medieval lords and town officials, few of whom normally expected to see any major building projects that they commenced anywhere near complete in their own lifetime. Clearly many projects such as town walls were as much to do with status and authority as practicality. Originators of schemes must have hoped that they would long thus be honourably remembered. Town walls were often depicted on seals (eg those of Canterbury, Colchester, London and Shrewsbury) and in heraldry and in manucripts, although with little attempt at realism.

Doorways into the Tile Tower at Carlisle

Near Fishergate on the walls at York

At Hereford, Northampton, Nottingham and Worcester the 13th century stone walls enclosed more space than the original Saxon or Danish earth and timber defences. At Abergavenny, Bristol and Shrewsbury the areas originally enclosed in the 12th century were quite modest and considerable extensions to the walled areas were made in the 13th century. Coventry, Edinburgh, Newcastle and Scarborough are other places where the area eventually walled was considerably greater than that originally envisaged when stone walls were begun. At Lincoln and Durham the original circuits of walls mainly contained high status and administrative buildings rather than trading or industrial premises and this phenomenon may have been more common than is now apparent. At Rochester the castle and cathedral priory between them took up half the space within the original Roman walls and the later extensions created more space for the cathedral priory rather than for any trading or living premises. Commonly large suburbs were left unwalled. At Oswestry the only parish church was left just outside the walls. Towns usually controlled far more land than that around the dwellings and industrial premises so town walls only defined inner trading areas rather than the outermost boundaries of townships. Bars for collecting tolls well in advance of town walls or market places existed in many places, Temple Bar in London being the best known. Industrial premises likely to cause pollution or to need extra space were commonly placed well outside any walls.

The building of town walls sometimes went hand-in-hand with land drainage and reclamation schemes, as at Bristol. At Dunwich and Hastings seaward facing walls may have been as much to do with controlling tidal flooding than keeping out sea-borne raiders. Ditches at Beverley may also have been as much for drainage as for defence.

Whilst the English Crown tended to encourage towns to be independent and walled, towns controlled by bishops and abbots (representing about a fifth of 250 English towns possessing charters by 1520) were rarely walled. Bath, Durham and Hartlepool are the only English towns held by bishops with remains of stone walls. The walls at Bath are of Roman origin and thus existed well before the abbey did, being maintained by royal command, whilst the vanished defences of other church-held towns at Bury St Edmonds and Newark were of Saxon origin. Some towns only began to build walls after freeing themselves of obligations to overlords, as at Coventry, where priory lands were the last part of the town to be enclosed with stone walls. Only in districts very vulnerable to cross-border raids were towns closely controlled by resident lords likely to aspire to the construction of fortifications, especially lasting structures of stone or brick.

Not all walled towns flourished. Some were crippled by the plague epidemics of the mid 14th century whilst others suffered a silting-up of their port facilities as at Winchelsea, or erosion by the sea as at Dunwich. Fortified settlements in Wales and the Marches that never became true towns are Clun and New Radnor, now just villages, Caus and Richard's Castle, now just a farmhouse or two, and Dolforwyn, Dryslwyn and Dynevor, all now deserted. They lay in exposed places, far from main trading outes, and were dependent on castles left decaying by absentee lords after c1360. The Scottish town of Roxburgh was once one of Scotland's greatest towns but ultimately failed and vanished because of the loss of its port at Berwick to England and its vulnerability to English attacks. Several towns in SW England such as Barnstaple prospered but did not see a need to maintain any defences after the Norman period.

Commonly plans for building walls proved over-ambitious even for flourishing towns. Schemes of wall building at King's Lynn, Sandwich, Scarborough and Stafford appear to have been left incomplete. At Dover only one of the two parishes was fully enclosed by walls, although the original intention was probably to enclose both. At Ipswich, Salisbury, Winchelsea, and perhaps Oakham, stone walls may have been planned but were never actually built, although gates existed at each of these places.

The South Gate at Winchester

The Netherbow Port at Edinburgh

In Warwickshire the citizens of Coventry finally completed their town walls in the early 16th century. By then the citizens of Warwick seem to have ceased to maintain their walls although there is no evidence that the town had failed economically, and it long retained its county-town functions. Lincoln and Winchester both have wide south-facing late medieval gateways without any obvious means of securing the passageways, one bearing a guildhall above it and the other one a chapel.

Swanswell Gate at Coventry

By the 16th century cannon could quickly breach a stone wall unless it was backed by an earth rampart. Walls of the 1540s at Stirling are the last of the medieval style town defences. Lying outside the scope of this book are the systems of stone-faced earth ramparts flanked by arrow-head shaped bastions first introduced in a town-defence context in the 1560s at Berwick-upon-Tweed, and continued throughout the late 16th and 17th centuries with a series of newly founded fortified towns in Ireland (see page 222). Eventually some southern English ports, particularly Portsmouth, also gained such defences but the Cromwellian fortifications at towns such as Ayr and Inverness in Scotland took the form of purely military citadels rather than town defences.

Old print of the Pilgrim Gate at Newcastle

The Heber Tower at Newcastle: crossloop and latrine projection

One aspect of town walls that casts some doubt on their military strength is the piece-meal way in which they were usually constructed and maintained. On the rare occasions when they were needed militarily they were usually either incomplete or badly in need of repair. Commonly the same circuit of walls would include sections that were strongly built with deep ditches and flanking towers and other sections that were low or flimsy. The integrity of defensive circuits would often have depended on castles and ecclesiastical precincts being both properly maintained and manned, which in practice was far from the case, and the adequate stopping up of any private posterns. At Worcester in 1263 invading forces came in through a derelict royal castle in church hands.

Few towns in England actually withstood a full scale attack for more than a few hours at any point between the reigns of the first and eighth Henrys, although there must have been occasions when the strength of defences and the assumption of a well-prepared garrison forstalled an attack. Only a few border towns had full time garrisons. Carlisle and Berwick held out against the Scots on occasion, and Exeter defied a rebel force in 1549. However no attempt was made to hold Canterbury or London against the peasant revolt of 1381, or Ludlow or Stamford against Lancastrian attacks in 1459 and 1461. French raids on southern ports such as Hastings, Rye, Sandwich, Southampton and Winchelsea were nearly always successful. Even in Wales men and materials had to be urgently supplied especially for the occasion when the Welsh threatened to revolt.

Many towns needed their medieval walls augmenting by more up-to-date outworks in the civil wars of the 1640s, as at Carmarthen, Gloucester, Kingston-upon-Hull, Newark-on-Trent and Oxford. In the 1660s Charles II ordered the demolition of walls of towns with Parliamentarian sympathies at Coventry, Gloucester and Northampton. In the 18th century town gateways were often removed to ease traffic flows. The walls themselves were often robbed for valuable stone. Sections of walls only survived when needed as boundaries or when incorporated in buildings. Eventually railways began to bring tourists to seaside towns such as Conwy and Tenby and their walls were then appreciated as attractions and preserved. In more industrial places such as London, Newcastle and Southampton remains of the walls have only been properly exposed and preserved in the last few decades following redevelopments after wartime bombing and the decline of port facilities and heavy engineering works close to their centres.

FEATURES OF TOWN WALLS

Fifty English towns eventually had medieval stone walls enclosing those sides of them not well secured by water or cliffs, and another thirty had stone or brick gateways of some pretension connected by earth ramparts and ditches. Quite a number of other towns present difficulties in deciding whether intended gates or walls were actually built, whether gates were in any way defensible, and also whether ditches were boundaries or for drainage or an attempt at fortification. Because the word gate meant a street in Danish, some towns in northern England have the name gate appended to roads.

In England most of the towns with obvious remains of walls lie on or near to the coast or within raiding distance of Wales or Scotland. Of all the walled towns located well away from any vulnerable borders or coasts only five, Coventry, Norwich, Oxford, Warwick and York, currently have particularly impressive standing remains of their walls or gates. Of these only York still has anything like a complete circuit.

York is the best preserved medieval walled town in England. The walls and towers are quite low, but the principal gateways all still survive and they are lofty and impressive. Of other walled towns in NE England Newcastle has substantial remains of walls, but without surviving gateways. There are more minor remains of the medieval walls at Berwick, Durham and Hartlepool, and just single gateways at Alnwick and Warkworth. In NW England only Carlisle has any remains of walls. The existence of any medieval walls at Lancaster and Penrith is doubtful and there is no evidence that any other towns in that region such as Appleby were ever walled, despite the obvious risk of Scottish raids.

In East Anglia there are considerable remains of town walls at Colchester, Great Yarmouth and King's Lynn, as well as Norwich, already mentioned above. The flanking towers at Great Yarmouth are more numerous and impressive than those of any other English town, although no gateways survive. In SE England Canterbury and Southampton each retain about two thirds of their circuits of walls with numerous towers and fine gateways. Southampton is the only walled town in England other than York with more than two medieval gateways surviving, The rather plain circuit at Chichester is even more complete but lacks any gateways. There are more fragmentary remains of walls and towers at London, Rochester, Rye, Sandwich, Winchelsea and Winchester. Exeter takes pride of place in SW England, with a nearly complete circuit, although no gateways have survived. Otherwise the main remnants are gateways at Bristol, Langport, Launceston and Totnes, and minor fragments at Bath and Poole.

Chester is the best preserved of the English walled towns bordering with Wales although it lacks any medieval gateways. Much altered gateways remain at Bridgnorth and Ludlow, low walls with two bastions at Hereford, lengths of wall at Shrewsbury and Worcester, and just the bases of former gatehouses at each of Gloucester and Caus. See pages 158, 184 and 190 for summaries of remains in Wales, Scotland and Ireland.

The NW walls of Carlisle, near the castle

The Heber Tower at Newcastle   *Length of crenellated wall on the SW side of Newcastle*

Few sections of town walls in Britain now seem sufficiently thick, high and well-flanked to stand up to a full-scale assault by a well-trained, motivated and properly equipped attacking force. However one should allow for former ditches in front of them. Retaining walls set against a face cut into a natural slope were common, as at Durham, Exeter, Ludlow, Malmesbury, Pembroke, Rye, Shrewsbury and Totnes. This provided quite a strong form of defence, being difficult to breach, and might result in the internal height being little more than that of the parapet. Bath and Shrewsbury have sections of wall-walk now used as pavements beside roads almost at the same level. Sometimes the wall-walk was actually upon an earth bank behind the wall-face, as at Chichester. Commonly the wall-walks of town defences in Britain only lay two or three metres above the internal ground level. A height of six metres or more to wall-walk level for extensive sections as at Caernarfon and Conwy was quite exceptional. Sometimes the main wall was arcaded, the recesses usually being on the inside, as at Bristol, King's Lynn, Great Yarmouth, Norwich, and also Clonmel and Drogheda in Ireland, but arcades occur on the outside at Southampton where piers to carry a wall-walk were added against a wall formed from older buildings. Some portions of walling were not thick enough to support both a parapet and a wall-walk, as in the sections which joined up with the castles at Caernarfon and Conwy.

Town walls usually had crenellated parapets but these have often been lost through ruination or later rebuilding with plain parapets, as at Canterbury and Chester. Long sections with original crenellations remain at Caernarfon, Conwy, Oxford, Tenby and York, and shorter lengths at Great Yarmouth, London, Newcastle, Norwich and Southampton. No original town wall crenellations remain in Scotland or Ireland, but there are recently restored examples on town walls beside the churchyard at Fethard in Tipperary. Crenellations at Oxford and Winchester are referred to in the mid 13th century documents. Stone for crenellation was purchased at Berwick in the 1390s and at Sandwich in 1471, and royal permission specifically for crenellated walling was granted to Penrith in 1345 and Winchelsea in 1415. The merlons were occasionally pierced by loops for archers, as at Conwy, but outside of North Wales it would have been rare to see a town wall in Britain well equipped for a heavy discharge of volleys of arrows or bolts. A notable exception was an arcaded section of walling bounding a Templar preceptory at Bristol, but this may have been more for display than for military necessity.

An earth rampart was usually a cheaper option than a stone wall, requiring mainly only unskilled labour rather than a lot of expensive materials. In some places earth ramparts remained in use right though to the end of the medieval period, as at Sandwich. The eastern parts of the defences at Lewes may have remained of earth and wood. In 1363 jurors at Southampton were prepared to accept construction of a wall of either stone or earth, and at Salisbury in 1377 just a ditch was considered adequate. By a strange quirk of fate, partly owing to the way boundaries have been used and preserved over the years, long and impressive lengths of town ditches tend to only survive in places where there was never much in the way of a stone wall, as at Castle Acre, Sandwich, Wallingford and Wareham.

Some of the towns were a lot better fortified than is now apparent. King's Lynn, Kingston-upon-Hull and York appear to have had very good water defences. At low-lying towns such as Canterbury, Chichester, Coventry, Stafford and York dual-carriageway ring-roads have taken the place of former wet moats. Coventry was clearly regarded as defensible against rebel peasantry in 1450-1 even though its circuit of stone walls was then far from complete. In some cases rivers have over the last two centuries been diverted or culverted like the River Frome has on the north side of the old centre of Bristol. On the other side of that city extensive former marshes have been drained and built upon, thus disguising the original strength of the defences there.

The Goblin Tower at Denbigh

Projections from medieval town walls in Britain tend to have the circular or D-shaped form in vogue during the 13th and 14th centuries. To properly flank a wall they needed to be provided at intervals of not more than about 100m and on all corners. However not many towns could afford to build such a lavish provision of flankers. Long sections of wall with regularly spaced D-shaped towers now only survive in England at Great Yarmouth, London, Newcastle, Norwich, Oxford and also Canterbury and Southampton, where some of the towers were square in plan. In Wales series of D-shaped towers remain at Caernarfon, Conwy and Tenby. Polygonal towers were rare (they were never common in castles). One example remains at Denbigh, where half of the castle towers were also polygonal. Great Yarmouth has another. A small bastion with unusual corner pilasters at Exeter probably dates from King John's reign and thus would predate all the D-shaped towers and bastions elsewhere. Polygonal towers once existed at London, Norwich and Oxford, whilst York has several semi-hexagonal towers and Chester had a gateway with two polygonal fronted towers like those of the castles at Caernarfon and Denbigh.

Flanking bastion with a gunport at Stirling

Interior of a flanking tower at Oxford

Originally there were twenty-four towers (excluding gateways) in a two mile circuit of walls at Newcastle. Southampton and Hereford respectively had twenty-nine and seventeen flanking projections in circuits of just over a mile each, Great Yarmouth had sixteen towers in a circuit of a mile and a third, and Conwy has twenty-one towers in a circuit of two thirds of a mile. Only at Caernarfon and Conwy does the whole circuit of a town wall have towers placed as close together as one might expect on a castle wall. The provision of towers was as much about status as about defence, and where towers were fully enclosed structures the rooms within them were often leased out and put to all kinds of uses. Usually the tenants not only had to pay rent but maintain their tower, allowing full access as needed in a time of war. In the 13th century at least two of the towers at London were inhabited by religious hermits. Tenants commonly made alterations and additions to the towers that sometimes compromised their usefulness as military strongpoints, but which in some cases has led to the survival of individual towers. The upper chambers of gatehouses were also put to various uses such as meeting rooms and prisons, and, as already noted, were occasionally used as places of worship.

Most towers on British town walls are about 7 to 8m in external diameter. Commonly they were open backed, the open gorges being crossed at wall-walk level by plank bridges as at Conwy. At Newcastle and Norwich the main wall-walk passed through the flanking towers. At Oxford the wall-walk ascended a few steps and then continued round the summit of the towers. There was a similar arrangement at Chepstow on bastions that were little higher than the main wall. Second storey rooms in fully enclosed towers on town walls were usually accessed from the main wall walk, from which ladders might give access to any third storey rooms and the tower wall-walks. External stairs up to the main wall-walk survive in places, notably at Conwy, whilst at Newcastle several towers on the west side have staircases leading out of their basement rooms and up within the thickness of the main wall to reach its wall-walk. Internal stairs in the towers are uncommon but a brick example remains in the Black Tower at Norwich.

The late 14th century towers at Canterbury are a mixture of enclosed rectangular structures and open-backed D-planned examples. Both types have keyhole-shaped loops suitable for guns. Circular and D-shaped towers at Waterford have stirrup-shaped gunloops. There are other gunloops in the Catchcold Tower at Southampton and in the unusually tall towers containing several levels of habitable rooms at Great Yarmouth. There the main wall is pierced by firing loops about halfway up its height and these must have been reached by a timber walkway. Other loops halfway up the height of walls opened out of arcading at King's Lynn and Norwich. The Cow Tower of the 1390s at Norwich has cross-shaped gunloops. There are vertical gunloops in a bastion at Edinburgh and horizontal gunloops on the walls at Stirling. Some loops were more for show than use, two at York having poor fields of fire and being obstructed internally.

Loops suitable for discharging crossbows or longbows rarely survive in town defences in England apart from at Newcastle, Norwich and Southampton. Some loops of this type remain at Conwy and there are others below wall-walk level in the main wall at Tenby and a row in a short section at Denbigh. It was unusual for firing loops to be inserted into older walls, and most walled towns in England and Wales already had a complete circuit before guns came into common use in the late 14th century. The corporation of Southampton purchased a gun in 1382. Guns are mentioned in 1386 at King's Lynn and Norwich and at Canterbury in 1403, when stone cutters were paid to make stone balls for them to fire, and again in 1461 when further guns were purchased. There are also mid 15th century references to guns at Coventry, Exeter and Rye.

The word bastion is used to describe projections which do not rise significantly above the main wall, like the D-shaped examples at Chepstow. They may be similar in size to towers or larger and do not normally contain habitable chambers. As already mentioned solid bastions were common in the late Roman period. They reappeared in the later medieval period as mounts for cannon, eventually transforming into the very large arrow-head shaped projections of late 16th century and 17th century artillery fortifications at Berwick and Londonderry not fully described in this book.

Gunloop at Tenby

Gunloop in a tower at Canterbury

Gunloop in the Cow Tower at Norwich

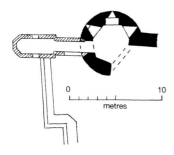

Southampton: plan of Arundel Tower

Bastion and crenellated length of wall at Chepstow

Larger and fully circular towers or donjons up to 13m across were occasionally provided to serve as strong-points at sharp corners. The prime example is Reginald's Tower at Waterford where there may have been a second such tower elsewhere on the circuit. Footings of a mid 13th century tower of similar size have been exposed at Dublin. The Tower Harratz built by the Templars on the Portwall at Bristol was also a building of this type. The Cow Tower and Black Tower at Norwich are smaller and later examples and Barnard's Tower at Pembroke is another. The only fully circular tower at Conwy is at a sharp corner in an elevated position above the rest of the town. Caernarfon also has a single full round tower at a right-angled corner. It later contained the vestry of a church added within the corner. Small projections less than 5m in diameter as at Worcester (and also the square examples at Rinndown) are referred to in this book as turrets. Turrets took other forms, such as those projecting from the wall-heads only at Newcastle.

Interior of the Cow Tower at Norwich

The last remains of the walls at Carmarthen

The former North Gate at Shrewsbury

Town gateways were natural focal points, gathering around them activities and services from trading stalls and inn-keeping to street preaching by friars and begging and prostitution by less fortunate individuals. Despite a tendency for narrow arches to be removed in the late 18th century to improve traffic flows, medieval gatehouses of some substance have survived at thirty towns in England and Wales and ten in Ireland, in addition to a few minor fragments and small simple posterns elsewhere. Town gateways often displayed civic pride. Those facing major roads were made as elaborate as funds would allow. They could be adorned with statues of saints or legendary figures such as King Lud and his sons upon Ludgate at London and Brennus and Belinus on the outlying gate of a suburb at Bristol. Displaying statues of monarchs or the royal arms on gateways was seen as a sign of loyalty. Most of the gateways surviving in England are still roofed. In several places a gatehouse is the only or principal remnant of former defences. Beverley, Castle Acre, Sandwich, Warkworth and Winchelsea have gatehouses but were never fully walled. There is evidence from Newcastle and Norwich of gateways being built slightly earlier than the adjoining sections of town wall and in any case gatehouses usually replaced simple bars where tolls were collected.

Most English and Irish walled towns originally had between four and six gates in addition to minor posterns leading out to quays, cemeteries, friaries and gardens. Southampton and York each still have four impressive gateways, Conwy has three good examples and Winchelsea three small and weak specimens. Two gateways remain at each of at Caernarfon, Coventry, Sandwich, Totnes, Warwick and Winchester. In Ireland Drogheda and Fore each have two gateways remaining. Those at Fore are simple archways, as are the gateway at Dundee and one of those at Totnes. Lincoln still has ruins of three Roman gateways. One of two Roman gateways remaining at Colchester is larger in area than any gatehouse built in the medieval period.

Bootham Bar at York

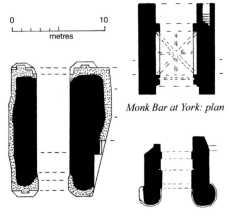

0 ⌞ ⌟ 10
metres

Monk Bar at York: plan

East Gate at Warwick: plan

Gate at Castle Acre

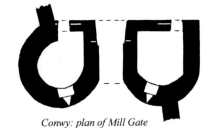

Conwy: plan of Mill Gate

Some of the surviving gatehouses are simple in form, commonly a modest square tower pierced by a passageway, as at Chepstow and Launceston and the two at Coventry. Occasionally a small guardroom flanked the passage, which usually had grooves for a portcullis raised and lowered from a room above and a least one pair of strong wooden doors secured by a draw-bar. Gatehouses with external machicolations now only survive at Canterbury, Rye, Southampton and Winchester and on the bridge-gate at Monmouth, but others are known from old prints. Internal machicolations or murder holes are not that common either, but appear in heavily fortified gatehouses at Conwy and Denbigh.

Gateways at Bristol, Warwick and Winchester have churches above them which would have compromised their military value, although this was a common and ancient custom, going back to Saxon times. Several later medieval town gateways were more like those of abbeys or colleges, as at King's Lynn and Lincoln.

The West Gate at Warwick, surmounted by a church

The South Gate at Launceston

Mill Gate on the south side of Conwy

Upper Gate at Conwy

West Gate at Canterbury

Caernarfon, Conway and Denbigh between them have six late 13th century gate-houses each with a long central passage flanked by pairs of round-fronted towers about 8m in external diameter. Rye has a gateway of this type but with a shorter passage leaving little space for rooms above it and with the towers more of a full circle in plan. Ludlow and Sandwich have much more altered twin-towered gatehouses, and just the base of one tower of such a gateway is now exposed at Gloucester. Twin towered gatehouses at Coventry, Edinburgh, Exeter and Great Yarmouth are now known to us only from the evidence of old prints. Kidwelly has a 14th century gatehouse with rooms either side of a central passage but with the overall shape of the building more of a plain rectangle rather than with distinct projecting towers. The upper level was a court-house. The 15th century Hotspur Gate at Alnwick is similar. Canterbury had two gatehouses with pairs of round towers projecting from the outer corners of a square main body, whilst one of the three small gateways at Winchelsea has tiny round turrets at all four corners of a rectangular main body. A water-gate at Hartlepoool has an archway set between two triangular turrets. It is uncertain what sort of superstructure (if any) it might have once had.

The Strand Gate at Winchelsea

The Bar Gate at Southampton had a pair of round towers added c1280 on each side of an older arch. An extension behind the towers provided enough space for an upper room servng as a guild hall, a common use of upper rooms in large town gatehouses. An outer front with machicolations was later added between the round towers. Town gates often had work of various building periods, as at Canterbury, King's Lynn, Warwick and Winchester.

Bar Gate, Southampton

God's House Gate, Southampton

Probably the largest medieval town gateway in Britain was the north gate at Durham, another example of later additions grafted onto an older core. Like many town gateways it served as a prison from the 15th century onwards. The gateways at York are simple square towers in plan but have pairs of round bartizans high up on the outer corners. They had long barbicans in front but these restricted traffic flows even more than the gateways and only one has survived, it too having a pair of round bartizans on the outer corners. The Five Arches at Tenby is an open-planned barbican in an unusual D-shaped form protecting a gateway that was itself no more than a plain arch in the main town wall. Caernarfon and Conwy also each have one gate with a barbican. Newgate at Newcastle had one, and in 1377 it was ordained that each of the gates at London was to have a portcullis and a barbican. The West Gate at Canterbury had a drawbridge over a moat just in front, as did the North Gate at Durham. One of the gates at Newcastle had a turning bridge, but other such bridges seem to have been uncommon. Recesses for raised drawbridges appear at Conwy and Launceston but were not otherwise common on British town gates. There were probably instances of drawbridges forming a separate barrier just in front of a stone gatehouse. Gateways at Beverley and King's Lynn are built of brick and footings of another remain at Kingston-upon-Hull.

West Gate, Southampton

The castle and walled town of Caernarfon

Most towns with stone walls also had a castle with a stone walled court. All of the county towns in Wales except that of Merioneth had some sort of defences and a castle, and half of those castles were royal. Twenty five of England's county towns were walled and fifteen of them had royal castles, the rest having castles held by barons or bishops. At Stafford the castle lay a mile outside the town, and there was a similar relationship between the walled town of Cowbridge and the castle of its lords at Llanblethian. Apart from Bath and Bury St Edmunds which were both church possessions, walled towns in England without an associated castle tended to be coastal ports such as Great Yarmouth, King's Lynn and Poole. At Coventry and Worcester former castles had been abandoned by the time the towns were fully walled, and this was also the case at Perth, where visiting royalty lodged instead in monastic guest apartments.

Only at Caernarfon, Carlisle, Conwy, Denbigh, Durham, Exeter and Southampton are there remains of town walls actually still joined up to castle walls. Often there was a physical separation because of water features, as at York, or a natural ravine, as at Berwick and Chepstow, or the castle lay at a much higher level, as with the exceptionally large royal castles above the ports of Dover and Scarborough and the smaller royal castle at Montgomery. Town walls at Edinburgh and Carlingford in Leinster also lay considerably below the castle buildings. At Norwich and Old Sarum royal castles lay isolated in the middle of roughly circular layouts of town walls but normally a castle would fill one corner, as at Dublin, Exeter, Ludlow and Rochester, or project from one end as at Bristol, Caernarfon, Carlisle, Conwy, Oxford, Pembroke and Totnes. At Launceston the castle bailey projected diagonally from the straight side of a D-shaped layout. The towns of Durham, Shrewsbury and Warkworth each had a good natural defensive site almost completely surrounded by a loop of a river with the castle occupying about half of the width of the narrow neck of solid land.

ACCESS TO REMAINS OF TOWN DEFENCES

By their very nature as public works the remains of town walls and gates tend to be easily accessible or at least visible. They generally adjoin public rights of way or lie within spaces set aside for public recreation. Complete circuits of town defences with access onto at least some sections of wall-walks are actively encouraged by signs and information boards at Berwick, Chester, Chichester, Conwy, Exeter, Southampton and York. Old Sarum Is a national monument. There is good public access to significant remains at Caernarfon, Canterbury, Carlisle, Chepstow, Colchester, Coventry, Denbigh, Edinburgh, Great Yarmouth, Hereford, King's Lynn, Lincoln, London, Newcastle, Norwich, Pembroke, Rochester, Rye, Sandwich, Stirling, Tenby and Winchester, plus in Ireland: Cashel, Clonmel, Drogheda, Dublin, Fethard, Galway, Kilkenny, Waterford and Wexford and gateways at Carlingford, Fore, Kilmallock, Loughrea and Trim. Gateways normally lie beside or across public roads. Upper rooms are only ever accessible when in use as either a place of worship (as at Winchester) or as a museum (as at York).

Places where sections of town walls with towers lie hidden away in private areas are Durham and especially Oxford. The sites of deserted towns at Caus and Clonmines are not on public land. Remains at Athenry can only be viewed at a distance. Remains at Rinndown lie on private farmland but are accessible on foot.

FURTHER READING

M.W.Barley, Town Defences in England and Wales after 1066, 1976
C. Beresford, New Towns of the Middle Ages, 1967
J. Bond, Urban Archeology in Britain, 1987
John Bradley, Walled Towns in Ireland 1995
R.A. Brown, H.M. Colvin, A.J.Taylor, A History of the King's Works, 1963
Oliver Creighton & Robert Higham, Medieval Town Walls, 2005 (good bibliography)
Eileen Gooder, Coventry's Town Wall, 1971
John Kenyon, Medieval Fortifications, 1990
S. Reynold, An Introduction to the History of Medieval Towns, 1977
Avril Thomas, The Walled Towns of Ireland, 1992
Hilary Turner, Town Defences in England and Wales, 1970 (thorough references)

Ancient Monuments inventories for certain English, Welsh, Scottish and Irish counties contain good descriptions of town defences and medieval buildings within them at: Caernarfon, Colchester, Conwy, Cork, Drogheda, Edinburgh, Hereford, London, Northampton, Oxford, Stirling, Waterford, Wexford and York.

Guide pamphlets to castles, etc, including information on town defences exist for: Denbigh, Dryslwyn, Conwy, Newport, Rhuddlan, Old Sarum.

The Victoria County Histories include much historical information on town defences in England, especially on post-medieval usage and demolition dates of gateways.

The Buildings of England series and similar series for Wales, Scotland and Ireland give descriptions of standing remains & other medieval buildings within town walls.

Amongst many articles in archaeological and historical journals of great interest are:
Late-Saxon Christchurch & Burghal Hidage, J.Haslam,Medieval Archaeology 53, 2009.
The Town Defences of Exeter, Ian Burrow, Trans Devon Assn. Advent Science, 109.
The Town Walls of Pembroke, D.J. King & M. Cheshire, Archaeologia Cambrensis

All the castles associated with town defences are fully described in many other titles by Mike Salter. He also has four titles describing or including friaries, and twenty titles which describe medieval parish churches at about two thirds of the walled towns included in this book.

GAZETTEER OF WALLED TOWNS IN ENGLAND

ALNWICK Northumberland

Alnwick was often the first place attacked whenever the Scots raided or invaded England, although it was an unlucky place for Scottish kings, Malcolm III being defeated and killed here in 1093, and William the Lion being defeated and captured here in 1174. It was also attacked by Wallace in 1297. The town grew up to serve the needs of the large and important castle which in the early 14th century became the chief seat of the Percy family, earls of Northumberland from 1377. They were constantly at war with their Scottish counterparts the Douglases. Town walls were begun after a raid by the Douglases in 1428 and murage was obtained in 1434. The surviving Hotspur Gate or Bondgate must have been under construction when a Scottish raid took place in 1448. William, Bishop of Norwich, left £10 towards the work in 1449 and in 1450 the mason of Alnwick Abbey was paid £1 10s for carving the worn figure of a lion on the gate. From 1452 an annual sum of £20 from customs duties was to be made available for completing the walls.

There is uncertainty as to whether walls ever linked Hotspur Gate with the castle, which fills the NE corner and overlooks the bridge over the River Aln just NW of it. West of the castle the wall probably enclosed St Michael's church in the NW corner but excluded St Mary's Chantry. Pottergate is now an ornate 18th century rebuild. The wall went south down Dispensary Street to a gate over Clayport Street and continued down Tower Lane, then turned east down Green Ball and went NE along Hotspur Street.

Hotspur Gate has a passage 3.5m wide with a portcullis groove in a four-centred arch running between two towers 5m wide each with both their outer corners chamfered off above pyramidal bases. Each tower contains a guardroom originally entered off the passageway and having loops facing the field. There are two upper storeys and there are corbels for arching the former parapet across between the towers with machicolations behind it. A trace of the 1.8m thick wall itself survives on the SW side.

Alnwick: plan of Hotspur Gate

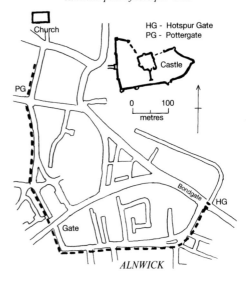

HG - Hotspur Gate
PG - Pottergate

Church

Castle

PG

0   100
metres

Bondgate   HG

Gate

ALNWICK

Back view of Hotspur Gate at Alnwick

Outer front of Hotspur Gate at Alnwick

ARUNDEL   West Sussex

Earthworks in the private park NW of the castle represent a fortified Anglo-Saxon burgh. The footings of a gateway with Caen stone facings on the north side are probably of the Red Gate mentioned in 1570 and which still partly stood until 1851. The presence of this gate suggests this area may have been still at least partly occupied when the castle was founded in the late 11th century. A continuation to the SW of the northern rampart dates from the Civil War period when the castle was captured in turn by the Royalists and the Parliamentarians and then left in ruins. The palisade which was decayed and fallen down in 1275 was probably in this area. The town was granted an annual fair in 1285. It declined following fires in 1338 and 1334 and the Black Death of 1349.

The new town defences which resulted from a ten-year grant of murage in 1295 enclosed an area further south which was 400m wide and extended 500m SW from the castle. The rampart of the south side of the Saxon burgh was given a new ditch on its northern side to form the northern line of defence between a north facing gate close to the castle ditch and the NW facing Mary Gate across the then re-routed main road from London. Only the jambs of Mary Gate survived by 1780 and the existing building lying in the castle grounds to the west of the large late medieval collegiate church of St Nicholas is a 19th century folly made up of old and new parts.

From Mary Gate the defences went down Mount Pleasant, Park Place and School Lane to the March Gate or Water Gate across Maltravers Street. References in the early 15th century to a new ditch in the vicinity of Tarrant Street suggest the defences were either left incomplete or were later extended down to the river bank. There is no evidence of a stone wall forming part of the defences. The south side was protected by the river, on the bank of which are remnants of a Dominican friary. The castle formed most of the east side but there appears to have been an undefended gap in the SE corner and there is no record of a gate on, or facing towards, the bridge.

BARNSTAPLE   Devon

The original fortified burgh of Alfred's day seems to have been at Pilton, now a small northern suburb rising up from a crossing of the Yeo to a medieval parish church which once also served a small Benedictine priory. In the late 10th century, under King Athelstan, Barnstaple had its own mint. By the time of Domesday Book in 1086 a wedge-shaped area about 400m across with the wide River Taw on the SW side seems to have had defences with the outer edge of the ditch now defined by Boutport Street on the SE and NE, and along North Walk towards the Yeo on the NW. It had 40 burgesses within the borough and another 9 outside and the parish church of St Peter and St Paul on the east side must have existed by then. It appears that the ramparts were stone faced and a short section of wall footings 1.5m thick have been revealed in Joy Street. A jamb of the NW gate remains in Youings on the corner of High Street and Boutport Street. Other gates faced NE to Bear Street, and south towards a causeway leading to the sixteen-arch bridge over the Taw, which although widened later is still essentially a 13th century structure. The defences were decayed by 1140. Excavations showed evidence of the wall having been robbed of stone by the late 13th century and it was "almost clene faullen" c1540 when John Leland found the suburbs greater than the town.

Domesday Book also records the destruction of 23 houses to make way for Judhael's new castle of which the motte remains, raised partly over a Saxon cemetery, at the SW end of the town. It had a bailey towards the junction of the rivers and documentary evidence suggests a second bailey towards the town. Judhael also built a Cluniac priory just outside the northern edge of the town. The lack of any friaries here or anywhere else in North Devon is remarkable. An attempt in the mid 14th century to establish Augustinian friars at Barnstaple was strongly resisted by the Cluniac priory. Only one or two buildings close to the Taw hint at the town's former importance as a port.

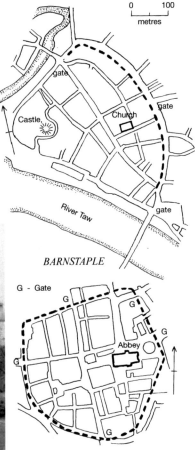

BARNSTAPLE

Section of the north wall at Bath

BATH

BATH   Bath and NE Somerset

The walls of Bath enclosed a roughly pentagonal area of 23 acres about 330m across each way set within a loop of the River Avon enclosing all but the north and NW sides. On the SW and SE the river lay 200m away and only on the NE did it come close to the walls. They were built in the Roman period when Aquae Sulis was a spa drawing sufferers of rheumatism and other ailments from all over Britain to its famous baths, although the Roman town was quite small and had no military or political importance.

By the late Saxon period remains of the Roman baths were covered in enough depth of soil for use of the area as a cemetery although there is a mention in the 9th century of men bathing in hot springs within the walled town. During that period Bath ranked as a burgh with its defence maintenance supported by an allocation of 1000 hides, and it had a mint in the time of Edward the Elder, whilst King Edgar was crowned here in 973. The defences are not mentioned in Domesday Book and the next note of them is in 1138, when King Stephen ordered the walls to be heightened, i.e. built up again from ruin. The walls were repaired in the early 13th century but by 1270 people were being accused of taking stone from them. Murage for repairs was granted in 1369.

The only surviving medieval church within the walled area is that of the Benedictine abbey, an early foundation, the precinct of which took up all of the SE quadrant. Now an early 16th century building, the church briefly ranked as a cathedral in the late 11th century when Norman bishops were encouraged to transfer their sees to walled towns. By the 12th century the bishops had returned to Wells, but the see has long been known as that of Bath and Wells. Four parishes within the walls were amalgamated in 1583 and the other churches were then closed. A fifth medieval church lay 200m to the north.

Set far below the existing street level is the East Gate, a modest simple-arched postern giving access to river-side quays. Most of the rest of the wall and the other gateways all disappeared during the mid 18th century. From East Gate the wall ran NW for 90m before turning WSW just north of Bridge Street for 50m to the site of North Gate. Excavations in this area showed that a 2nd century rampart had its northern face cut back for the building of the Roman stone wall. Saxon outworks beyond the ditch were removed in the 13th century. By the 18th century tenements had been built over the former ditch, using the town wall as a back wall to build up against.

The East Gate at Bath

From North Gate wall then ran for 240m along the north side of Upper Borough Walls. Between Vicarage Lane and Brideswell Lane one short section with late medieval battlements still remains, the wall-walk being the road pavement. The lower part is probably Roman, but is now buried, the external height to tops of the merlons currently being less than 3m. The wall eventually turned south for 100m down to the West Gate. Continuing past two further slight angles for 200m the wall then ran down the south side of Lower Borough Walls to the site of the South Gate. An image of Edward III was one of three statues in niches over the outer arch of this gate. From there the wall ran ENE for 80m and turned to run NE. War-time bombing revealed a 50m long section of the base of the wall here but in the 1960s it vanished under what until recently was Woolworths store. East of the abbey church the wall turned NNW up to the East Gate.

BERWICK-UPON-TWEED   Northumberland

Berwick was originally the chief town of the Scottish county of Berwick and served as a port to the royal burgh of Roxburgh further up the Tweed. The castle existed by the 1160s and was surrendered to the English in 1174 as part of William The Lion's ransom but nothing is known of any early defences of the town. In 1216 it was razed to the ground by King John, but soon recovered. The existence of no less than six friaries here by the end of the 13th century attests to the town's wealth and importance by then. None of the friaries remain and Holy Trinity is the only survivor of three parish churches, although it was wholly rebuilt in 1650-52. Berwick supported John Balliol in his treaty with the French against England. In retaliation Edward I stormed the town in March 1296. Some 8,000 people are said to have then been slaughtered although estimates of the late medieval population are around 5,000. The king then began rebuilding the castle and started building a town wall of stone. The medieval walls were 3.3km long, enclosing an area 1100m long by 550m wide and are said to have had nineteen towers or bastions and five gateways. They seem to have been complete by 1318 when the Scots captured Berwick and heightened the walls, which were regarded as too low, in an attempt to retain it.

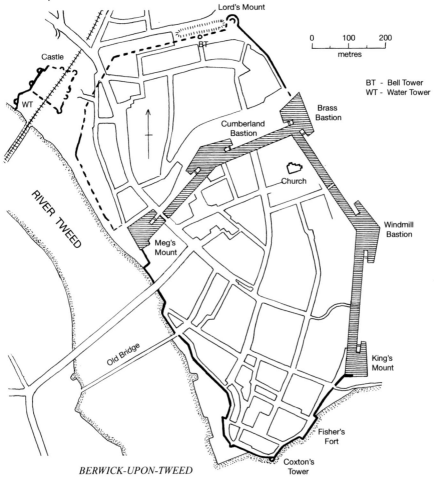

BERWICK-UPON-TWEED

Interior of the Lord's Mount Bastion of c1540 at Berwick

Murage for walling Berwick was first granted by Edward II of England in 1313 and other grants and allowances came later in the 14th century. Berwick was annexed to England in 1333. The Scots held the town briefly in 1377 and 1384 and for a longer period during the 1460s and 70s after Margaret of Anjou handed it over in return for Scottish support for the exiled Lancastrian Henry VI. After being recaptured in 1482 by Richard, Duke of Gloucester, Berwick remained permanently in English hands. Until 1746 the town had a semi-independent status, being mentioned separately in Acts of Parliament, and from 1551 it ranked as a separate county, only being included within Northumberland in 1885. The Jacobite risings of 1715 and 1745 prompted further work on the defences. Berwick has what are said to be the earliest purpose-built barracks in England, built on the east side of the town in 1717-21 and a new magazine was built in 1749. Berwick remained a garrison town under military law until the mid 19th century.

Henry VIII had an artillery bastion added to the vulnerable north corner in 1539-42, and a new citadel on the east side with four triangular corner bastions was begun under Edward VI in 1550. This work was abandoned in 1558 when Elizabeth's new government began what was intended as an enclosure of about 480m by 400m with six huge arrowhead-shaped bastions occupying most of the area of the SE end of the town. The NW end became a suburb retaining its pre-Elizabethan defences, including the castle until that was sold off and dismantled in James I's reign. The medieval town wall was retained along the river bank, where the intended Elizabethan wall higher up with a southward-facing bastion was never built. Only three of the Elizabethan corner bastions were completed in the form intended with two deeply recessed flankers containing cannon commanding the 4m high walls backed by wide earth ramparts fronted by shallow water-filled ditches, beyond which was a counterscarp. A full analysis of the Elizabethan defences, which to the Queen's dismay had cost almost £130,000 when left unfinished in 1569, lies outside the scope of this book. Based on systems developed at Verona and other Italian towns in the 1530s, the Elizabethan walls at Berwick designed by Sir Richard Lee are of quite exceptional interest, the early 17th century town walls at Londonderry and Pendennis Castle in Cornwall being the only comparable pre-18th century works now surviving so completely in Britain. The upper ramparts, although part of Sir Richard Lee's original design, were not added until the Civil War period. The bastions are carefully shaped so that their outer faces were covered by cannonfire from flankers on each side of each adjacent bastion. For maximum effectiveness the guns were down almost at moat level, hidden behind screen walls within the pit-like flankers.

Berwick: Black Watch Tower by Kings Bastion

Not much remains of the castle isolated by a natural ravine at the NW corner of the town and the site is now bisected by the railway of the 1840s. Descending from the castle to the Tweed is the White Wall of 1297-98 built to prevent access along the river-bank. The wall now ends in the Water Tower, rebuilt c1540 to contain three casemates for cannon. Just east of the castle lay the main gateway towards Scotland. Further east the line of the medieval wall is marked by a rampart and ditch in open ground and the octagonal Bell Tower of the 1570s stands on late 13th century footings. Originally there were two other intermediate towers here and the Dominican and Franciscan friaries lay fairly close to the wall.

The Lord's Mount at the north corner is a large circular ashlar-faced artillery bastion of 1539-42 containing six casemates for cannon each with a magazine in a side-wall and a smoke-vent above. The original guns on swivel mounts were later replaced by guns in wheeled carriages. Only the bottom level of the bastion survives. From it the ruinous lower part up to 2m high of the medieval wall 2m thick extends for over 220m to the SE to the ditch outside the Brass Bastion at the northern corner of the Elizabethan defences. Not far behind the bastion lies Holy Trinity Church. From Brass Bastion the Elizabethan walls extend 200m WSW to the Cumberland Bastion and 250m SE to the Windmill Bastion, past the Cowport on the site of a medieval gateway. Windmill Bastion has a flattened arrow-head shape and measures 160m across at the widest extent. The Elizabethan wall then heads south past a magazine to the King's Mount, which was left as a demi-bastion because of the intended south and SW walls not being built.

The southern face of King's Mount is actually medieval walling left in situ with one original projecting turret (the Black Watch Tower) about 5m in diameter. More medieval walling survives SW of the gateway near the bastion. Fisher's Fort by the shore is a gun battery of 1522-23 remodelled in the 18th century. The wall then runs SW to what is now called Coxton's Tower at the southern angle of the town. The upper parts of this circular structure are 18th century but the basement has an early 14th century vault with chamfered ribs rising from corbels and window embrasures with shouldered lintels. Most of the walling beyond the tower facing the river mouth is 18th century work with a parapet 1m high above a battered base 2m high with a roll-moulding between the two. At the foot of Sandgate is the Shore Gate with rusticated voussoirs and doors of the 1760s. SE of here lay the Carmelite friary in the Palace Green area.

The English Gate demolished in 1825 faced the old bridge, rebuilt in 1611-26. North of it lay the house of the Friars of the Sack and beyond that the Trinitarian friary. East of them lay the Maison Dieu Hospital and to the west was the hospital of St Edward the Confessor. As rebuilt with two re-entrant angles in the 18th century, the wall then follows the shore before climbing back up to meet Meg's Mount, like King's Mount only completed as a demi-bastion. The principal surviving Elizabethan gateway, Scotsgate, lies close to Meg's Mount through the wall connecting it to Cumberland Bastion. The gateway was widened in 1815 and further altered in 1858. A fragment of the medieval wall remains to the NW of Meg's Mount, and a longer section with an angled corner remains 200m further NNW, both these parts being visible from a public path. This takes us back to the edge of the natural ravine which isolated the castle from the walled town.

BEVERLEY   Humberside

Immediately after a Scottish raid in 1321 the townsfolk petitioned parliament for grants for the provision of better defences. Edward II replied that he needed to see the town's charters and consult the Archbishop of York. There is no evidence of further action then, and gates and ditches seem to have already existed. A commission of array issued in 1371 to "provide against the dangers which may happen to the town, and to the inhabitants by reason of the defect of the fortifications" suggest the defences were regarded as inadequate. Beverley was then one of England's largest and wealthiest towns but was gradually overtaken by Kingston-upon-Hull, which was then newly walled. No murage grants for Beverley are recorded and John Leland found no evidence of a wall as such.

A ditch and rampart called the Bar Dyke once enclosed a large space 1200m long from north to south. The cathedral-sized minster established as a collegiate church by Athelstan in 935 lies in the eastern end of the 750m wide southern part, with the Dominican friary NE of it, beyond the ditch. East of the friary was a preceptory of the Knights Hospitallers. This part of the town had just one main gateway, the South or Keld Gate facing west. The main trading area and the large parish church of St Mary lay in the more densely populated northern part about 400m wide with the surviving North Bar and two other gates, Norwood facing east and Newbiggin facing west. SW of the latter, outside the ditch, lay the Franciscan friary. Traces of the rampart and ditch can be made out going west from North Bar along York Road and then south to the site of Newbiggin Bar across Westwood Road. Excavation evidence suggested they were a 12th century creation and were in a poor condition by the late 14th century and had never had much of a defensive character, the ditch being shallow and the rampart wide and low.

The gatehouse known as North Bar was built in 1409-10 at a cost of nearly £98 under the direction of William Rolleston and other town council members. Almost square at 7m by 6.7m, and a rare instance of a town gateway of brick in Britain, it has buttresses flanking the outer arch, in which is a portcullis groove. The passage is rib-vaulted in two bays, and there is one upper storey, formerly reached by an external staircase. The battlements are carried on a moulded string-course with remarkably tall stepped merlons and the corner merlons have the extra elaboration of thin pilasters carried on corbelled courses and ending in tiny gablets. The building is said to incorporate 125,000 irregularly-shaped bricks, mostly about 50mm thick and 250mm long. Three shields and three ogival-headed blank recesses on the south side are all executed in brick, an elaboration unequalled anywhere else in England at so early a date. See plan, page 35.

The North Bar at Beverley

BRIDGNORTH   Shropshire

High Town, so called to distinguish it from the later medieval suburb of Low Town east of the River Severn, has one of the finest defensive town sites in Britain. It lies on a sandstone promontory with sheer cliffs both to the River Severn on the east side and to a tributary valley on the west now partly filled by the railway station. The sandstone is, however quite soft and contains caves made into it at various dates. Undermining was possible and accounts for the incredible lean of the remaining parts of the keep of the early 12th century royal castle occupying the southern point of the promontory, a classic piece of slighting by Parliamentary forces following capture in 1646. During the siege much of High Town was destroyed by fire, a new Town Hall being built in 1648-52.

The castle was a baronial foundation of 1101 possibly on the site of a burgh built by Aethelfleda in 912 after a Danish army had camped further south in 896 at Quatford. The latter was also the site of the late 11th century castle and collegiate church moved upstream to Bridgnorth in 1101. East Castle Street and West Castle Street are thought to represent the site of the early 12th century town. In the 1150s Henry II is assumed to have taken this area for an outer bailey for the castle and laid out new burgages on either side of the present High Street. The church of St Leonard in a close to the NE may actually be of Saxon origin although most of it now is Victorian. The church of St Mary Magdalene near the castle keep was originally the castle chapel, and only later became a parish church, being rebuilt in 1792. Royal visitors were frequent until the early 15th century but by the early 16th century the castle was ruinous and the townsfolk had begun to build wooden houses within the former outer bailey as mentioned by Leland.

When Henry III granted timber for town defences in 1220, and then made the first of a series of murage grants, the town was modestly sized, extending 300m north beyond the castle to the North Gate, with a maximum width of 450m from the West Gate to the NE corner by St Leonard's Church. Squeezed in beside the river bank far below the church are remains of a Franciscan friary. The murage grant of 1257-72 probably refers to when a stone wall was added to the outside of the original clay bank, part of which between Whitwell Gate and North Gate was excavated in the 1990s and shown to have had a ditch 8m wide in front of it. Of the wall there remains a three-sided bastion in Pound Street just north of the site of West Gate. A small fragment remains further

Bastion on the west side of Bridgnorth

south in Hollybush Road. Another small fragment remains behind a house at 93 Cartway. Bishop Percy's House dated 1580 appears to incorporate a medieval structure possibly associated with a former gateway at the foot of Cartway. This gave access to the bridge, upon which there was once a gateway near the eastern end like that at Monmouth but in this case large enough to contain a chapel dedicated to St Osyth. Until a bridge was built further downstream at Bewdley in the 1440s the bridge here was the only one between Shrewsbury and Worcester.

North Gate is now mostly a rebuild of 1910 of a brick structure of 1740. Part of the defensive enclosure in the area of St Leonard's Church continued to be a palisade rather than a stone wall and it was here that Parliamentary troops assaulted the town in 1646.

BRIDGWATER   Somerset

In 1200 King John granted William Briwere charters allowing refortifying of the already existing castle and the establishment of a borough and a Saturday market. The town lies on low ground west of the lowest bridging point of the River Parrett and had wide tidal ditches. Short sections of them on the south side were located by excavations in the 1970s and 80s. It appears that property boundaries served to enclose an area about 350m by 300m around the town, which was granted murage in 1269. Little remains of the large castle filling the NE corner apart from the Water Gate. The parish church occupied the SW corner and there was a Franciscan friary east of it. By the end of the 13th century the town had already outgrown the defences. The South Gate is mentioned in the 14th century and survived until the early 19th century. The other three gates are all mentioned in the 13th century, and the East Gate facing the bridge over the river is also mentioned in the 16th century. The West Gate was repaired in 1556 and has a sandstone structure with habitable upper rooms. The North Gate was rebuilt in the 17th century but removed in the 18th century.

BOSTON   Lincolnshire

There are slight traces of a 12th century ditch east of the town, and excavations found part of a 1.8m thick brick wall dated by pottery as early 14th century. The Worm Gate faced north, the Bar Gate NE, and the St John Gate faced south. The town served as a port for Lincoln until the River Witham silted up, and the Hanseatic League had warehouses here. Many medieval buildings lie hidden around the town. The friaries of the Augustinians, Carmelites, Dominicans and Franciscans and the huge parish church of St Botolph are evidence of 13th and 14th century prosperity at Boston.

Beverley: gate plan

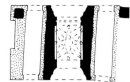

Bristol: plan of North Gate

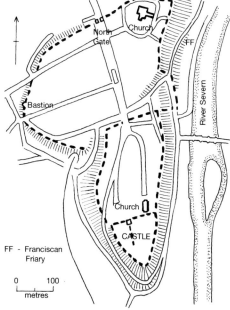

FF - Franciscan
     Friary

0   100
metres

BRIDGNORTH

North Gate at Bristol

BRISTOL   Bristol

Bristol was a prosperous town as early as 1020 when it had a mint stamping silver pennies with its own name. In 1067 the burgh resisted an attack by Irish raiders led by sons of the late King Harold. It was granted a charter by Henry II in 1155 and by then already had a retaining stone wall cut into the natural slopes, enclosing an oval area about 390m long from east to west with a greatest width of 300m defined by Bristol Bridge, Baldwin Street, St Stephen Street, Nelson Street and Fairfax Street. The east end was only about 100m wide and adjoined the Saxon quayside by the Avon. Beyond New Gate at this end lay St Peter's church, now gutted, and the large castle which was retained as a royal fortress after the rebellion of 1173-4. Short fragments of walling on the north side near the castle have been exposed between Narrow Wine Street and Fairfax Street east of Union Street and to the west of Union Street and north of Wine Street.

The church of St John the Baptist adjoins the 15th century North Gate with its tower and spire standing over the gateway passage, which is fan-vaulted and has a portcullis groove. The side passages are of 1820. Under the church is a 14th century crypt built against the town wall. The church of St Nicholas also lies over a medieval crypt built against a hidden section of the wall. The adjacent South Gate was destroyed in 1762, prior to a new church being built over the crypt. This gate faced towards a bridge rebuilt in stone in 1247, and again in the 1760s. The West Gate demolished in 1770 was associated with a church of St Leonard. The roads from these gates met at a market cross, near which were grouped the churches of All Saints, St Ewen, and Christchurch. Other churches within the inner circuit of early walls were St Werbergh towards the West Gate and St Mary-le-Port associated with a gateway towards the original quayside.

The town continued to expand rapidly and on the basis of tax receipts it soon ranked alongside Lincoln, Norwich and York. Bristol became a major port trading with many European cities and Ireland, and was also a major supply base for Edward I's campaigns in Wales. From 1232 murage was granted almost continuously until the late 15th century, and about that time marshy land between the northern wall and the now culverted River Frome was reclaimed by building an outer wall up to 80m out from the older one. Originally the River Frome also flowed by the western and southern sides of the core of the town but it was diverted further west in the 13th century, allowing a further expansion onto former marshland and the development of a new set of quays on its new east bank. In the 1260s the south end of the promontory thus created between the Frome and the Avon was cut off by a new wall with two gates and several D-shaped towers. Excavations at St Nicholas Almshouses in King Street in 1970 revealed the 8.5m wide lower part of one tower or bastion with three deep embrasures with loops.

A larger extension, doubling the walled area, was the enclosing of Redcliffe south of the River by the Portwall of 1239-47. The eastern end had a regular series of firing loops set 5.7m apart set in embrasures later blocked up, possibly symbolically after the fall of the Templars in 1307. The circular donjon called the Tower Harratz on this section was their treasure store and status symbol. Nearby lay a water gate and their circular-naved church. Also in this district was the church of St Thomas. The huge church of St Mary Redcliffe lay outside the wall. On the south side of this area was the Augustinian friary. Another suburb which existed by the 12th century east of the castle had a gateway called Lawford's Gate but no wall as such. Statues from Lawford's Gate depicting Edward I, Edward III and Geoffrey, Bishop of Coutances now lie at St Nicholas Church.

Bristol was raised to county status in 1373, previous to which the town north of the Avon was in Gloucestershire whilst the southern suburbs were in Somerset. Ship-building was a major industry. For the 1346 attack on Calais Bristol sent as many ships and crews as London. The population in late medieval times is estimated at about 10,000.

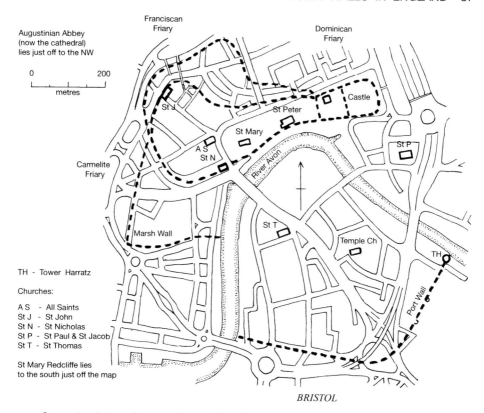

Augustinian Abbey
(now the cathedral)
lies just off to the NW

0   200
|____|____|
    metres

Franciscan Friary

Dominican Friary

Carmelite Friary

St J

St Peter

Castle

St Mary

A S
St N

River Avon

St P

Marsh Wall

St T

Temple Ch

TH

TH - Tower Harratz

Churches:

A S   - All Saints
St J - St John
St N - St Nicholas
St P - St Paul & St Jacob
St T - St Thomas

St Mary Redcliffe lies
to the south just off the map

Port Wall

BRISTOL

Several religious houses lay north and west of the Frome, outside the walls. There are considerable remains of the Dominican friary north of the castle. To the NE lay the Benedictine priory of St James and the Franciscan friary, whilst St Michael's church, the Carmelite friary and the hospital of St Mark lay to the west. Still higher up to the NW are the churches of St Augustine the Less and of the Augustinian Abbey founded in 1140. The latter was raised to cathedral status in 1542, thus making Bristol a city, although its nave was only completed in the 1880s. The location of the house of the Friars of the Sack is unknown.

When the Royalists attacked Bristol in the summer of 1643 the southern walls were strong enough for the Cornishmen under Prince Maurice to be repulsed with heavy losses. Forces led by Prince Rupert found a blind spot in the newly erected outer defences on the rising ground to the north. After heavy fighting around the Frome Gate facing north near the castle the town was surrendered by its commander Nathaniel Fiennes and remained in Royalist hands until 1646.

Excavated tower base, Marsh Wall, Bristol

BURY ST EDMUNDS   Suffolk

The grid plan of this town suggests a deliberate foundation, probably of the early 12th century since a charter of the 1120s or 30s states that both knights and burgesses were to contribute to the maintenance of the now-vanished defences. Murage grants were received in 1304 and 1330. A stone wall is mentioned in documents of 1400 and 1467, whilst it was called a dykewall in 1570. The town was controlled by the Benedictine abbey on the east side of it which has facing the town a fortified precinct wall with two very fine show-piece gatehouses, one 12th century and the other 14th century.

CAMBRIDGE   Cambridgeshire

Excavations in the Red Lion car park at TL 450583 found evidence of a 13m wide ditch descending 4m to the bedrock. It appeared to be 16th or 17th century and no trace was found of a wall or rampart or anything of the period of Henry III. In 1267 he had gates and ditches made with great haste against rebel knights hiding out in the fenland marshes. On the townward side of the ditch were found traces of an earlier ditch 5m wide and 3m deep associated with Saxo-Norman pottery. These defences enclosed a vesica-shaped area east of the River Cam, which filled the ditch. The bridge is first mentioned in 875. From it Bridge Street and Sidney Street ran down to the Barnwell Gate, passing the churches of St Godmund and Holy Sepulchre (on the site of that of St George). A branch street heading south to the Trumpington Gate passed by the churches of All Saints, St Edward, St Benet and St Botolph, whilst St Mary the Less lay outside the gate. This street passes most of the medieval colleges, several of which fill an area between it and the River Cam which is devoid of private houses or retail premises. The friaries of the Augustinians, Carmelites, Dominicans and Franciscans were also all clustered within the southern part of the town, whilst the Friars of the Sack had a more central location. The royal motte and bailey castle built in 1068 replaced 28 houses on the site of a Roman fort on the other side of the river north of the bridge. It was rebuilt in stone by Edward I and given new corner bastions in the 17th century. West of it lies the church of All Saints. Jesus College of 1497 to the NE beyond the King's Ditch was formed from the buildings of a former Benedictine nunnery which by then had fallen on hard times.

Canterbury City Walls near the Dane John Mound

CANTERBURY   Kent

The Roman town of Durovernum Canticorum was walled c270-300, having previously had a 2nd century fort at the southern end. The Roman wall was 2.5m thick and 6m high and formed the footings of the thinner 14th and 15th century wall on the same line. It enclosed an oval area of 120 acres and had at least six gateways, whilst there was an earth rampart round the inside. The existing name derives from after the Jutes arrived, when it was called Cantwareburgh, stronghold of the people of Kent. St Augustine arrived in 597 in the time of King Ethelbert and established the cathedral in the east corner of the walled area and a large Benedictine abbey to the east outside the walls, where Saxon footings remain amongst the Norman and later medieval remains. Coins were minted at Canterbury in the early 7th century and in 672 the Synod of Hertford confirmed the see of Canterbury as having authority over all the other sees in England. The city was damaged by Danish raids in 842, 851 and 991. In 1011 the Danes only captured Canterbury after a siege of twenty days but the eleven houses built in the ditch noted in the Domesday Survey of 1086 suggests subsequent neglect of the defences.

Shortly after 1066 an ancient burial mound at the south corner of Canterbury was re-used as part of a royal motte and bailey castle. A few years later a stone keep was built further west, using the Roman wall for the SW side of its rectangular bailey. During this period the cathedral-priory was rebuilt on a much larger scale. In the 13th century the friars arrived. There are remains of the houses of the Franciscans and Dominicans respectively in central and northern locations beside a minor branch of the Stour running through the walled area. A precinct is named after the Carmelite friary on the SE side, and there was also a short-lived house of the Friars of the Sack. Parish churches of Holy Cross and St George were associated with town gateways. Other ancient churches further within the walls are those of St Alphege, St Margaret, St Mary Magdalene and St Peter, all probably of Saxon origin but without surviving remains of that period.

Structural or documentary evidence of work on the walls is lacking for the two hundred years after minor maintenance noted in the Pipe Roll for 1166-7. In 1363 a commission of inquiry found the defences in a poor condition due to stone-robbing and gradual infilling of the ditch. Murage was granted in 1378, 1379, 1385, 1399 and 1402. Major work on the walls and gates was in progress at the time of the Peasants' Revolt of 1381 when the castle and archbishop's palace at Canterbury were sacked and the Archbishop Sudbury himself was executed by the rebels after their capture of London. An earlier archbishop, Thomas Becket, had been murdered in his own cathedral in 1170 and his shrine at Canterbury had become a major place of pilgrimage, as recalled in Chaucer's late 14th century Canterbury Tales. In 1386 work on the walls was being directed by Sir John Cobham and the royal master mason Henry Yevele, who is generally credited with the design of the West Gate and the cathedral nave.

A document of 1403 makes it clear that Henry IV, who was buried in Canterbury cathedral ten years later, was concerned about the still incomplete state of the city defences, the citizens being exhorted to speed up the work. In 1448 the city was granted a charter creating the still-surviving offices of mayor and high sheriff. Work on the walls was still in progress in the 1490s. All the late 14th and 15th century towers and gates were liberally provided with keyhole-shaped loops suitable for guns and small cannon.

In 1647 the citizens rebelled against Puritan rule after Charles I's defeat but surrendered to Parliamentary forces without a siege after a Royalist defeat at Maidstone in 1648. Most of the wall facing the River Stour along the NW side was then demolished by Colonel Ireton. The gates were removed in the 1780s as an impedance to coach travel except for the West Gate then in use as a prison. The city was badly damaged by wartime bombing, especially in 1942, and parts of the east walls were rebuilt in the 1950s.

The West Gate at Canterbury from the south

About two thirds of the circuit of the walls at Canterbury still survive, with seventeen of the twenty-one towers mentioned c1800 by Hasted. Although restored and lacking gateways the sections from the castle around the SW, SE and NE sides up to the cathedral and North Gate are almost complete and clearly visible from an encircling ring-road replacing the Roman and medieval ditches. Near the station at the SW end part of the city wall lies by the Norman castle keep. Here lay the Worth Gate, latterly part of the castle. It was blocked up in 1548 and demolished in 1791. It was replaced by the Wincheap Gate further east. Passing the site of a lost tower and one complete one the wall goes east to a corner tower by the ancient Dane John Mound which was landscaped in the 1790s. There are two more D-shaped towers as the wall goes NE to the site of Riding Gate marked out in the road. These series of four towers are all open-backed and of two levels with gunloops. The third tower is still crenellated and a buttress here hints at the former height of the wall, here 0.9m thick and revetted by an earth bank.

The Riding or Red Gate opened onto the original road to Dover and was the only Roman gate at Canturbury with two carrageways, beyond which were rectangular towers projecting internally. The southern carriageway was disused by the early 10th century and the tower beside it later contained the chancel of the late 11th century church of St Edmund which was removed in the late 14th century. A round tower 7m in diameter was then built against the outside of the other Roman tower and a new gateway opened out in 1430. It was blocked during Wyatt's rebellion in 1553 and only re-opened the following year. By 1560 it was ruinous and the gateway was removed in 1782.

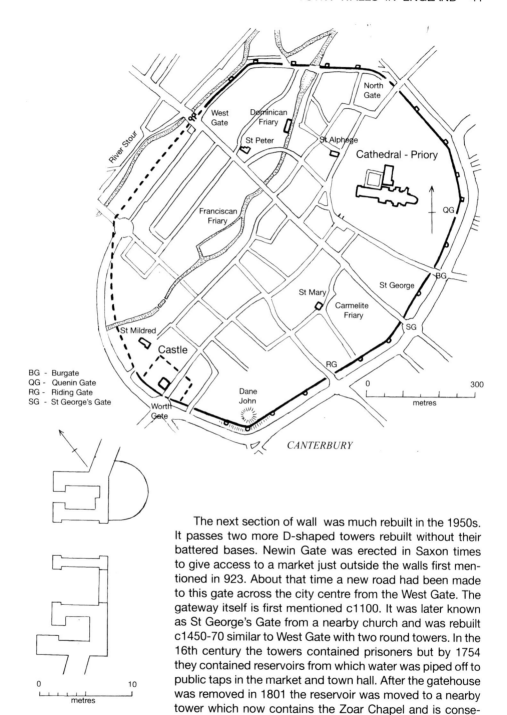

BG - Burgate
QG - Quenin Gate
RG - Riding Gate
SG - St George's Gate

*Canterbury
Riding Gate; plan*

The next section of wall was much rebuilt in the 1950s. It passes two more D-shaped towers rebuilt without their battered bases. Newin Gate was erected in Saxon times to give access to a market just outside the walls first mentioned in 923. About that time a new road had been made to this gate across the city centre from the West Gate. The gateway itself is first mentioned c1100. It was later known as St George's Gate from a nearby church and was rebuilt c1450-70 similar to West Gate with two round towers. In the 16th century the towers contained prisoners but by 1754 they contained reservoirs from which water was piped off to public taps in the market and town hall. After the gatehouse was removed in 1801 the reservoir was moved to a nearby tower which now contains the Zoar Chapel and is consequently mostly rebuilt above the battered base.

See pictures on title page and pages 10 and 18.

Tower by the cathedral-priory precinct at Canterbury

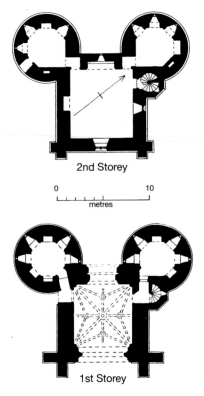

2nd Storey

0   10
metres

1st Storey

The West Gate at Canterbury: plans

Excavations beside the wall in the Burgate Lane area suggested that the medieval wall here was built on the base of the Roman wall, which partly survived over 2m high, and that the D-shaped tower here was an addition of the 1390s to an older wall face. Further NE the outline of Burgate is marked out in the roadway. It was rebuilt in brick with stone quoins in 1475 and repaired in 1538 using materials from St Augustine's abbey. The southern tower was removed in 1809 and the northern one went in 1822.

Beyond Burgate the walls formed part of the precinct boundary of the cathedral-priory, which took responsibility for their maintenance. The first section was rebuilt in the time of Prior Sellinge (1472-94) and has two D-shaped towers with battered bases. The first has just two levels with quatrefoil shaped gunloops on the upper one. The other tower has three gunloops in the bottom level and single-light windows in the upper room, string-courses marking the divisions between three levels. Next to it is a blocked-up Roman arch known as the Quenin Gate,

Further along, where the wall seems to date from Prior Chillenden's time in the 1390s, the four towers are rectangular. Each had a gunloop in each face of each of two levels, the lowest of which is now inaccessible because of the bank added against the wall. The wall-walk passed through the upper level. Open stairs led to the battlements above the roof, but only the first tower still stands to that height. These towers and the cathedral behind them are shown on a seal of the prior and convent dating from 1418, proof that they were completed by then.

Tower on the east side of Canterbury Town Walls

Beyond North Gate, demolished in the 1780s, the wall followed St Radegund's Street and Pound Lane round the north corner of the city and was under construction c1388-1403. Two towers here are D-shaped but the third is a rectangle of three storeys with stone quoins and modern windows. The wall-walk passed though the second storey. This may have been the tower which was rebuilt in 1467-8.

The West Gate is one of England's finest town gateways and is built of rag-stone in contrast to the rest of the defences which are faced with knapped flints. Archbishop Sudbury had it begun c1378 as a show-piece towards the road to London to replace an older gate associated with a chapel which was replaced by the nearby church of Holy Cross. The embattled gateway has a two storey main block 10m square with buttresses on the corners within the city and drum towers 7.2m in diameter on the outer corners, these towers being well supplied with keyhole-shaped gunloops and fireplaces on three levels. The passageway has a rib-vault and the outer arch has a portcullis groove and is covered by external machicolations. From it a spiral staircase rises on the NE side to the upper room which has a fireplace on the SW side and a two-light window facing SE. No scars remain of where the walls adjoined the gateway but a doorway leading south out of the southern tower second storey room must have led to its wall-walk.

The eighteen perches (roughly 90m) of walling beyond West Gate was completed in 1392 and destroyed in 1648. One square tower still remains, adjoining a house, and consequently much altered, but with three gunloops in the basement.

Tower in St Radegund's Street at Canterbury

CARLISLE   Cumbria

William II began a castle at Carliisle in 1093 after retaking Cumbria from Scotland and made the town a borough. During the Saxon period it seems to have been the capital of the kingdom of Rheged. Just north of the town once lay a fort called Petriana for 1000 cavalry forming part of the garrison of Hadrian's Wall begun in AD123. The castle partly overlies the site of a small earlier Roman fort associated with Lugavalium, the tribal capital of the Carveti which had been fortified by the Romans, and later refortified in the Hadrianic era as a supply base. Henry I was at Carlisle in 1122, shortly after which work probably began on building the castle keep. In 1133 Henry I divided off part of the diocese of York to create a new see of Carlisle, the church of the Augustinian priory he had founded in the city then becoming a cathedral. This church also served a parish in the northern half of the city, whilst the church of St Cuthbert served the southern half. In later years there was also a chantry chapel of St Alban. During King Stephen's reign Cumbria reverted to Scotland. The Scottish King David I was a frequent visitor, completing the castle keep and dying there in 1153. Henry II recovered Carlisle and began providing the castle with stone walls. He and Richard I spent small sums on the city gates.

Walling in stone of the north and east sides of the city may have begun in the early 13th century. The first of a long series of murage grants dates from 1232. The city was devastated by a great fire in 1292 which destroyed parts of the cathedral-priory, the Franciscan friary near the SE end, and the Dominican friary on the SW side. Several documents of the period 1324-45 refer to the need to repair damage to the city wall sustained during Scottish sieges. A petition to parliament from the citizens in the 1340s refers to six perches of walling (about 30m) being about to collapse, and one part had already fallen. Edward III granted the city a charter in 1352 allowing various privileges including markets on Wednesdays and Saturdays and a fair lasting sixteen days. William of Windsor spent £162 on repairing the castle and city walls in 1367-8 but a second petition of 1376 suggests the defences were still in a poor condition. It was said that neither could the gates be closed nor the drawbridges raised and the number of inhabitants had dropped far below the number needed to man the walls. Some repairs were carried out in the 1390s and in 1409 the citizens were allowed an annual grant of £13 for ten years towards the defences, and in 1410 for the same purpose they were allowed to keep fines and the profits of justice. Almost £287 was spent on repairs to the castle and city walls after a survey by William Stapilton and Christopher Boynton in 1421. Another annual grant of £80 for three years was obtained in 1438. About that time the county assizes began to be held again in the city after being moved elsewhere.

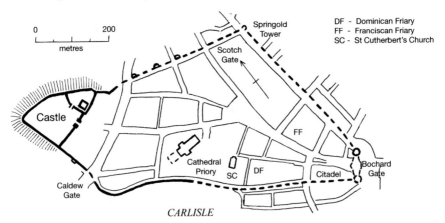

CARLISLE

Sallyport through the West Walls at Carlisle

Carlisle claims to be the most besieged town in England. It withstood Scottish attacks in 1173 and 1174 but was captured by Alexander II in 1216. The city held out against the Scots in 1296 and withstood a ten day siege in 1315 by Robert Bruce. Other unsuccessful raids and assaults took place in 1337, 1345, 1380 and 1385. The next time it fell was in 1461 to a Scottish force supporting the deposed Henry VI. It was also attacked by rebels under Nicholas Musgrave in 1537. A small Scottish force managed to break into the outer ward of the castle in 1596 and rescue a Border reiver named Kinmont Willie Armstrong. In June 1645 after a short siege by General Leslie the city was surrendered, having previously held out against an attack in May 1644. The Scots dismantled most of the nave of the cathedral to provide materials for strengthening the city defences. During the 1745 rebellion the city was captured by Jacobites under Charles Edward Stuart but was recaptured by the Duke of Cumberland in December.

The walls enclosed a flattened triangular area of 45 acres with a maximum width of 400m and a length including the castle in the NW corner of 900m. Carlisle had a reputation for being a difficult fortress to capture yet neither the castle nor town walls were properly flanked by projecting towers or bastions and the town gateways were comparatively modest affairs. A short length of the wall 2.5m thick survives in good condition continuing the line of the west end wall of the castle. Just south of the dry ditch in front of the castle is the Tile Tower, a rectangular structure 9m by 8m possibly of 12th century origin but refaced in brick in 1483 by Richard III. A spiral stair leads to an upper room over a basement with a loop in each outer wall face. Excavations in 1997 failed to locate traces of the Caldew or Irish Gate, a square tower with a roll-moulded outer arch about where the inner ring-road now goes through. The wall then projected out, came back with a re-entrant angle to pass the cathedral priory precincts and then headed SE to the Bochard Gate. A much rebuilt length of about 240m still survives as a retaining boundary wall. This wall has a double chamfered plinth and existed by 1238 when the Dominican friars were allowed to make a hole through it to bring in their water supply. The only tower along this side was the D-shaped Collier's Tower near the SE end. The ground outside this side may have been marshy until the railway was built.

Tile Tower and city wall at Carlisle

In 1541-3 Henry VIII had the defences of Carlisle much strengthened. The castle walls were lowered and made suitable for mounting cannon and at the SE end of the city a new citadel isolated by a deep ditch was created by building a U-shaped blockhouse on the city side of the square tower of the Bochard Gate, which was replaced by a plain arch called the English Gate further west. On either side of the new blockhouse was a small walled court with a large circular bastion with two levels of gunports with wide external splays. The central parts of this citadel were removed to allow a road through in 1804 but the bastions were rebuilt in 1810 to contain circular courtrooms for the assizes. Parts of the lower level of the original bastion remain on the north side. A well serving the citadel was discovered in 1883.

From the citadel the walls ran straight along Lowther Street for about 400m with one projection in the middle to the D-shaped Springold Tower at a corner. West of it lay the Rickard or Scotch Gate, which measured about 9m by 11m and is shown by Nutter as having two low upper levels over a round-arched gateway passage. From this gate the wall ran along West Tower Street past three D-shaped open-backed towers to a re-entrant angle with a fourth tower where the ring-road lies, and then back to the Queen Mary Tower at the east corner of the castle. Just before the re-entrant angle a mostly buried fragment 17m long remains by a car-park in Bitts Park in Finkle Street. The stone-work here is quite different and it is possible that this section dates from John's reign.

CASTLETON   Derbyshire

This village far below the clifftop royal castle guarding lead mines was made a borough in 1196 and has a ditch around its east and north sides. It was too isolated to thrive as a trading settlement.

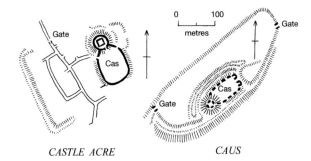

CASTLE ACRE   *CAUS*

Gateway at Castle Acre (see also page 20)   *Remains of the Wallop Gate at Caus*

CASTLE ACRE   Norfolk

SW of the 11th and 12th century motte and bailey castle of the Warennes lies a contemporary town enclosure 180m square, the two of them controlling where the ancient road of Peddar's Way crossed the River Nar to the south of them. The town enclosure has a well preserved ditch and rampart on the west side. A stone wall crosses the castle ditch at the castle SW corner, suggesting a possible intention to wall the whole enclosure. It has on the north side a gatehouse 7m wide called Bailey Gate assumed to date from c1200 since the passage has two plain pointed arches, the outer one with a portcullis groove behind it. The northern corners have round turrets 2.5m in diameter. The castle passed to Richard Fitz-Alan, Earl of Arundel in 1374 but may have been mostly abandoned by then, and the town would have decayed with it. By 1582 there were just eighty-eight houses here, seventeen of them empty. Some houses still occupy the enclosure but the main street of the existing village and all trading activities lie further north. The parish church lies outside to the west, beyond which is the Cluniac priory.

CAUS   Shropshire

Possibly originally the site of an Iron Age fort, Caus is a deserted township on a steep sided ridge 15km WSW of Shrewsbury. The site is 390m long from SW to NE by 140m wide but nearly half of its area and more than half of its width is taken up by half-buried ruins of a castle with 12th century earthworks in the middle of the SE side. Named after the Corbets' estate of Pays de Caux in Normandy, in the 12th and 13th centuries Caus formed a vital part of the chain of fortresses along the Welsh Border. Occasionally there were royal grants towards fortifications here. The rest of the site was occupied by a small fortified town granted a weekly market in 1200. The town gates are mentioned in 1371, by which time the castle was held by the earls of Stafford. At the SW end part of the base of the Wallop Gate still remains, and there was another gateway at the NE end. The town may have been stone walled by 1300 and had 58 burgesses in 1349, but the plague and Welsh revolts led to a decline. Just one farm now occupies part of the town enclosure, the same level of occupation that existed in the early 17th century, when the castle gained a new lease of life under the Thynne family until taken and destroyed by Parliamentary forces in 1645. A chapel of St Nicholas remained in use until that period but the chapel of St Mary founded in 1272 is last heard of in 1447.

CHESTER   Cheshire

A lead water pipe stamped with the name of Agricola dating from AD79 probably marks the period of the completion of the original earth and timber fort of Deva begun two or three years earlier by the previous governor, Frontinus, against the Ordovices of North Wales. It became the headquarters of the Twentieth Legion and soon after AD100 was rebuilt with a stone wall enclosing a rectangle 480m long from north to south by 320m wide. The Roman walls were repaired in the early 4th century and again under Athelstan against the Danes in the early 10th century.

In the late 11th century Chester became the power-base of the earldom of Chester. A mention of Ship Gate in 1121 suggests that by then the walled area had been expanded southwards and westwards to the banks of the Dee extending the area enclosed to about 750m by 500m. The SW corner has a rather irregular outline to enclose the castle founded by William I within the bend of the river. Occupying the NE corner of the original Roman enclosure is the precinct of a Benedictine abbey founded in 1090 by the first Earl of Chester and made a cathedral by Henry VIII in the 1540s. There were three friaries of the Carmelites, Dominicans and Franciscans within the western part of the walled area. A fourth friary, of the Friars of the Sack, did not survive the 13th century. There were also several parish churches and chapels, all of them now much rebuilt since the medieval period. About twenty stone cellars of medieval houses also remain. The major

major collegiate church of St John lay outside the walls. During the 13th century Chester was used by Henry III and Edward I as a supply base for their military campaigns in North Wales and the construction of their castles there. Murage was granted in 1249 and much work was done between then and the 1320s, including the provision of new twin-towered gateways, that on the east being a particularly fine structure. Although the city record books have been damaged it appears that the walls were well maintained right through the whole medieval period, although they were reported to be ruinous at the outbreak of the Civil Wars of the 1640s. See photo on page 4.

The Water Tower at Chester

Bonewaldesthorne's Tower and Spur Wall at Chester

Almost the entire circuit of nearly two miles of medieval walls still remains. None of the original main medieval gateways have survived, although there are later and wider replacement arches to maintain a continuity of the wall-walk, which is open to the public at all times. Most of the towers have had their upper parts rebuilt or removed, and the main wall parapet is mostly of the early 18th century. Chester was a Royalist stronghold and was besieged by Parliamentary forces for several months until it was surrendered in February 1646, by which time a great breach had been made in the east wall. Several of the gates and much of the original parapet on the main wall had also been wrecked by cannon-fire. Fortunately an order for partial demolition of the town walls was never executed, whilst the castle also long remained in use as a prison and military depot.

West of North Gate the wall passes a rectangular projection called Morgan's Mount, near which lay the NW corner of the Roman enclosure at St Martin's Gate, and then the Goblin Tower or Pemberton's Parlour, now a semicircular structure mostly of 1894 but originally a full circle projecting both outside and inside the wall. An inscription on the tower commemorates the murengers or officials responsible for collecting the murage tax. At the NW corner of the walls, beyond where new arches have had to be made across a railway, is a turret called Bonewaldesthorne's Tower. It commands the access to a spur wall 3.3m wide with a parapet on both sides extending 30m out to the Water Tower. The latter is the best preserved tower on the walls and was built in 1322-26 by John Helpstone at a cost of £100 to defend the harbour lying south of it, for in those days the River Dee came up right alongside the western walls of Chester. The racecourse now lies on the southern part of the harbour site. The tower now stands 21m high above a public park and is a circular structure 10m in diameter containing two octagonal rooms over a solid base. The numerous cross-shaped loops opening from the rooms have now all been widened out into slit-windows but there are two better preserved ones in the parapet. A spiral staircase lies south of the entrance doorway facing the walk over the spur wall, and there is a latrine on the other side of the entrance passage.

Interior of the wall west of the North Gate at Chester

The wall-walk on the west wall is barely 2m above the ground outside, where the outer face of the wall has many buttresses, and the inner face is now flush with the level of City Walls Road and Nun's Road. Only at the north end and at the Watergate of 1788 is the wall-walk higher above ground level. There are gaps in the wall on either side of the castle, around the southern side of which is a low section of wall following an irregular outline. One short section SE of the castle is entirely 19th century work. The arch of the Shipgate SW of the castle has been re-erected in Grosvenor Park.

The Bridge Gate in the eastern part of the south wall dates from 1782 and adjoins a minor part of the medieval gatehouse. It faces the late 14th century bridge over the river. The bridge originally had a tower between the sixth and seventh arches at the south end, where there was a drawbridge. The existing seventh arch is later, and the bridge was widened in 1826. East of the gate the wall passes a small semicircular tower and then turns through an angle. After another 130m there is a second angle where the wall-walk ascends a set of late 18th century steps to reach the higher level of the east wall. This second corner has quite high walling dramatically set on a sandstone outcrop. Overlooking a park with an assortment of Roman remains, the wall then continues to Newgate, opened as part of the new ring-road of the 1930s, and the nearby Wolf Gate, dating from the early 17th century.

Wolf Gate lies just south of the former Roman SE corner, footings of which remain together with a square internal corner tower beside the medieval wall. Next is the semi-polygonal Thimbleby's Tower measuring 5.2m in external diameter and probably of c1290-1320. Two stories remain, under a modern roof. North of here the wall is hemmed in by high buildings to the east for a short section.

East Gate is a rusticated elliptical arch of 1768. An old print shows that the medieval gate had a pair of similar polygonal fronted towers three or four storeys high with a series of three elliptical arches over the passageway, above which were three niches for statues. Beyond here is a set of modern steps rising up to the wall-walk from parkland over the base of a small semi-circular tower. This section of the wall has its wall-walk less than 2m higher than the ground outside.

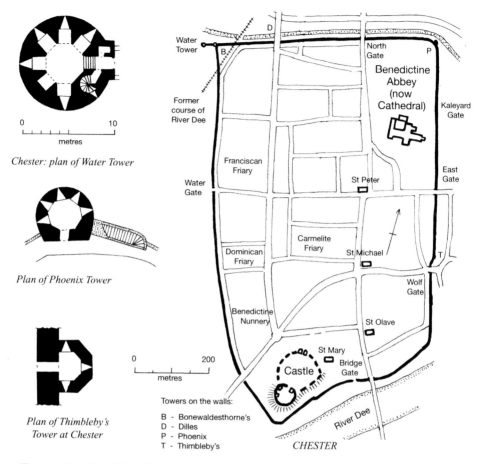

Chester: plan of Water Tower

0   10
metres

Plan of Phoenix Tower

Plan of Thimbleby's
Tower at Chester

0   200
metres

Towers on the walls:

B - Bonewaldesthorne's
D - Dilles
P - Phoenix
T - Thimbleby's

CHESTER

The section of wall beside the abbey (now cathedral) precinct contains the Kaleyard Gate, a small postern cut through the wall by permission of Edward I in 1275 to allow the monks access to a vegetable-garden lying outside the walls. The king's order that the gate should be locked at night was still enforced until recent times. At this point footings of the Roman wall lie just outside the wall, here probably mostly 13th century.

Near the NE corner stands the Phoenix Tower, also named after King Charles, who in 1645 is said to have stood on this vantage point to see his army being defeated on nearby Rowton Moor. The tower is circular to the field, where it is 16m high and 6.3 in diameter above a stepped and battered base, but it has a flat face towards the main wall-walk. Most of the upper parts of the tower appear to be 18th century rebuilding but it retains a plaque of 1613 over the doorway commemorating use of the tower by a city trade guild. The room at wall-walk level has five loops and was once used as a museum. West of here the north wall has a dramatic sandstone rock cutting in front of it, apparently a deepening and widening of a formidable ditch originally cut during the 1260s to accommodate an 18th century canal, now giving the appearance of a wet moat far below the wall. East of the North Gate dating from 1808-10 (replacing a medieval structure used as the city prison until the early 19th century) a section of Roman walling still stands nearly 5m high. This part of the wall appears to be a rebuilding two centuries after the wall was originally built since it contains older memorial stones reused.

CHICHESTER   West Sussex

By the end of the 2nd century the Roman town of Noviomagus Reginorum was given a rampart faced externally by a stone wall around a polygonal area of 100 acres, about 700m across. By the mid 3rd century the wall had been strengthened by sixteen solid D-shaped bastions, five of which still remain. The four main streets meeting at a crossing now marked by a fine market cross of 1501 perpetuate the Roman street layout. The four gateways were all destroyed in the late 18th century but almost all the circuit of the wall survives apart from wide gaps around the sites of the West Gate and the East Gate. The latter faced towards Stane Street, the Roman road to London, whilst the North Gate faced towards a road to Silchester. About half of the rampart-walk can still be perambulated, mainly as a result of 18th century landscaping, and indeed the parapet on the wall and much of the facework below it appears to be 18th and 19th century work, as are two minor gateways through the rampart, alhough the very nature of flintwork makes work of different periods hard to distinguish. The wall is mostly 6m high to the top of the parapet. The defences were repaired in 1204 and a murage grant was obtained in 1261. Fears of French raids saw a considerable amount of work on the defences in the late 14th century, when the ditches were improved and made into water-filled moats.

Chichester was one of King Alfred's burghs of 878-9, maintenance and manning of its walls being supporting by a generous allocation of 1500 hides. A Danish army was defeated close to the town in 894. There was a mint at Chichester in the 10th century and Domesday Book in 1086 records 300 tax-payers, suggesting a population of 1500 or more. The see of Sussex had then just been moved here from Selsey and a new Norman cathedral was under construction by the 1090s. The cathedral and its other buildings such as the bishop's palace and deanery occupy the SW part of the walled city, the smallest of its four quadrants. Diagonally opposite, in the NE quadrant, is a Norman castle mound, near which is the choir of the Franciscan friary. Also in this quadrant, but closer to the East Gate, was a Dominican friary, and there were also parish churches of St Andrew and St Olave. The SE quadrant contains the churches of All Saints and St John, and the NE quadrant contains the church of St Peter. All existed by the 11th century but the last two have been rebuilt. There was also a leper hospital just outside the East Gate. The city was given its first charter in 1135 and in 1353 was made one of the Staple Ports. It held a Royalist garrison during most of the Civil War period, when a circular-naved medieval church of St Sepulchre outside the West Gate was destroyed.

Chichester City Wall

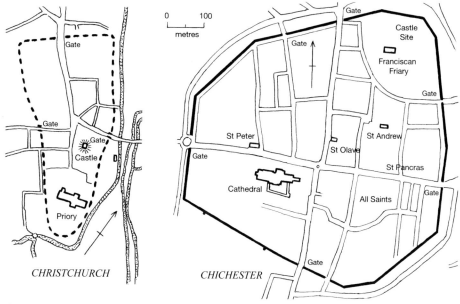

CHRISTCHURCH

CHICHESTER

CHRISTCHURCH   Dorset

It was probably in 878-9 that Alfred, King of Wessex provided his royal manor of Twyn-ham with an earth rampart 6m wide with a berm separating it from a ditch. The Burghal Hidage gives a figure of 470 hides for maintenance of the defences, which enclosed an area 500m long by 220m wide roughly the shape of a pre-historic hand-axe, and set on low-lying ground within the confluence of the River Stour and the River Avon. The eastern causeway and bridges over the Avon, plus the street layout, may also be of that period. Renewed Danish raids in the 890s may have stimulated the adding of a stone wall cut into the front edge of the rampart and recutting the ditches. The whole length of the wall seems to have been toppled and material from it used to fill the ditch as part of a slighting of the defences. A likely context for this is in 1017 when the Danish leader Cnut consolidated his power over Saxon England after taking the throne at the end of 1016.

The Normans filled the SE end with an Augustinian priory, the church of which served the parish and replaced a Saxon minster. A motte was raised further north with a bailey extending NE across the line of the late Saxon defences towards a mill stream parallel with the River Avon. The motte ditches encroached upon the original central crossing of streets and resulted in the 12th century East Gate across Castle Street replacing a Saxon gateway on a different alignment. The medieval Bar Gate closing off the NW end of the High Street lay near the centre of the straight NW side of the Saxon defences. The West Gate lay across Wick Lane in alignment with Quay Road which has replaced part of the ditch to the SE, towards where the west gate of the priory close lay. Aligned with the West Gate to its NW, and within the Saxon defensive line, was a new ditch cut either c1085-1110, or perhaps in the 1140s, but filled in by the end of the 12th century.

CLUN   Shropshire

Murage was granted in 1277 for enclosing a small area bounded by the castle of the Fitz-Alans on the west, Newport Street on the north and Ford Street on the east. The-River Clun lies on the south side, beyond which lies the parish church. It is doubtful if much of the wall was actually built. Clun is now just an average sized rural village..

COLCHESTER Essex

Immediately after the Roman invasion of AD43 a legionary fortress was established on the site of the present town to dominate the existing town of Camulodunum just to the west. Originally surrounded by an earth rampart 8m wide, the fortress soon became a colonia with its military buildings adapted for civilian use. The town was destroyed by Boudicca in AD60-1 and soon afterwards work began on surrounding a 108 acre rectangular area 900m long by 500m wide with a stone wall 2.8m thick and about 4.5m high to the wall-walk. There were six gates, one at each end and two on each of the north and south sides. Eight internal rectangular towers are known to have existed and probably there was one at each of the rounded corners and at the end of each street. About two thirds of the circuit still survives in some shape or form, and long sections clearly retain Roman facework to a good height with bands of brick between coursed septaria.

Evidence of occupation during the Saxon period is limited to three houses found in excavations and the surviving west tower of Holy Trinity Church. An English force took the town from the Danes in 917, slaughtering all those found within, and a Danish force captured and burnt the town in 1071. A huge royal castle keep was later built over the remains of a Temple of Claudius begun cAD54. The keep was surrounded by a bailey whose vanished southern defences resulted in a southwards kink in the line of the High Street running between the east and west gates. There was a 12th century moot hall on the site of the present town hall and a stone 12th century house survived in Foundry Yard on the north side of High Street until 1886. Six churches of medieval origin still lie within the walls, two more having been lost in 1878 and 1955 respectively. Footings of a church of as early as c330 have been excavated at Southway, just outside the walls.

In 1377 Colchester was the ninth largest town in England with an estimated population of 5,000, prospering mainly from cloth-making. From about that time the more centrally placed town of Chelmsford gradually took over the function of county town of Essex although Colchester castle keep continued to serve as the county gaol until 1668. Crouch Street is named after the vanished house of Crutched Friars outside the SW corner of the town. Ruins of the Augustinian priory church of St Botolph, used as a parish church until the siege of 1648, lie close to the SE section of the walls, whilst a gatehouse is all that remains of the Benedictine Abbey slightly further out from the walls on the south side. A Franciscan friary stood within the walls, just NW of the East Gate.

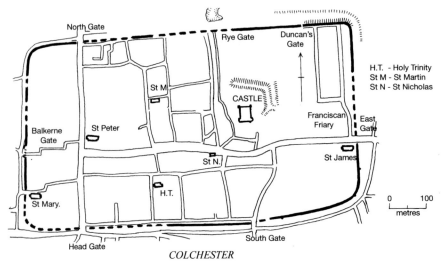

COLCHESTER

Bastion on the south side at Colchester

King John granted the town some wood from a royal forest towards defensive works in 1215. Several people were prosecuted during the early 14th century for taking stone from the walls, which suggests they were then not properly maintained. On several occasions between 1382 and 1410 Colchester was exempted from the duty of sending someone to represent the town in parliament so that his allowance could be spent on repairs to the walls. The four small semi-circular solid bastions added around the SE quadrant are assumed to be of that period. No part of the wall has clearly identifiable remains of a wall-walk or parapet either of the Roman, medieval or Civil War periods and no medieval posterns have survived.

A plaque at the junction of High Street and East Hill marks the site of the East Gate, which collapsed in 1651, probably because of damage sustained during the 76 day siege by Parliamentary forces led by Sir Thomas Fairfax during the summer of 1648. The last remains were removed in 1675. A long section of wall extends from here around the SE corner of the town, the first part being over 4m high and retaining the churchyard of St James. There is a small late medieval bastion projecting 2m from the wall about 70m from the gate site, and another after a second similar interval, west of which the wall has seen more rebuilding and strengthening with buttresses. A lower section runs past a car-park towards another bastion. West of the site of South Gate the wall is up to 4.5m high and retains ground on which are built shops opening off Eld Lane. On the north side of St John's Street the entrance to a service area below the Culver Centre cuts through the wall, part of which has been rebuilt at right-angles to the original line. The section of wall west of the site of Head Gate and around the SW is missing, having been breached during the siege of 1648, but a good length of wall 4m high then runs from the west side of the churchyard of St Mary up to the Balkerne Gate in the middle of the west side. Outside of the SW corner lay the house of the Crutched Friars.

The Roman Balkerne Gate at Colchester

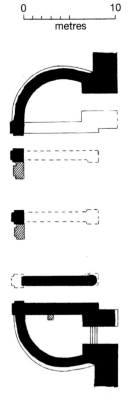

0   10

metres

*Colchester: plan
of Balkerne Gate*

The Balkerne Gate was a very impressive structure 33m wide projecting 9m beyond the main wall. A screen wall containing two 5m wide and 6m high archways for wheeled traffic existed here by c50AD. A dozen or so years later these arches became part of a gateway with additional pedestrianways on either side with beyond them quadrant-shaped towers. By AD300 the main archways had been blocked up but in a reduced form they may have been open during the medieval period, although they lack obvious defensive arrangements. Parts of both towers still stand 5m high, together with the vaulted southern pedestrianway, but the northern one now has a public house built over and against it. From the gate the wall descends quite steeply northwards. There are three gaps before a long section 2.5m high goes round the NW corner. On the steep slope the courses of Roman brickwork lack the regularity seen on the southern sections of wall. The wall is missing to the east of the site of North Gate. To the east of West Stockwell Street a 100m length of footings of the wall appear below the north side of Northgate Street, the houses just beyond the wall starting from a level one and half stories below the existing roadway. East of here is the site of Rye Gate, a medieval addition to the town's gateways. The next section through a park is much reduced in height and has been much patched over the years. Along this section lies the base of Duncan's Gate, a square tower projecting internally with a passage 3.4m wide. The wall rounds the NE corner and extends another 70m further south but has mostly been rebuilt and is nowhere more than 2m high. House gardens back onto the inner side, whilst there is parkland externally. The final section past the site of the Franciscan friary to the East Gate is missing. See p5.

COVENTRY   West Midlands

Murage was first granted in 1329 but no work appears to have started on stone walls or gates until New Gate was begun in the 1350s when Richard de Stoke was mayor. By then Coventry was one of the leading towns of England. Newly founded in that period were the collegiate church of St John and several new guilds of merchants. A few under-crofts of medieval merchants' houses still survive. There had been a large castle of the earls of Chester in the town centre during the 12th century but this had gone by the 14th century, being replaced by Cheylesmore Manor House to the SW. The manor was held by Edward II's consort Isabella, and she persuaded her son Edward III in 1345 to make her part of the city a corporation with a mayor, resulting in a reduction in the influence of the priory. Immediately north of the castle stood two large parish churches, Holy Trinity (serving the prior's part of the town) and St Michael, (serving the earl's part of the town). Beyond them lay the large Cluniac Benedictine priory, the enormous church of which shared cathedral status with that of Lichfield. The bishops of the see of Coventry and Lichfield based themselves at Coventry from 1102 until 1188. Regarded as superfluous, the priory church was mostly destroyed after the Reformation. To the SW and SE of the centre respectively lie remains of the friaries of the Franciscans and Carmelites.

Work on the two mile long circuit of walls slowly proceeded along the south and west sides until the end of the 14th century. A royal licence to crenellate the walls was obtained in 1363 and murage was granted again in 1364. Another crenellation licence for completion of the work was obtained in 1385. Cheylesmore Manor House was then in the hands of Richard II and he was keen to see it enclosed by the city wall, with some justification, for in 1395 an abortive attempt to capture the city was made by a small force of rebels under Sir William Ba-got. In the 15th century work began on walls around the priory lands north of the River Sherborne. In 1482 Prior Deram complained that although the priory had long paid £10 murage to-wards the construction of six perch-es of walling each year, yet only two perches a year had been built around the priory lands. He claimed the rest of the money had been spent on oth-er parts of the wall. The NE side of the city was only finally enclosed in the first third of the 16th century. The wall then extended for two miles and had twelve main gates plus posterns in some of the twenty flanking tow-ers, most of which lay on the earlier parts of the walls away from the pri-ory lands. Sandstone for building the walls came from quarries at Allesley and Cheylesmore and also from cut-ting the ditch outside the wall, part of which was water-filled. Documents of 1430 and 1456 suggest the wall may have been backed by an earth rampart.

Cook Street Gate at Coventry

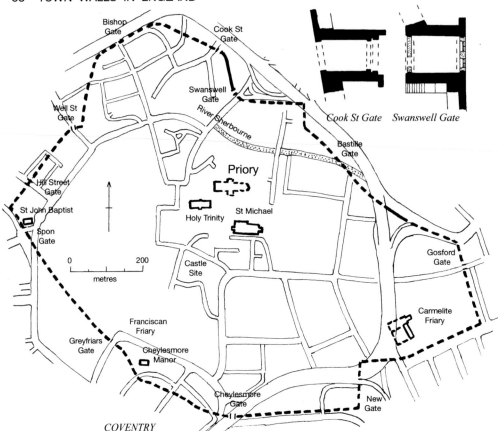

Cook St Gate   Swanswell Gate

COVENTRY

In the 1660s Charles II charged the Earl of Northampton with the task of dismantling the walls because of rebels being harboured within them. The city had been a Parliamentary stronghold and in 1642 had defied a Royalist force which withdrew after firing a few token cannon-shots. Nine of the gates were then blocked up, only New Gate, Bishop Gate and Gosford Gate being left open and well fortified with new outworks of earth, whilst a new bastion was added on the south side in 1644. Much of the medieval circuit still stood in 1672 when the removing of materials was stopped and some repairs were then carried out, mainly to allow the towers and gatehouses to be rented out as dwellings. By the early 19th century most of the circuit had gone and today the main surviving parts are the Priory and Cook Street gates and most of the wall between them.

New Gate was begun c1355 and removed in 1762. It stood just south of the Carmelite friary in a re-entrant angle of the wall around the north and west sides of where there is now a roundabout as London Road leaves the ring-road. From here the wall went round a corner and headed west for 400m, passing three intermediate towers and the Little Park Gate to reach the Cheylesmore Gate, this section being built c1355-85 and lying south of the ring-road. The next section headed NW for 230m passing two towers and then went round a corner to run NNW for 160m first beside Cheylesmore Manor House and then the Franciscan friary to reach Grey Friars Gate, demolished in 1781. An illustration of 1840 shows this gate as a three storey structure with round turrets on the outer corners linked at the top by a machicolated parapet, below which was a niche for a statue. The passageway appears to have had a fan-vault.

A section of wall built in the 1380s, interrupted by two towers, one set over the River Sherborne, headed NW for 400m from Grey Friars Gate to Spon Gate which was built c1392-9, and demolished in 1771. It adjoined Bablake Church and had two polygonal towers facing outside with polygonal stair-turrets behind them. The passage was extended inwards by a single storey section with its own parapet with decorative blank-panelling on the merlons. Behind it rose the gable and a pair of two-light windows of the higher outer part. During the disturbances of 1450-1, when the city was carefully guarded, the ditches cleaned out and temporary dams provided across the River Sherborne, this gate was furnished with a new portcullis and provided with four brass guns made in Bristol which were mounted on trestles. From Spon Gate a section of wall built in the 1390s headed NW for another 50m before turning NE for 40m to Hill Street Gate. The wall continued NE for 180m crossing Radford Brook to Well Street Gate. Both these gates were square structures of the 1420s each with just one upper storey. The next section ran NNE for 180m before turning through an angle to meet Bishop Street Gate. First recorded in 1411, and rebuilt in 1689, this gate was also square with one upper storey lighted by a row of four windows towards the city, and the inner arch was flanked by buttresses. Within the parapet was an attic room.

The next section of wall dating from c1430-60 headed east for 190m with a slight in-bowing at an intermediate tower to reach the still surviving Cook Street Gate which has one upper room with doorways out to the wall-walk over a passageway with moulded four-centred arches, the outer one having a portcullis groove and being flanked by buttresses. Most of the 110m length of wall from here to Swanswell Gate still survives in a public garden, although reduced in height. This wall cut in half the prior's orchard and a "mud wall" subject to frequent collapse was later built across the ditch by Cook Street Gate to secure the part of the orchard left outside the wall. Swanswell Gate, originally called Priory Gate, has a modern parapet like that on Cook Street Gate. It has one upper room, and that was probably the original form, but an illustration of 1840 suggests that latterly there were as many as three habitable upper levels, under a double-hipped roof with a high chimney-stack on one side.

A length of wall built c1460-1500 went almost east for 230m before arriving at a corner tower and heading south to the River Sherborne (now here culverted under the ring-road). This part enclosed the priory gardens. The wall then went SE along the south bank of the river for 150m to the Mill Lane or Bastille Gate built in 1512-4 and demolished as late as 1849. An illustration of 1840 shows it with a row of three shields over a moulded archway. There were then two upper storeys, but the upper one, under a hipped roof, was probably made up from the former parapet level in the 17th century. Constructed with difficulty on water-logged ground, most of the 350m of wall running SE from here to the Gosford Gate was not built until the early 16th century, although the last portion, after turning a corner, may have dated from c1480-1500. A section of ashlar-faced wall base 1.8m thick was excavated in 1970 to the east of the end of Grove Street together with evidence an older rampart probably of the 12th century and a long low section also remains in parkland below flyovers.

First mentioned in 1411, Gosford Gate had one upper room and a pair of circular bartizans. It was demolished in 1765 along with a former guild chapel of St George adjoining one corner. The 200m section of wall running SSE from the gate was only begun in the 1430s. An agreement with the Carmelite friars for building it had been reached as far back as 1365, the wall only to be accessible to the townfolk in times of strife. The wall turned at a corner tower and ran WSW for 240m past one tower to another corner tower. Another section of 120m dating from the 1350s and with two towers ran west to New Gate. Part of the wall here was rebuilt in 1636 after it collapsed. The tower next to the gate contained the friars' shrine-chapel of St Mary, probably built c1370.

CRICKLADE Wiltshire

First mentioned in 903, Cricklade is thought to have been founded in 879 by King Alfred to control where the Roman road Ermin Street crossed the River Thames. Different versions of the Burghal Hidage refer to 1400 or 1500 hides allocated for maintaining defences around a rectangular area 550m by 510m south of the river. The defences originally had a double ditch system around a clay and turf rampart with stone walkway on the inner side and four corner towers. A stone wall 1.2m thick at the base was later added against the outer face of the rampart. Levelling of the rampart as a means of slighting the defences probably took place in 1017 as King Cnut consolidated his power over England after taking the throne at the end of 1016. A palisade later took the place of the rampart, probably during the 1140s. There is no evidence of later maintenance of the defences. Much of them are delineated only by a very slight rise but a better preserved section remains on the south side. The parish church of St Sampson lies west of the middle where Calcutt Street intersects with High Street to divide the town in quarters. The former church of St Mary may have been a second Saxon foundation associated with the north gate towards where a causeway led out to a bridge over the river.

DEVIZES Wiltshire

There was no significant settlement here before the Bishop of Sarum built a castle in the 1080s, the motte and inner bailey of which had stone buildings and defences by the 1120s. NE of them lay a large outer bailey 200m wide and 440m long. The original town simply served the castle's needs and formed an arc extending around this bailey. Made a borough by the Empress Matilda in 1141 during her struggle against King Stephen, the town was enclosed by a ditch 7m wide and 3m deep and had three gates which faced SE, east and NW. The burgages extended around New Park Street, Monday Market Street, Sheep Street and Bridewell Street and the market south of the parish church of St Mary lay just outside the main gate of the castle outer bailey. In 1292 the town was important enough to send two members to parliament. In the early 14th century the Crown allowed the town to take over the former outer bailey of the castle, the defences of which were probably then levelled. It appears that fresh burgages were laid out and a second (Thursday) market was established, for which a large space was left on the north side. The former castle chapel of St John served this area as a parish church.

DONCASTER South Yorkshire

The large church of St George is a later medieval enlargement of what was originally the chapel of the 12th century castle, otherwise destroyed in the 1170s and now vanished. The street layout was partly dictated by the water-filled ditch around the town, which was originally a Saxon burgh and was given a charter of privileges in 1194. There was no wall as such but stone gates are recorded at St Mary's Bridge, St Sepulchre's, Hall Gate and Sunn Bar. The Victorian Corn Market stands on the site of the original parish church later replaced by a large market place close to the quays. A Carmelite friary lay near the centre whilst the Franciscan friary lay on an island to the NW between the two rivers.

DUNWICH Suffolk

Six parish churches (three existing in 1086), a Dominican friary and a preceptory of the Knights Templar have all been lost to sea erosion which has destroyed one of England's wealthiest medieval towns. The only survivals are part of the Franciscan friary, a hospital chapel and a fragment of the Pales Dyke, a 14m wide ditch now thought to be of 10th or 11th century origin. Murage raised from a grant of 1253 may have been spent on sea-defences rather than landward defences but a South Gate is mentioned at that time.

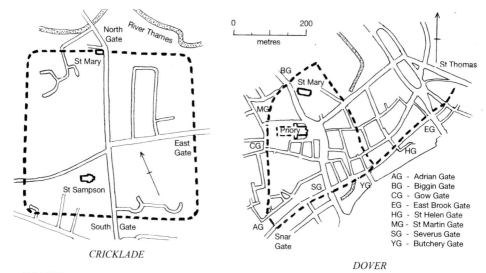

CRICKLADE

DOVER

AG - Adrian Gate
BG - Biggin Gate
CG - Gow Gate
EG - East Brook Gate
HG - St Helen Gate
MG - St Martin Gate
SG - Severus Gate
YG - Butchery Gate

DOVER   Kent

Dover was one of the original Cinque Ports and at the time of the Domesday survey was obliged to provide the king with twenty ships each with a crew of twenty-one men for fifteen days annual service in return for various privileges. It had been the site of a Roman fort and a Saxon burgh, and the Roman lighthouse attached to the Saxon church in the castle grounds attests to its early importance as a port. The town lies low down between the castle high up on the site of an Iron Age fort to the east, and the Western Heights with impressive 19th century fortifications on the other side. Almost continuous murage grants are recorded from 1324 until 1483, the tax being applied to travellers using the port rather than goods being brought into it as was usual. Heavy expenditure on walls is recorded in accounts surviving from 1365 onwards, but as much effort seems to have been on defences against the sea as against sea-borne raiders, and the 1435 murage grant specifically mentions damage cause by recent storms.

On the south side of the town the seaward wall extended west for 480m from the site of the East Brook Gate giving access to the original harbour, itself about 300m west of the castle. The wall itself started still further east, south of the church of St Thomas. The next feature of the wall was St Helens Gate, and then followed Fishers Gate, Butchery Gate, Severus Gate and Old Snar Gate. At the SW corner lay the Snar Gate built in 1370 along with a minor extension of the wall here, and demolished in 1683. The wall then went up the cliff to the Adrian Gate. Next along was the Cow Gate, demolished in 1776, so called because cattle were then grazed on the Western Heights. The Monk's or St Martin Gate was a mere postern. The wall then headed round to the Biggin Gate across the road to Canterbury and London which was demolished in 1762. It was probably intended to extend the wall from here all the way back to the foot of the castle but as completed the wall only went as far as a nameless corner tower before turning SE past the Tinker Tower and over the River Dour back to the Fisher Gate. A section of this eastern wall and part of a gate were uncovered by excavations in Dolphin Lane. The area thus fully enclosed by walls corresponding to the parish of the church of St Mary near the north wall, was just 320m long from north to south by 250m wide, a considerably smaller area than that enclosed by the castle outer walls. The lack of a NW or inland-facing wall for the part of the town roughly corresponding to the parish of the now-ruined church of St Thomas may have confused Leland, who doubted that the town was ever walled.

DURHAM   County Durham

Viking raids caused the removal of St Cuthbert's relics and the see from Lindisfarne to Chester-le-Street in 883, but in 995 they were transferred yet again to an elevated promontory at Durham which is 550m long by up to 230m wide and encircled by a loop of the River Wear, one of the finest sites both defensively and visually of any British city. There is some evidence houses stood on the site by the early 10th century. Vanished Saxon defences were sufficient for the city to be successfully held against Malcolm, King of Scotland in 1006, and another attack by King Duncan in 1038. By this period the bishops also functioned as earls, thus creating the County Palatine with semi-independent prince-bishops which officially survived until the early 19th century. The first Norman bishop, Walcher, murdered in 1080, occupied a new castle on the neck of the promontory. His successor, William, went into exile in Normandy during 1088-91 but on his return the Saxon cathedral was replaced by a much larger new Norman building.

Ranulph Flambard, bishop from 1099 to 1128, continued work on the cathedral nave (although it was vaulted after his death) and is said to have enclosed the 58 acres of the whole peninsular with a stone wall. This whole area was administered by the castle constable and tended to be referred to as the castle in medieval chronicles and deeds. The castle and cathedral priory took up half the space within the wall leaving room for houses on either side of one north-south street along the eastern side. The northern part formed a parish served by the church of St Mary-le-Bow lying just north of an east-west cross-wall extending across from the cathedral. The collapse of the gate here in 1635 left the adjoining church derelict until 1671. Another wall curving round from the castle mound to the cathedral NE corner closed off this part known as North Bailey from the area now called Palace Green, from which is reached the cathedral north doorway, always the normal means of access for the general public. Until cleared by Bishop Flambard the Palace Green area contained private houses. The east wall contained two gates, Owen Gate at the north end and Lye Gate at the south end. In the west side of Palace Green lay a postern called Windy Hole, near to which excavations found the base of a round tower. Between the postern and the west end of the cathedral a 70m length of the outer wall was removed in 1661 for the construction of a grammar school.

At the NE corner lay the North Gate, rebuilt after the Scottish attack on Durham by Robert Bruce in 1312 as a huge three storey building 21m by 18m with a central passage between two towers rising from square bases as semi-polygons. There was a projection on the west side and a polygonal stair turret at the SE corner. Enclosing the drawbridge was an open barbican with polygonal turrets rising from square bases. In 1420-3 Bishop Langley filled in the barbican with a rectangular tower with a four-light window facing north out of the topmost room. It was later used as a prison, a new block and exercise yard being added on the east side in 1790. The building was demolished after a new county prison was built in Elvet in 1819. Hidden away behind 50 Saddler Street, between the site of the North Gate and the castle motte is a D-shaped tower 9m in diameter containing five embrasures with loops facing outside the wall. It is thought to date from the time of Bishop Anthony Bec, 1284 to 1311.

South Bailey was a separate parish served by the smaller church of St Mary-the-Less, beyond which the street bends round westwards down to Watergate, a circular arch of 1778 replacing a 12th century gate further south which led to a ford replaced by Prebends' Bridge. Except for a section south of King's Gate by Mary-le-Bow Church, the rest of the wall around the promontory appears to survive in a rebuilt and lowered state but the tree-clad steep slopes make the outside difficult to see and there is no internal access because of houses and gardens. King's Gate faced a bridge replacing the former Bow Bridge which itself replaced a ford. A 15th century postern lay further south.

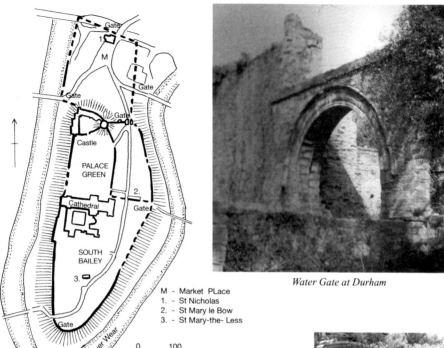

Water Gate at Durham

M - Market PLace
1. - St Nicholas
2. - St Mary le Bow
3. - St Mary-the- Less

0   100
metres

DURHAM

Durham: tower near North Gate

In 1315 and 1337 murage was obtained for enclosing the parish of St Nicholas to the north which contained the market place and was ruled by a bailiff appointed by the bishop. This area was a borough given a charter in 1179 by Bishop Hugh le Puiset. The only remnant of the wall in this part is a possible section along the river bank on the west side. From the market place Silver Street leads steeply down to the SW to the site of Framwell Gate demolished in 1760. Although it also had a postern on the south side giving access to the river bank below the walls of the castle, the gate faced a bridge over the river originally built by Bishop Flambard, much repaired in the 15th century and widened on the south side in 1828. Remains of a postern in Walkergate at the NW corner survived until the 1960s. The earls of Westmorland had a town-house here in the 16th century. On the north side of the market place, just east of the parish church of St Nicholas, was the Clayport Gate, which existed in the late 12th century. It was once a large 14th century tower with an east facing postern as well as the main gateway but was later reduced to just a wall with vehicular and pedestrian arches before being removed in 1791. On the east side was a postern and also a gate facing Elvet Bridge, which existed before the suburb of Elvet east of the river was made a separate borough sometime before 1195. By the end of the 13th century two chantry chapels of St Andrew and St James stood beside bridge. The two central arches needed rebuilding after flood damage in 1771, and in 1804 the bridge was widened northwards.

ELLESMERE   Shropshire

In 1258 Peter de Montfort was granted murage for five years for fortifying the town, which had recently been devastated by John de Grey. There are no remains but It is quite likely a ditch at least existed in the 12th century. Ramparts along Church Street, Watergate Road and Birch Street would give the best possible defensive position, enclosing the church and with the lake on the east and the castle to the SE. This small elevated area might just have been enough space for the 59 burgesses mentioned here in 1280. An alternative larger enclosure would use Willow Street as the NW boundary.

EXETER   Devon

Under the central part of the city lies the site of a Roman fort which accommodated the Second Augustan Legion from c55 to c75, the bath-house of which was found in 1970 under Cathedral Green. The site became a town which was given stone walls around a rather larger area measuring up to 800m long by 500m in the late 2nd century. Exeter was occupied by a Danish army in 877 but was soon recaptured and refortified by King Alfred, being made a burgh. It successfully defied another Danish army in 893 and the defences were repaired in 928 by Athelstan. Another Danish attack in 1001 was resisted but in 1003 a Danish army was admitted by order of Emma, queen-consort of Aethelred, who had been given Exeter as part of her dowry. The Benedictine monastery refounded by Athelstan was then destroyed by the invaders. It was subsequently rebuilt as a minster and in 1050 its church became a cathedral when Bishop Leofric was consecrated in it and the see of Devon and Cornwall then transferred to Exeter from nearby Crediton.

The Roman wall with its Saxon repairs was clearly still quite defensible in 1068 when Exeter defied King William I as a result of the influence of Gotha, mother of the late King Harold. An attempt to intimidate the defenders by parading a blinded hostage resulted only in a rude gesture. The city, estimated as then the tenth most populous in England, withstood eighteen days of siege before it was surrendered on generous terms under which the king agreed not to harm the citizens or increase the annual tribute due to the crown. The terms were honoured but a new royal castle was immediately built in the NE corner to control the city. The first Norman bishop was installed in 1072 but it was not until c1112 that a new cathedral was begun to the east of the Saxon minster..

Exeter: south wall beside former Holy Trinity Church

A market at Exeter is first mentioned in 1213 and by 1283 it was held on three days a week. By that period the city had a small Benedictine priory of St Nicholas in the NW quadrant, a Dominican friary in the SE corner, a Franciscan friary outside the south gate and about twenty parish churches within the walls. The eight surviving irregularly laid-out churches tucked in between other buildings are mostly late medieval now, but originate from the 10th and 11th centuries. Exeter was made a county in its own right in 1537. It held out against rebel forces in 1497 and 1549 but in 1643 was captured by the Royalists after a siege of eleven weeks. The city was blockaded by a Parliamentary army throughout the winter of 1645-6 and was surrendered before it could be stormed.

Exeter: SE corner bastion

King John granted the citizens 100 marks in 1215 towards fortifications and in 1216 they were instructed to make sure neither the ditch nor the wall were obscured by houses. There was another royal grant of 100 marks in 1218. The long series of mural grants started in 1224 and ended in 1369, but in anticipation of a French attack in 1377 the mayor and bishop were both instructed to ensure the defences were in good order. Evidence that the money was not always properly spent occurs in 1307-8 when the mayor and bailiffs were called to present their accounts before a royal commission. Considerable work was evidently done to the walls in the period 1404-7 when during each summer building season of twenty to twenty-five weeks an average of a hundred cart loads of stone was brought in,

Three quarters of the circuit survives, mostly much patched and lacking a wall-walk, nor are there many towers. There is public access to either the interior or exterior of most of the remaining portions of the wall, and a trail around the walls with appropriate new signs and plaques has recently been created. All four main gates have been lost and also a long section of wall around the SE corner. Roman walling stands high in several places but most of the wall is 13th and 14th century work on a Roman base.

A long gap marks the site of the East Gate demolished in 1784. It had two round corner towers containing small rooms with gunloops. Work on this gateway is recorded in 1361-2, 1376-7, 1403-4, 1460 and 1511-3. The wall then goes NW to a small circular tower with pilaster buttresses probably of c1210 at the east corner of the castle. Further along another small round tower has been added to the Early Norman castle wall. The wall is lower behind the courthouse in the castle bailey. The next portion as far as the square Athelstan's Tower, where the wall leaves the castle, preserves a unique set of presumed Saxon crenellations below Norman heightening. Beyond the tower the wall stands between 7 and 9m high as far as Queen Street and shows evidence of Saxon repairs on the outside face visible from Northernhay Gardens. Between Queen Street and North Street the wall is rather higher externally than internally towards a car-park.

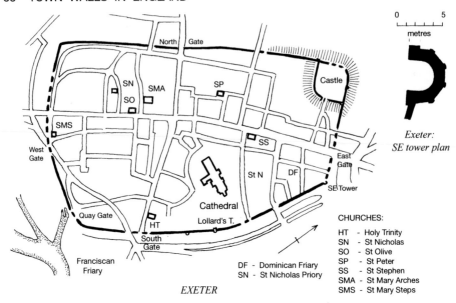

0   5
metres

Exeter:
SE tower plan

North Gate

SN
SMA
SP
Castle
SO

SMS

West
Gate

SS

East
Gate

St N   DF

SE Tower

Cathedral

Quay Gate
Lollard's T.
HT

South
Gate

Franciscan
Friary

DF - Dominican Friary
SN - St Nicholas Priory

EXETER

CHURCHES:

HT   - Holy Trinity
SN   - St Nicholas
SO   - St Olive
SP   - St Peter
SS   - St Stephen
SMA - St Mary Arches
SMS - St Mary Steps

The gate across North Street was demolished in 1769. It had two guard rooms flank-ing the passage so it was probably a twin-towered structure. Work on it is recorded in the 1370s and 80s and in 1498-9. Behind Bartholomew Terrace houses front onto the wall-walk and the wall retains the ground on which they are built, set above a valley. The corner of the wall here was occupied by the Snail Tower until the 19th century. Still basi-cally a retaining wall hardly rising above Bartholomew Street, the wall goes SE to the site of the West Gate, which is said to have borne the brunt of the attack of 1549. Here William of Orange entered the city in 1688. Repaired or altered in 1380-1 and 1388, this gate survived until 1815.

A section of wall 3m high then leads to where the new Western Way cuts through the old street plan. Next comes a higher section which is mostly still Roman work and then the site of the Quay Gate or Water Gate rebuilt in 1566 in a slight re-entrant angle of the wall behind the old Custom House. The next section of wall above Commercial Road is about 4.5m high and has a chamfered base-course, making a 13th century date likely. The western part here is of rubble. Ashlar blocks appear further along but are irregularly coursed and perhaps reused. The last part of this section is of oblong blocks regularly coursed and a short section of the wall-walk remains.

A modern bridge goes over Western Way, east of which stood South Gate, a 14th century building similar in form to the East Gate. It was used as a prison from at least 1354 and survived until 1819. The receivers' accounts record work on it in 1403-14. There is then a long stretch, much of it up to 6m high, with two bastions, as the wall passes the cathedral precinct and bishop's palace. The first bastion projects about 5m from the wall and is 10m in diameter. It was mostly rebuilt in 1912 and the wall east of it was repaired in 1673 after being in a poor condition for some time. The second projec-tion was probably originally a mid to late 13th century open bastion similar in size to the other one. It was later given a back wall which contains a spiral staircase to two upper storeys opening off the entrance doorway into a vaulted basement with one north facing window. This converted it into a tower used until 1469 by the bishops to incarcerate religious dissenters, hence the name Lollards' Prison. At this point the wall is up to 9m high and has a rampart on the inner side, thought to be an addition of the 1650s.

Exeter: walls west of the former South Gate

Along the northern side of Post Office Street the wall retains an outer face but the core has been removed. This section ends at a corner capped by a bastion probably of c1215-20 about 6m in diameter, circular internally but a half-octagon with the rare feature of angled pilaster buttresses externally. The parapet on the bastion dates from the Civil War period. In 1642-3 the Parliamentarians spent over £4300 on repairs to the walls, much of it probably in reinstatements of crumbled away parapets and strengthening the naturally weaker southern line of walls. From here back to the site of the East Gate the wall is missing.

Exeter: bastion on the south walls

FARNHAM   Surrey

Excavations have located the town ditch mentioned in the 1215-16 Pipe Roll in Borelli Yard, The Borough and at the junction of Castle Street and Bear Lane. With the church in the SW corner the ditch would have enclosed an area about 400m by 350m on the north bank of the River Wey. There was no rampart. In 1247 Farnham was granted a charter by the Bishop of Winchester, whose castle lay further north up the slope, separate from the town.

Old print of the West Gate at Exeter

GLOUCESTER   Gloucestershire

Set by the former lowest bridging point of the River Severn, Gloucester has always been of strategic importance. The city centre developed from a Roman fort which superseded an earlier fort further north at Kingsholm. After the 2nd Augustan Legion moved forwards to a base at Caerleon in Wales the Gloucester fort became the colonia of Glevum, originally settled by retired army veterans. By the early part of the 2nd century a stone wall 1.4m thick was added in front of the original rampart enclosing an area 480m by 400m with the corners set to the cardinal points so that the East Gate actually faced SE.

The Saxons captured Gloucester along with Bath and Cirencester in 577 and it was then ruled by the Hwicce as a sub-kingdon of Mercia. What later became the Benedictine abbey straddling the NE side of the Roman wall, burial-place of Edward II and later elevated to cathedral status in 1541, originated as a minster church founded c679. The priory of St Oswald further north was founded by King Alfred's daughter Ethelfleda, who is assumed to have refortified Gloucester against the Danes in the early 10th century. About this time Westgate Street and Eastgate street were re-aligned further north. Parish churches which originated during the 10th century were St John and St Aldate near the North Gate, St Michael and St Martin near the central crossing of main streets, St Mary-de-Crypt beside Southgate Street, St Kyneburgh by the South Gate and St Mary-de-Lode north of the western part of Westgate Street, ie beyond the Roman walls.

In the 11th century there was a royal palace 800m north of the town at Kingsholm which was much used by Edward the Confessor and William I. The latter erected a motte and bailey castle in the west corner of the Roman walls. In 1100-20 it was replaced by a stone castle further west, later a royal fortress. Remains survive of the Dominican friary on the older castle site and of the Franciscan friary in the southern corner, whilst the vanished Carmelite friary lay just outside the North Gate. Undercrofts of several medieval merchants houses remain in Westgate Street. At The Cross in the middle of the town stood a medieval cross, the lower stage of which acted as a conduit for a public water supply by the mid 15th century. Henry II granted the town a charter in 1155 and John in 1200 gave it another charter making the citizens free from toll anywhere in England. In 1483 the town was made a county in its own right by Richard III.

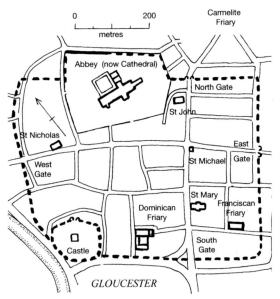

Base of tower on east side of Gloucester

The first of a series of murage grants extending until the end of the 14th century was in 1226. The east and south walls are generally assumed to have been rebuilt in this period on the old Roman base, although the medieval wall was probably thicker than the Roman one. The embattled precinct walls of the abbey projecting beyond the line of the Roman wall formed part of the circuit. Not far from them lay the North Gate which was used as a prison and had a gaoler's house added on the SE side in 1590. The wall then followed St Aldate Street to the SE before turning SW down to the East Gate, described as new in 1253. The base of its southern D-shaped tower has been uncovered and left on display in a glass-covered pit. This gate was used to keep female prisoners in 1560, and was demolished in 1778. The wall then went down the inner side of Brunswick Road passing a tower and postern mentioned in 1509. A length of wall which survived until the 19th century then headed NW along Parliament Street to the site of the South Gate. The wall then went past the Dominican friary to join up with the castle walls. The alignment on the NW side and the location of West Gate with its four corner turrets remain uncertain. There may only have been a palisade and ditch. In 1641 this part of the city was described as unenclosed and a part of the northern wall had fallen down.

A depleted Parliamentary garrison under Colonel Edward Massry held out against a Royalist attack during August and September 1643 until a relief force under the Earl of Essex arrived. After the siege huge earth bastions were erected to reinforce the East and South gates and the south and east corners, whilst a new line of defence with five more bastions was built out to the NE and NW sides of the city. Both these new defences and parts of the older stone walls were demolished by order of Charles II in the 1660s.

Tower at the NW cornr of Great Yarmouth

Blackfriars Tower at Great Yarmouth

GREAT YARMOUTH   Norfolk

Great Yarmouth was a major fishing port until comparatively recently. It was settled by people from the Cinque Ports as a place for the landing of fish and had 70 burgesses by the 11th century, being a royal possession. King John's charter of 1208 gave the town privileges and allowed for a merchant guild. The town provided naval vessels for the king's use, having three galleys in 1205 and providing 43 ships for Edward III's siege of Calais in 1347. The town is unusual in that it had just one church, St Nicholas, which grew to be one of the largest ordinary parish churches in England. Three friaries, of the Carmelites, Dominicans and Franciscans, are evidence of 13th century prosperity here. A bridge across the River Yare was first built in 1427.

A six year murage grant was obtained in 1261, but in 1279 a commission was appointed to look at the accounts of the collectors. Little or no work probably took place on defences until another grant for seven years was made in 1285. Continuous grants were made between 1321 and 1448 and most of what now stands is clearly of that period. Much of the £20 grant from the fee farm of the town in 1457 seems to have gone on harbour defences. Further murage grants were made in 1458 and 1462. The accounts suggest long sections were under construction simultaneously rather than the completion of short sections each year. Two thirds of the circuit of over 2km enclosing 133 acres still survives, along with eleven out of the sixteen towers, but the ten gates have all been lost. The walls enclosed an area 1400m long on the east bank of the River Yare which was 300m wide at the south end but up to 550m wide towards the north end. A characteristic of the town layout is the presence of three main north-south streets which by the 16th century were connected by narrow lanes called The Rows, onto which many of the houses opened. The walls are of flint and brick with Caen stone used for dressings and features such as gunloops. Much of the wall had a wall-walk built over a series of arches forming an arcade as at King's Lynn and Norwich. A rampart was added on the inside face to strengthen the wall in the 1540s when French raids were expected. A new fort was also built outside the wall at the south end in 1590.

The circuit started with a boom-tower at the south end by the river bank. This tower controlled a boom or chain which could be raised to prevent hostile ships coming into the quayside areas, which were without defences. Not far east of the boom-tower lay the South Gate, beyond which is the Palmers Tower, with a chamber at wall-walk level and another room higher up in which three loops face from east to SE. Originally three more probably faced south to west. The wall is then obscured externally by houses as far as the Blackfriars' Tower whilst the inner face is partly buried. The tower stands 9m high with the adjoining wall up to about half that height and has a modern passage through it. Three loops remain in the outer face.

Great Yarmouth town wall, showing evidence of arcading

Loop in the main wall at Great Yarmouth

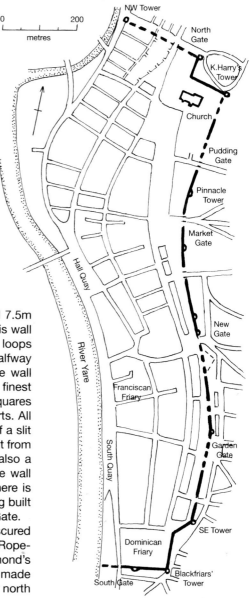

GREAT YARMOUTH

From the tower a section of wall 7.5m high runs north to a re-entrant angle. This wall may be that heightened in 1342 and has loops at the summit and another row about halfway up which open out of the arcades. The wall then heads NE to the lofty SE Tower, the finest of those remaining. It has patterns of squares made with tile and flint on the upper parts. All three levels have gunloops in the form of a slit with a central roundel, each one being cut from a single block of Caen stone. There is also a high gabled attic room.   From here the wall goes due north to Alma Road, where there is a gap, a modern church of St Peter being built across the line. Here stood the Garden Gate.

The wall then heads NNW and is obscured by houses. It passed the White Lion or Rope-makers' Gate, demolished in 1745, Symond's Gate and the Lancaster Gate, an opening made in 1758. Only the lowest stage of a tower north of Lancaster Road survives as part of a house. The wall here is 3.5m high. The next lengths of wall stand up to 9m high in places and again have a double row of firing slits, although those here are blocked up. Along here were the Ames Gate and the New Gate, a 16th century insertion. A tower north of St George's Road is much obscured by adjoining buildings. Also much altered is the Pinnacle Tower by a retirement home in Alexander Road. It measures 6m in diameter over walls 1.2m thick and has squinch arches where the wall adjoins it. The upper storey has square windows of later date. The next feature was the Ravelin, a triangular 17th century bastion, now gone.

Pinnacle Tower at Great Yarmouth

Three towers remain of the next section, one in the middle of the Market Gates Shopping Centre, the second by Coopers Car Park, and the third by the Dissenters' graveyard near the Co-op. There was also a gate here. After a gap the wall re-appears in back gardens north of St Nicholas Road near the site of Pudding Gate. The next tower went sometime between 1660 and 1730 and the St Nicholas Gate was destroyed in 1642. Beyond lay two more towers shown on old drawings. The octagonal lower storey 3.5m high of King Harry's tower stands at the NE corner of the churchyard. This chamber is said to have been vaulted. Passing the site of two lost towers the wall runs west along the churchyard and then turns north to Maygrove Tower at the NE corner, which has been refaced, as no original loops remain. A short section of wall runs to the west to the site of the North Gate, a mid 14th century structure with two round towers similar to the Landgate at Rye. There is then a big gap as the wall ran past the Ramp Tower. Standing on the end of the River Bure (which below here flows into the Yare) is the conical-roofed NW tower standing about 9m with evidence of the wall-walk passing through its lower storey.

King Harry's Tower by the churchyard at Great Yarmouth

The SE Tower at Great Yarmouth

GRIMSBY   Humberside

The town was already a major port by 1201 when it was granted a charter by King John and a royal castle was begun, but never completed. Henry III granted a second charter to the town in 1226 and parts of the large church of St James are of that period. Originally there was a second parish church of St Mary further east and there were Franciscan and Augustinian friaries, a Benedictine nunnery and a leper hospital, plus a house of Augustinian canons to the SW. Murage was granted in 1261 and 1268 and account rolls show evidence of small sums on defences in Henry V's reign. There is no evidence of what form the defences took. Marshy ground around the town offered some protection.

NE corner tower at Great Yarmouth

GUILDFORD   Surrey

A rampart and ditch probably of Saxon or Early Norman origin extended round from the Dominican friary by the river, along North Street and South Hill to connect with the ditch of the castle by New Castle Street. Excavations have revealed a 30m length of a thick clunch wall parallel with the south side of the High Street. A wall on this alignment would have included St Mary's Church and a small nucleus of the town next to the castle. It might in fact represent a former northern bailey of the castle, abandoned to the townsfolk in favour of palatial but hardly defensible royal apartments south of the motte. The town lies where the River Wey flows through a gap in the North Downs. It had a mint in 978, and was a small borough at the time of Domesday Book in 1086. A charter allowing a weekly market and an annual fair was granted in 1257 by Henry III, a frequent visitor to the castle.

The Sandwell Gate at Hartlepool

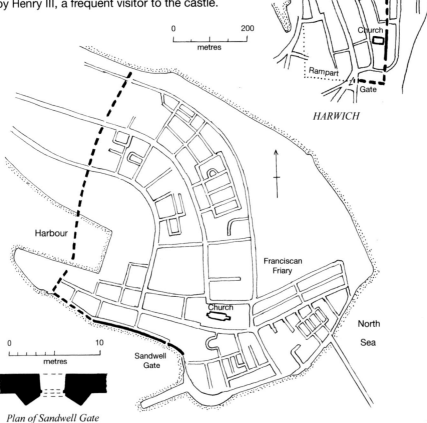

HARWICH

HARTLEPOOL

Plan of Sandwell Gate at Hartlepool

Distant view of the walls and gate at Hartlepool

HARTLEPOOL - Co Durham

Murage was granted in 1315 for the protecting of the town against a recurrence of what the Scots under Sir James Douglas had just done to it. The irony is that it was the Bruce family, who had recently forfeited their English possessions in a successful bid to win the Scottish throne, who had founded the town and probably intended the parish church of St Hilda as their burial place. In 1201 King John had confirmed the town's earlier charter. Flanked by numerous rectangular and semi-circular bastions, and about 5.5m high, the wall not only cut off the 400m wide neck of the peninsular site measuring 750m by 600m but continued across the mouth of the 260m wide medieval harbour (now mostly silted up), leaving just a narrow entrance gap between two towers. The main gateway lay just north of the harbour. The wall then continued SW for 80m and then headed ESE along the shore for 300m. The eastern section of this part still remains and contains the Sandwell Gate, a double-chamfered shouldered archway flanked by two solid triangular buttress-turrets of ashlar each 3m wide. An offset appears about 4.5m up on the structure, which is 7.5m high outside. It is uncertain whether it ever stood significantly higher. A later breach in the wall immediately to the east has now been blocked up again. A Franciscan friary stood NE of the church. Hartlepool was Co Durham's only port in medieval times but by 1725 was little more than a fishing village, having lost its port functions to Stockton. The modern port of West Hartlepool dates only from the 1840s and 50s.

HARWICH   Essex

The town was given a royal charter in 1238 and has a planned layout on a peninsula between the River Orwell and the River Stour with parallel main streets running from NW to SE. A murage grant of 1338 was revoked because of protests by Ipswich. However a licence to crenellate a wall at Harwich was issued in 1352 and sometime during the late 14th century a wall of septaria was built down the eastern side of the town past the parish church (where a possible small fragment of it adjoins the churchyard) as far as the South Gate towards Colchester. The wall connected a large round tower at the NE corner and several seaward facing gates. A rampart and ditch cut off the marshland to the SW to enclose an area about 400m by 200m. The defences were strengthened in the 1550s and a bulwark called the Queen's Mount added at the SE corner, whilst the palisade connecting stone buildings facing the quays to the NW seems to have formed part of further works carried out during the Spanish invasion scare of 1588.

HASTINGS   East Sussex

The Burghal Hidage lists a Saxon burgh here, which had a mint, and in the 12th century it became the chief of the Cinque Ports. The town had seven churches in 1291, although only two medieval ones now remain. The castle has a good cliff-top site but the town in the valley extending NE of it would have been difficult to defend from an inland attack. French raiders sacked the town in 1339 and 1377 and the short sections of wall behind flats in Hastings Walls, between East Street and Winding Street, and between Pleasant Row and East Bourne Street, are probably works of c1375-1400 against sea-raiders.

HEREFORD   Herefordshire

Excavations have revealed remains of a timber-revetted rampart and ditch erected around the city in the 9th century and the see is of still older origin, but the local centre in Roman times was Magna at Kenchester several miles to the NW. What was probably originally a square defended area about 370m across was later extended eastwards to enclose the former church of St Guthlac and in the early 10th century the rampart was externally faced with stone, but probably still with a wooden superstructure. Although the castle may then have been newly founded (with ramparts enclosing St Guthlac's church), the city defences appear to have been in a neglected state in 1055 when the Welsh captured and sacked Hereford, burning the cathedral. Harold Godwinson then rebuilt the defences and Hereford held out against an attack by Eric the Wild in 1067. King Stephen captured Hereford in 1138 from Geoffrey Talbot after a siege of about a month, during which much of it was burned down. Stephen's enemies recaptured Hereford in 1140, although only the castle seems to have been besieged on that occasion.

Widemarshe Gate, Hereford

Richard I's charter to the city in 1189 and the threat of further Welsh attacks prompted new work on the defences. Four new gates were built and the enclosed area was extended to the north to take in the market place now known as High Town and the churches of All Saints and St Peter, resulting in an enclosure of about 75 acres measuring about 600m by 540m which originally had three other churches. The Row Ditch extending westwards from the Victoria Bridge by the castle may also date from this period to enclose a suburb beyond the river south of the old bridge further to the west. Hereford was captured by Hubert Walter from Prince John in 1197.

City wall with pilaster buttresses on the west side of Hereford

Old view of Bye Street Gate, Hereford

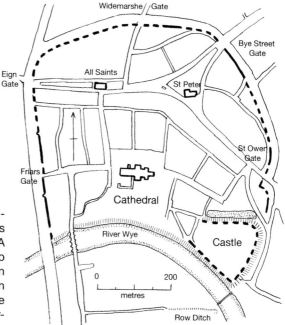

HEREFORD

The citizens were granted timber from a royal forest towards work on two gates in 1216. A long series of murage grants up until the late 15th century began in 1224. A new keep was built on the motte of the then royal castle and the city was gradually surrounded by a wall said to have been 2m thick and 5.5m high with six stone gatehouses, seventeen D-shaped bastions and a deep moat filled with water from the Yazor Brook. Before the Civil War period there were still five medieval parish churches within the walled area.

Quite a lot of the wall was probably completed by 1264, when Hereford supported Simon de Montfort against Henry III. and withstood an attack by Roger Mortimer, against whom the ditches on the west side were cleared of obstructions. De Montfort briefly governed England from the city whilst King Henry and Prince Edward, captured at the battle of Lewes, were kept in the castle.

Bastion near site of Friars' Gate, Hereford

Subsequent royal visits were rare and the castle was soon allowed to decay but John Leland in the 1530s found the city walls in good order, certain prominent citizens each taking responsibility for maintaining a short section known as a loop. Considerable works were required to make the city defensible in the 1640s. The city submitted to roving Parliamentary armies in October 1642 and April 1643 without resistance but a Royalist garrison under Barnaby Scudamore made a much more determined resistance against a Scottish army under the Earl of Leven in the summer of 1645. Most of the castle had gone by 1677, but the circuit of city walls remained almost intact when Taylor's map was made in 1757. All the gateways were destroyed at the end of the 18th century. A modern ring-road system now takes the place of the former moats.

Bastion and walls south of the site of Eign Gate at Hereford

The walls of Hereford are best preserved on the west side. A gate across St Nicholas Street was called Friars Gate because the Franciscan Friary lay outside it. South of here lies a bastion about 4.5m high with loops set fairly high up in outer facing of sandstone blocks. A length of wall beyond it south towards the Wye has small pilaster buttresses suggesting a possible 12th century date for this part, which is nowhere more than 1m thick at present. A round corner tower by the river was demolished in 1806. Further long sections of wall, much patched and reduced in height and thickness, extend past a featureless second bastion to the site of the Eign Gate. A high section of new walling behind Tesco's continues the line of the wall around the NW corner. Further east are other thin and low bits of walling of doubtful authenticity extending round to the site of the north-facing Widemarsh Gate, shown on old drawings as having a main body recessed between two rectangular turrets with corbels for a former machicolated parapet.

East of the gate a bastion was excavated in the 1960s and shown to be 6.4m in diameter over walling 1.8m thick, with a projection of 3m beyond the main wall, with which it was bonded. Remains of the walls in this section are hidden away as far as Commercial Street, across which stood the Bye Street Gate, shown with an arch of many orders recessed between two flat turrets of slight projection with windows for upper rooms. To the north lie remains of the Dominican friary. SE of here is a high section of wall, although its lack of significant thickness casts doubt upon its age. Further south is the site of another bastion excavated in the 1960s. Pottery dated the rampart against which the bastion was built to the late 12th century. Other short sections of wall appear to remain as property boundaries on either side of a former gate across St Owen Street, south of which are the moat and ramparts which are the main remnants of the castle. In 1596 a tower near St Owen Gate was rented to William Wellington on condition that he kept it in repair. The steep bank of the Wye west of the castle, passing the cathedral precincts, was never walled but a sixth gatehouse stood at the south end of the old bridge.

ILCHESTER   Somerset

The defences of of the Roman town of Lendiniae were at least partly serviceable during the early medieval period since Robert Mowbray was unable to capture the town during his rebellion against William Rufus in 1088 and the walls are mentioned in 1200. The town was once prosperous enough to support a Dominican friary, an Augustinian nunnery and a leper hospital, whilst a 13th century mace or staff of office (oldest of its type in England) survives in the town hall. Only one medieval church survives (St Mary Major) but two others stood in a derelict condition in the early 16th century and five others are known to have once existed. The town served as one of King Alfred's burghs and had a mint in 973 and 1082 which appears to have survived until the mid 13th century. The county gaol for Somerset was established here in 1166, moved to Taunton in the 13th century and then returned to Ilchester, where it remained until 1843.

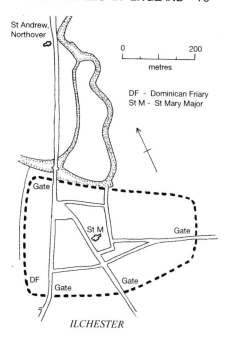

ILCHESTER

An excavation in 1969 in the area of the South Gate prior to the building of a bungalow on the site found evidence of a stone wall added in the 4th century to a 2nd century rampart and stone gateway. One D-shaped tower was found of the gateway which remained in use until a dismantling of the defences in the 16th century. A church of St Michael lay over the gateway. The Roman wall was demolished in the early 13th century and a new wall built just in front of it. The East Gate closes off Limington Road and is mentioned in 1242 and 1426. North Gate facing towards the bridge of c1200 over the River Yeo is mentioned in 1304. West Gate is mentioned in 1200, 1387 and 1557 and part of it stood until at least 1605. The defences enclosed a rectangular area 460m long with a greatest width at the west end of 300m.

IPSWICH   Suffolk

The town still has a dozen churches of medieval origin. Friaries of the Carmelites, Dominicans and Franciscans lay along the south side and there were two Augustinian priories, whilst Cardinal Wolsey, born in Ipswich in 1471, established a college in the town. Domesday Book records nine churches in the town but says the number of burgesses was greatly reduced from the five hundred here earlier in the 11th century. Danish raids on the town are recorded in 919, 991, 1010 and 1069. Evidence from excavations shows that a substantial rampart and ditch were created in the 13th century on the site of 11th century earthworks. The street named Tower Ramparts gives an indication of the route of the defensive line enclosing an area about 750m each way with a short-lived castle on the west side. A vertical sided trench probably for foundations for an intended wall was later cut into the rampart, either after a murage grant of 1299, or following a licence to crenellate of 1352, which was however revoked in 1354. A document of c1302 refers to the possibility of a piece of land being crossed by a wall if one was built. Gatehouses certainly existed, West Gate surviving until 1780, and North Gate until 1794, and the NW side of the town was possibly stone walled. By 1477 another gate faced Stoke Bridge which seems to have been rebuilt c1440.

KING'S LYNN   Norfolk

This major port, third only to London and Southampton, was called Bishop's Lynn throughout the medieval period as it belonged to the bishops of Norwich. The Saturday market was established c1100 beside the huge church of St Margaret, next to a Benedictine priory. This lies near the west end of the original narrow borough which was enclosed on the north by the Purfleet and on the south by the Millfleet. From St Margaret's the High Street runs north to the site of the later Tuesday market, established c1150-70 beside St Nicholas, which was originally just a chapel of ease, although huge. South Lynn beyond the Millfleet was a suburb with its own church of All Saints. A warehouse of the merchants of the Hanseatic league still survives, along with a 15th century guild hall. Friaries of the Carmelites and Franciscans lay at the south end, of the Dominicans on the east side, and of the Augustinians at the north end. A mayor and corporation were established in 1524.

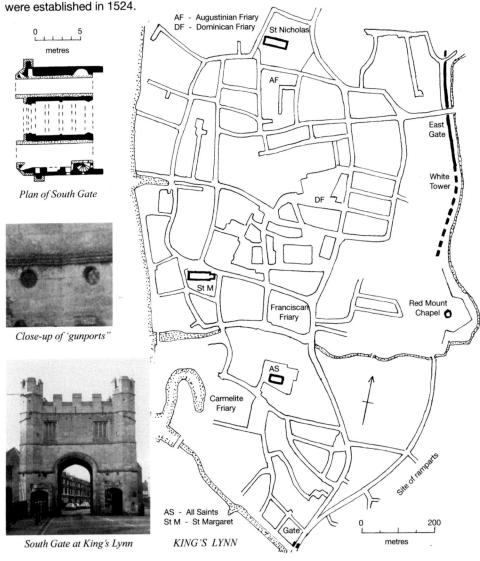

0   5
metres

Plan of South Gate

Close-up of 'gunports'

South Gate at King's Lynn

AF - Augustinian Friary
DF - Dominican Friary

St Nicholas

AF

East Gate

White Tower

DF

Red Mount Chapel

St M

Franciscan Friary

AS

Carmelite Friary

Site of ramparts

AS - All Saints
St M - St Margaret

Gate

0   200
metres

KING'S LYNN

Remains of arcaded town wall at King's Lynn

Murage was first granted after an attack on the town by de Mortfort adherents in 1266 and seems to have resulted in the construction of a rampart and ditch around the north, east and south sides of a huge area 1300m long by 850m wide including all three parishes. Further murage grants in 1294, 1300 and 1334 saw sections of wall built along the east side of New Land (St Nicholas parish). The 1290s saw disagreements between the townsfolk and bishop over the recent creation of sluices for filling ditches with water. Local taxation for work on defences was authorised in 1376 and 1385 and again in 1386 when there is a mention of "guns, springalds (huge crossbows) and other armaments". All townsfolk were required to contribute to a scouring out of the ditches in 1403.

Building of the Alexandra Dock and railway access to it has destroyed any northern barriers, which may anyway have been more to prevent flooding than invasions. A North Gate is first mentioned in 1373 when it was repaired. Walling of 14th century date is first encountered beside Kettlewell Lane. Here a long arcaded section survives facing the River Gaywood. The outer face is up to 3m high but no wall-walk or parapet survives, nor any bastions or turrets, although there are buttresses. The wide variety of material used suggests it was built of ballast taken from ships. Another section of wall in a more defaced condition remains further south on the east side of Wyatt Street. There is then a wide gap for the railway and there is uncertainty as to whether the next section of rampart was ever walled. Here lies the Red Mount which has the shape of a mid 16th century artillery bastion but must be older since it bears an octagonal brick pilgrimage chapel of c1485-90. Further south short sections of wall adjoin the Guanock Gate, a folly arch built of old parts of a two storey structure with four polygonal corner turrets. Small sums were spent on repairing a still older gate here in 1331.

From East Gate the town ditch at least (there is no evidence of a wall in this section around South Lynn) continued south and then turned SW down Guanock Terrace. Straddling the road to London is the South Gate begun c1416 by the London mason Robert Hertanger. The job was completed more cheaply by another mason after the money ran out, the passage having a simple barrel-vault on cross-ribs instead of the tierceron-ribbed vault that was intended. A previous gateway on this site was provided with a new key in 1335. The ashlar facing of the south front with polygonal corner turrets was added in the 1520s. In the 19th century pedestrianways were broken through the two narrow rooms flanking the passage, which has a portcullis groove. An upper room with pairs of three-light windows on either side is reached by a spiral staircase in the NE corner. Six circular openings on the upper level have been described as gunports, although no cannon could ever have been mounted behind them and they are too big for the use of hand fire-arms. The River Nar seems to have provided enough protection for the next section past the Carmelite friary and the quays had only water-gates.

KINGSTON-UPON-HULL   Humberside

The Kingston part of the name refers to Edward I, who purchased a village then called Wyke from the Cistercian monks of Meaux in 1293 and then laid out a new town, giving it a charter under the new name in 1299. This explains why the parish church of Holy Trinity ranked only as a chapel-of-ease until 1661 even though it is the largest medieval church in England not of cathedral, minster or abbey status. A second medieval church at St Mary Lowgate also only ranked as a chapel-of-ease. Aided by such royal patronage the port became very prosperous, soon acquiring a merchant guild and friaries of the Augustinians, Carmelites and Franciscans, although the latter was short-lived. Probably the port was intended as a naval base for royal expeditions in Scotland, being sufficiently far south to be fairly safe from retaliatory Scottish raiding parties.

Murage and a licence for a town wall were granted in 1321 and accounts for the next two years show expenditure of £110 on a rampart and ditch, £142 on timber and £40 on stone and brick. The licence mentions a wall of stone and lime but in fact the wall and gates were built of bricks made locally at a works owned by the de la Pole family, one of whom became the town's first mayor. In 1332 the young Edward III was said to be pleased with the new wall and in 1333 there is mention of a wall facing the Humber. The east side by the River Hull was left open. For further works a five year murage grant was made in 1341, a seven year grant in 1348 and a sixteen year grant in 1355. The only visible part of the wall is the brick base of the NE facing Beverley Gate revealed by excavations in 1985-6. The line of a considerable part of the wall further south is marked out in modern paving beside Princes Dock Street, showing it to be 1m thick and flanked by alternate square and circular towers. The wall was also backed by an earth rampart, the enclosed area being about 800m north-south by 550m wide. Docks along the west side of the town centre replace former wet moats. Excavations behind Hull College in North Walls have revealed part of a second main gateway. From it the wall passed down the NW side of Guildhall Street, passing another gate on the way to Beverley Gate. A fourth gate lay further south on the west side and there were also four posterns.

Footings of the Beverley Gate at Kingston-upon-Hull

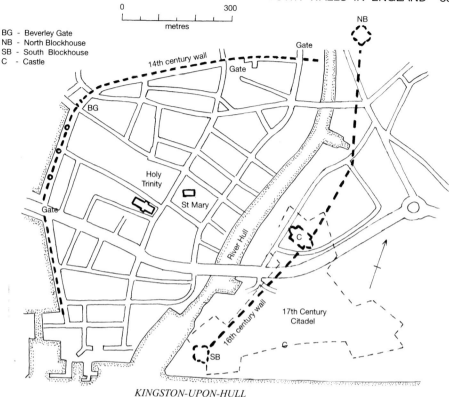

BG - Beverley Gate
NB - North Blockhouse
SB - South Blockhouse
C - Castle

0 300
metres

14th century wall

16th century wall

17th Century Citadel

River Hull

Holy Trinity

St Mary

KINGSTON-UPON-HULL

After the Pilgrimage of Grace of 1536, when Kingston-upon-Hull was occupied by rebels in protest against the closure of monastic houses, Henry VIII set about improving the defences of the town. A substantial new brick wall 3m thick was built to the east of the River Hull, thus protecting the anchorage. This wall had a quatrefoil-shaped blockhouse at either end and a central castle about 45m square externally with large bastions projecting east and west, parts of which have been excavated, the layout being clearly shown on John Speed's map of 1610. The castle had east and west bastions with beaks and accommodation in a central rectangular building isolated within the court.

The closure of the gates against Charles I by Sir John Hotham in April 1642 resulted in the first military action of the Civil War. The Royalists besieged the town throughout July that year but the attackers were kept at bay by the deliberate flooding of the landward approaches to the town and severely harassed by sallies by the garrison. During the siege the northern blockhouse of the Henrican defences was damaged by an accidental exploding of a magazine. Remains of it survived until 1802. The castle and southern blockhouse were incorporated into two bastions of a large triangular citadel of the 1680s which survived until 1864. By then the medieval walls had all been removed to make way for improvements to the port facilities, the moats becoming docks.

*Kingston-upon-Hull:
wall footings*

LANCASTER   Lancashire

A modest earthwork in Vicarage Field is thought to be a rampart created after the only known grant of murage in 1316. It appears that an attempt was made to build a town wall using material taken from a former Roman fort. Despite attacks by the Scots in 1323 and 1389 no effort was made to complete the town defences, although considerable work was done on the castle, which housed the county courts and gaol until recently. The castle lies on an eminence within the former Roman defences which do seem to have been used or maintained in the Saxon and later periods. Immediately north of the castle is a large priory church, now a cathedral, which served both Benedictine monks and the townsfolk. A Dominican friary in the town is evidence of 13th century prosperity. As a whole towns in Lancashire were noticeably lacking in either defences or friaries.

LANGPORT   Somerset

Langport was one of King Alfred's Burghal Hidage towns and retains a long length of rampart on the NE side, other sides being protected by the River Parret and marshes. The town had 34 burgesses at the time of the Domesday survey of 1086 and produced the then quite large annual taxation income of £79, suggesting a prosperous community. The man-made defences just enclosed the more elevated eastern part of the town, now hardly more than a large village, where the church lies. East of the church is a 14th century town gateway with a rib-vaulted passage lacking either a door rebate or a portcullis groove. It supports a room known as the Hanging Chapel since executions of rebels were held here in 1685. It is first mentioned as a guild chapel in 1344 but saw other uses later, being the town hall in 1570, and a grammar school in the 18th century. The lower and younger part of the town in Bow Street, a former causeway, was fired by retreating Royalist cavalry in 1645. There are traces of a possible rampart of that period to the NE of the town.

NG - North Gate
SG - South Gate
WG - West Gate

LAUNCESTON

0   200

metres

2nd Storey

0   5

Launceston
South Gate plans

Civil War Ramparts

Saxon Burgh

Medieval Extension

Gate

Church

River Parret

LANGPORT

Town gateway at Langport from the west

The South Gate at Launceston

LAUNCESTON   Cornwall

The name Launceston originally applied to the village further north with the church of St Stephen and the walled town containing what was originally a chapel-of-ease of St Mary Magdalene (now a spectacular early 16th century church) was known as Dunheved. No murage grants for the walls are recorded and they were probably built during the time of Henry III's brother Richard, when Dunheved with its major castle formed the main seat of his earldom of Cornwall. After the mid 14th century the castle served only as a shire court and county prison, Launceston being the county town until 1835 despite its increasingly inconvenient position for administration at the far east end of Cornwall. The nearly complete set of town records only contain occasional references to minor expenditure on the gates. The walls were said by Leland c1540 to be high, strong and well set but ruinous. They were later described as 6' thick and 6 furlongs in length.

The South Gate is a square structure of the late 13th or early 14th century with two low upper rooms over a chamfered-ribbed passageway, with buttresses flanking an outer archway with evidence of a portcullis groove. The three-light upper windows are 17th century and the parapet is of 1887 when a pedestrian passage was driven through the short length of wall to the east. The upper rooms had fireplaces on the east side and were reached from the west side. They were used as a prison for debtors and petty offenders until the early 19th century despite the lower of the two rooms having doorways out onto the main wall-walk. See picture on page 21.

From South Gate the wall followed the north side of Madford Lane, where one small fragment 2.3m high remains embedded in a building, round to the site of the West Gate. A fragment of walling found by the Cornwall Archeological Unit shows that the line of wall between the West Gate and the castle SE corner was not straight but bowed slightly to the east in the middle. The south and west walls of the castle formed part of the circuit. Beyond the north gate of the castle a section of clay-mortared town wall was found by an excavation in the grounds of the Eagle Hotel. Beyond it lay the North Gate, facing a narrow medieval bridge over the River Kensey. On the NE and SE sides of the town the wall followed Dockacre Road and Angel Hill back to the South Gate.

LEICESTER   Leicestershire

Excavation evidence has confirmed Matthew Paris' account of parts of the Roman walls (with rather meagre foundations) being undermined as part of the slighting ordered by Henry II after his capture of Leicester in 1173. This followed the Earl of Leicester having sided with the rebel princes. A 30m length of 3m thick footings of the Roman west wall facing the River Soar has been found in Bath Lane in conjunction with a kiln last used in the mid 3rd century. This section may have remained standing until the defences fell into ruin in the 16th century. A shorter section of Roman walling has been found of the north wall in Sanvey Gate. Murage grants of 1286, 1293 and 1316 tell of the later rebuilding of the defences and there are records of later leases of towers and gateway upper rooms as proof of substantial defensive works existing in the late medieval period. Leicester was a place of importance between the Roman and medieval periods, being one of the Five Boroughs of the Danelaw in the 9th century.

The medieval defences enclosed an area about 600m wide by 750m long from north to south and mostly followed the Roman lines. The motte and hall of the castle lie in the SW corner with the church of St Mary de Castro and the gateway which opened into the Newark, a later medieval southerly extension of the castle precinct. Further north lies the church of St Nicholas overlooking a set of Roman Baths with one high standing fragment of adjacent Roman walling. The church of All Saints lies just south of the former north gate and the church of St Martin, now a cathedral, stands just south of the middle of the town. Another major medieval church, that of St Margaret, lies just outside the NE corner of the walled area.

Town wall near the castle at Lewes

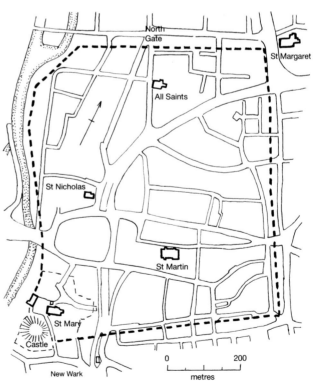

LEICESTER

LEWES   East Sussex

Set in a gap in the South Downs, and forming the county town of Sussex, Lewes was a place of importance in Saxon times, having a mint in the time of King Athelstan and a merchant guild as early as c1140. The Burghal Hidage assigns 1300 hides for maintaining its defences. In the 1070s Lewes became the administrative centre of William de Warrene's lordship, later the earldom of Surrey. His original motte south of the station soon became part of the precinct of a Cluniac priory and was succeeded by a stone walled castle with two mottes lying on the NW side of the town. Excavations on the west side of the town, which is roughly triangular with the SW and northern corners cut off, found evidence of a Saxon rampart fronted by a medieval stone wall. The Saxon burgh defences probably only went as far east as St Nicholas Lane. In addition to the surviving church of St Michael with a circular west tower, High Street once had three other churches, St Nicholas, St Mary-in-Foro, and St Peter the Less which existed before the castle took up most of the space north of the High Street. The School Hill area further east was more densely settled in the 12th century, having at either end former churches of St Nicholas and Holy Trinity. St Anne's served a suburb outside the west walls.

From the northern motte of the castle the wall went alongside Abinger Place and round the churchyard of St John sub Castle, east of which lay the North Gate. Green Wall may perpetuate the name of what was a rampart rather than a stone wall. It continued down Eastgate Street to the site of the East Gate at the end of School Hill which faced towards a bridge over the River Ouse. The defences then curved round following Friars Walk, named after a Franciscan friary beyond the walls here, to pass along the south side of All Saints Church. A wall continued westwards along the south side of Lansdown Road and Southover Road, and then along the north side of Town Wall. Just east of Keere Street are remains of the wall heading north towards the West Gate. This building had a pair of D-shaped towers 7.5m in diameter flanking a passage 3m wide and 5.5m long. Each tower had a doorway close to the east arch of the passage leading into a room with three loops in the outer part, which was polygonal internally, and a passage to a latrine within the main wall. Part of the northern tower lies hidden within the Freemasons' Hall of 1868 and part of the back of the south tower lies west of the Bull Inn beside the entrance passage to a chapel of c1700 behind the inn.

From the gate the wall went north another 90m, then headed NE to join the NW side of the castle, which has lost its stone wall.

Murage was granted in 1266, just two years after Henry III's defeat and capture by Simon de Montfort in the battle of Lewes, following which de Montfort's forces entered the town without resistance. The West Gate and the adjoining lengths of wall were presumably under construction in 1275 when there is a reference to the knights' fees of John de Warenne's earldom of Surrey being taxed to help pay for the work. Another grant of murage is recorded in 1334.

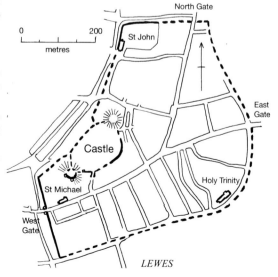

LINCOLN   Lincolnshire

A 40 acre Roman fort to house the Ninth Legion Hispana was built cAD60 just north of where the River Witham flows through a gap in the Wolds. Excavations showed the fort had a ditch and an earth rampart revetted with timber both internally and externally with wooden towers at regular intervals. The Second Legion Adiutrix was here from AD 71-8 when it moved to Chester. Eventually a self-governing colonia, one of just four in Britain, took over the fort and adapted it as a town. By the early 2nd century the rampart had been fronted by a stone wall 1.5m thick and the double-carriageway gateways facing the four cardinal points rebuilt in stone. The built up area soon extended southwards down the steep slope to the river. By the end of the 2nd century this area was also enclosed with a stone wall against the inner face of which towers were added in the 3rd century. Excavations have revealed the bases of single-carriageway gateways built in the 4th century from huge stone blocks from older buildings, one facing west lying just east of Orchard Street and the other (no longer visible) in Saltergate facing the river.

The town became largely depopulated after the Romans departed in the early 5th century but the discovery of a church probably of 5th or 6th century date at the junction of Bailgate and Westgate proves some level of occupation. In 628 St Paulinus came south from York to convert the settlement leaders to Roman Christianity. The Danes took over Lincoln in the 9th century and it became one of their Five Boroughs. With a long surburb extending on flat ground south of the river, Lincoln had become one of the largest towns in Britain at the time of the Norman Conquest, with a population estimated at 7,000. By the 13th century the walled areas and suburbs had nearly fifty parish churches, reduced to fifteen by the mid 16th century. No medieval churches now remain unrebuilt within the walls. There were numerous hospitals and five friaries, but only the Franciscans and Friars of the Sack lived within the walls, both in the SE corner. Two 12th century merchants' houses survive beside Steep Hill, and Deloraine Court in The Bail and St Mary's Guild Hall in the High Street are also 12th century buildings. As a trading centre Lincoln declined in favour of its port at Boston in the late medieval period, but it has quite a number of houses surviving from that era, most of them timber-framed.

The Roman Newport Gate at Lincoln

The west gate of the lower town at Lincoln

In 1068 The Bail or area of the original Roman fort on the hilltop was taken over as a huge royal castle with a large motte raised over the SW corner, no less than 166 houses then being removed from this district. The SE corner of The Bail was taken up by a new cathedral begun by Bishop Remegius in the 1070s, after the huge and wealthy see covering nine counties was moved here from Dorchester. The new cathedral had a large defensible block forming its western end. The existing castle bailey was probably only enclosed c1100-30, following which Bishop Alexander was allowed to adapt the East Gate of the Bail as his residence. The second motte may be a still later addition to allow the Earl of Chester a power base in the city overlooking an open space between the castle and cathedral. Lincoln played a major part in the wars of King Stephen's reign. Here in 1141 he was caught in a pincer movement between the castle garrison and a relief force, being defeated and held captive until ransomed several months later. As in other shire-towns in the later medieval period the castle was only sufficiently kept up to provide a county courthouse and prison. The Bail remained a separate administrative area until 1836, and to this day contains few houses and hardly any trading premises.

In 1137 King Stephen allowed the bishop to transfer his residence to a more private location on land extending beyond the south wall of the Bail, although a new palace may not actually have been built until the 1150s. This started the process of closing off the whole of the SE corner of the Bail and land beyond it to the east as a cathedral precinct with its own walls and gates. This process seems to have been mostly complete by 1327, royal licences for crenellating the precinct walls being issued in 1285 and 1316-18. The courtyard of the bishop's palace also had crenellated walls licensed in 1329.

Frequent grants for murage to maintain the wall of the lower city are recorded between 1225 and the early 14th century. In 1274 jurors reported that the collectors of the murage tax had profited from selling stone purchased for work upon the walls. They were probably ruinous by the Civil War period, when the castle was stormed by Parliamentary forces in 1644, and the bishop's palace was attacked in 1648, but no attempt appears to have been made to fortify or hold the either the Bail or the lower walled city. Whilst the castle and cathedral precinct still have medieval walls most of what remains of city walling which was the responsibility of the burgesses is in fact Roman rather than medieval, except for one southern gatehouse lacking any military character.

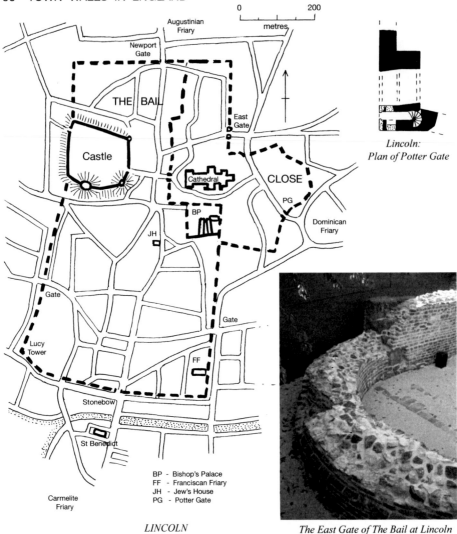

Lincoln:
Plan of Potter Gate

LINCOLN

The East Gate of The Bail at Lincoln

BP - Bishop's Palace
FF - Franciscan Friary
JH - Jew's House
PG - Potter Gate

The obvious place to start a tour of the walled area is the gateway known as the Stonebow across the High Street not far from the river. On the site of a Roman gate, and now of c1480-1520, the building lacks any defensive features and has pedestrianways on either side of a carriageway with four-centred arches. The room above is a guildhall. An adjacent block was used as a prison until 1809. From here the wall continued along the north side of Saltergate and St Swithins Road and headed north along the west side of Broadgate to pass just east of the Franciscan friary and climb the hill up to the bishops' palace. Of the part of the cathedral precinct projecting over 200m beyond the east wall of the former Roman fort, the principal remnant (other than hidden-away sections of wall) is Potter Gate, a restoration of the 1880s of a 14th century structure originally at a re-entrant angle but now isolated. A stair on the west side leads to a small upper room from which a portcullis was operated. The Priory Gate near the cathedral chapter-house is a folly archway of 1816 built from old materials.

Pottergate at Lincoln Cathedral Close

The Stonebow or south gateway at Lincoln

North of the cathedral lie the lower parts of the north tower of the Roman East Gate, a large structure with U-shaped towers either side of twin carriageways. In the 1130s this building was remodelled to briefly serve as the bishops palace until they transferred to a new palace in a more secluded location south of the cathedral. From the East Gate the wall continued north just east of East Bight, where a fragment remains with part of one of the Roman internal towers. The NE corner of the wall is missing but a more accessible section of the north wall remains in a park between East Bight and Church Lane.

The North Gate was similar in layout to the East Gate with towers set on either side of two carriageways. Part of the base of the western tower remains. The Newport arch is actually the inner arch of the eastern carriageway, and is the only Roman archway in Britain over a road still bearing vehicular traffic. The arch required rebuilding a few years ago after a lorry got stuck underneath it (the present road level being above that of Roman times). A section of wall further west lies behind a house in Cecil Street. The Roman West Gate is buried under the rampart and wall at the NW corner of the castle. The west and south sides of the castle lie more or less above the walls of the Roman fort, part of the south gate of which survives within the houses of nos 26 and 27 Steep Hill.

The west wall of Lower Town descended down the west side of Motherby Hill and then lay to the east of Orchard Street where there are substantial remains of another Roman gatehouse. The Roman wall turned a corner to travel east along the north side of Newland and Guildhall Street back to the Stonebow, but a new section of vanished medieval wall extended another 100m or so southwards from the corner to the riverbank.

Six medieval churches (three of them with Saxon west towers) survive in the suburb of Wigford extending for a mile southwards to where there was once a stone wall with a central gateway. Water features and earthworks protected the other two sides.

LONDON

Shortly after the Roman invasion of AD43 the River Thames was first bridged just above what was then the tidal limit. The town of Londinium quickly grew up by the northern bridgehead to be one of the largest conurbations in Britain by AD60, when Boudicca rebelled and destroyed it. Afterwards it soon outgrew the original core based around where Lombard Street and Fenchurch Street now are. Evidence of a huge public building straddling the north end of Gracechurch Street suggests London had attained local self-government status as a colonae or municipium by the end of the 1st century whilst there was a an enormous palace, possibly for the provincial governor, about where Cannon Street station now stands in the middle of the south side, immediately west of the Walbrook (now covered over), beyond which were public baths.

In the early 2nd century a fort was built in the NW corner, probably more for use as a barracks and transit camp than as a mighty fortress. In AD195 Clodius Albinus, then governor of Britain, drained the country of troops in an unsuccessful attempt to become emperor of Rome. It was either then or shortly afterwards that a wall 2.4m thick above its plinth and up to 5m high to its wall-walk was built to enclose an enormous area about 1700m long by 800m wide, one and a half times the size of Cirencester, the next largest Roman town in Britain, and only exceeded in size by four towns in Gaul. Right up to the mid 17th century Civil War period London remained by far the largest walled town in Britain. Of the six original Roman gateways Aldgate straddled the road leading NE out to Colchester, Bishopsgate closed Ermine Street leading north to Lincoln and York, New Gate faced the road to Silchester and the west, with Ludgate between it and the Thames. Aldersgate seems to have been a slightly later insertion to replace a former west gate of the smaller and older fort. It faced north from the narrower western part of the city, probably with a road out towards St Albans. Cripplegate never faced a major road and was simply the northern gateway of the older fort left open.

The former Cripplegate in London

Wall and bastion on north side of London Wall Road

The Saxons are thought to have originally mainly occupied the district between the western walls and Trafalgar Square rather than inside the walled area. Danish forces sacked the city in 842 and 851 and stayed in London over the winter of 870-1. King Alfred is thought to have repaired the walls after capturing the city from the Danes in 886. London was successfully held against the Danish leader Sweyn Forkbeard in 994, although he eventually occupied the city in 1013. Recovered by the Saxons it then withstood a siege by Sweyn's successor Cnut until relieved by Edmund Ironside. Cnut

Postern gate tower on Tower Hill in London

only obtained possession of London after Edmund was eventually defeated. Winchester had been the Saxon capital city but London assumed at least part of that role after the penultimate Saxon king Edward the Confessor built the palace and Benedictine abbey of Westminster a short distance further up the river in the 1040s. Duke William of Normandy's movements after his victory at Hastings in 1066 make it clear that London was then regarded as the capital of England and had to be taken and held at all costs.

St Paul's Cathedral was founded in the western part of the city in 604 although this early flourishing of Christianity here may have been short-lived since the next king was a pagan. There were eventually about ninety churches and chapels within the walls serving a population of about 40,000 by AD1300, whilst a similar number lived outside the walls. In spite of some losses due to war-time bombing over thirty churches still remain at least in part within the walls. Most of them were rebuilt after the Great Fire of 1666 and Saxon and Norman work only remains at All Hallows Barking. This church lies just west of the SE corner occupied by the Tower of London, named after William I's great keep of c1078-87, later surrounded by Henry III and Edward I's concentric lines of towered walls. The inner ward between the keep and the river used the Roman wall on its east side, although not much now remains of that section apart from footings of a solid Late Roman bastion, one of several added on this side. By the end of the 13th century Dominican and Franciscan friars were occupying the SW and NW corners of the walled area, the Carmelite friars had a house just outside Ludgate, Crutched Friars and Franciscan nuns had houses between Aldgate and the Tower and Augustinian friars had a house on the north side of the walled city. Part of the nave of the Augustinian friary remained in use by Dutch Protestants until bombed in the 1940s. Another church with medieval work still remaining is St Helen's, a former Benedictine nunnery.

Bastions near St Giles Church in London.

A new stone bridge across the Thames was built in 1176. King John donated funds for work on the walls of London in 1215 and allowed stone to be taken from the houses of Jews who occupied an area within the walls just NW of Aldgate until Edward I expelled them in 1290. Murage for maintaining the walls was first granted by Henry III in 1233 and continued until the early 14th century, the old Roman walls then being doubled in height and provided with several new bastions. Some of the gatehouses later served as prisons, particularly Newgate and Ludgate. All of them were rebuilt in the 17th century, and on old prints mostly appear as three storey structures each with a central passage closed by a portcullis and a pair of pedestrian side-passages. No attempt was made to defend the city of London (or the Tower) against the rebel peasants in 1381.

A tour of the walls of London starts on Tower Hill where the lower parts of an ashlar-faced rectangular tower of c1300 are on show below a pedestrianway. Lying with a slight lean northwards, the tower measures about 8m by 6.5m. The second level had two loops facing east and NE from the same embrasure, the NE corner being chamfered off beyond a portcullis groove closing a passageway with a dog-leg layout. Only the base remains of a turret on the NW corner probably containing a spiral staircase.

Not far to the north, just east of the entrance to Tower Hill underground station, is a good 35m long section of wall standing about 9m high, the upper half being medieval. Further north is a long section off Cooper's Row. Here the Roman work 4m high lies mostly below the present ground level inside the wall. About 40m of the wall stands high with a medieval upper part retaining part of the parapet and embrasures for windows and loopholes. None of the three bastions along this side remain. The wall then ran along the east side of Jewry Street to Aldgate, rebuilt in 1108-47 and again in 1215, ending up as a twin round-towered structure in which the poet Geoffrey Chaucer lodged when serving as a customs official between 1374 and 1386. The gate was rebuilt in 1606-9 and demolished in 1761. An Augustinian priory of Holy Trinity lay just outside the gate.

A length of the eastern part of the London wall in Coopers Row

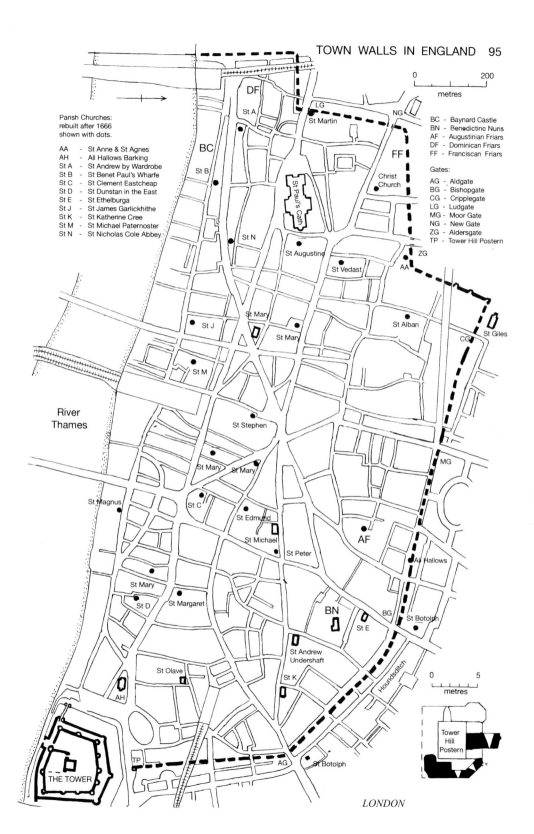

Parish Churches:
rebuilt after 1666
shown with dots.

AA - St Anne & St Agnes
AH - All Hallows Barking
St A - St Andrew by Wardrobe
St B - St Benet Paul's Wharfe
St C - St Clement Eastcheap
St D - St Dunstan in the East
St E - St Ethelburga
St J - St James Garlickhithe
St K - St Katherine Cree
St M - St Michael Paternoster
St N - St Nicholas Cole Abbey

BC - Baynard Castle
BN - Benedictine Nuns
AF - Augustinian Friars
DF - Dominican Friars
FF - Franciscan Friars

Gates:

AG - Aldgate
BG - Bishopgate
CG - Cripplegate
LG - Ludgate
MG - Moor Gate
NG - New Gate
ZG - Aldersgate
TP - Tower Hill Postern

River Thames

THE TOWER

Tower Hill Postern

LONDON

Section of the London wall on the north side of the churchyard of St Alphege

From Aldgate the wall ran along Duke's Place and Bevis Marks, parallel to which is Houndsditch, commemorating a custom of throwing dead dogs and other refuse into the ditch outside the wall here. This section once had five flanking bastions. Bishopsgate was rebuilt at the expense of the Hansa merchants in 1471 in return for Steelyard privileges. It was remodelled just twenty-five years before being demolished in 1760. Beyond Bishopsgate the wall continued along the north side of Wormwood Street, where there was another bastion. The church of All Hallows has a vestry (hidden from public view) which is built on the base of a bastion 5.7m in diameter projecting 4.7m beyond the main wall. West of the church is a much restored and reduced length of the wall. Beyond here the street is called London Wall and extends for 900m, although the western end bends round away from its original course behind the wall and is now a wide new road. The bending round occurs just west of the site of Moorgate, an addition of 1415 to the wall, replacing a 13th century postern just west of it. The gate was remodelled in the late 15th century, rebuilt in 1672, and demolished in 1762.

A good length of the wall remains on the north site of the churchyard of the former church of St Alphege between London Wall and Fore Street. The churchyard is at a rather higher level than the Roman base of the wall facing a sunken garden. Above is thinner 13th to 14th century work and then on top is a short section of a brick parapet built in 1476 under Lord Mayor Sir Ralph Jocelyn. The outer face of the Roman work is part of the 1.2m thick wall of the early 2nd century fort measuring about 270m by 220m. It was thickened internally when the 12 acre fort became part of the 330 acre walled city. West of here lay the Cripplegate. It was rebuilt in 1244 by the Brewers' Company, remodelled in 1491 and in 1663, and demolished in 1760. The area beyond it was known as the Barbican from an outwork in front of the gateway.

Recent redevelopment and landscaping following wartime bombing of London has provided a wide wet moat around the NW corner of the former fort. Excavation in 1966 of a bastion between Cripplegate and the corner proved that it was a 13th century addition. The wall once formed the southern boundary of the churchyard of St Giles outside the wall and has itself almost gone, but a round medieval bastion remains on the corner. South of here, down the west side of the former fort, brick ruins of post medieval date lie on the site of the wall in a public garden. After 45m there is the lower part of another bastion 8.5m in external diameter over walling 1.5m thick. A similar interval divides it from a third bastion just north of London Wall Road. This one stands 9m high externally and has been much altered internally, although traces of former original loops can be seen outside. In a car-park under the road to the south lies the northern carrageway of the fort west gateway with a guard room on the north side and two piers facing towards where the southern carriageway once lay. The base of the whole southern half of the west wall of the former fort lies in a sunk garden west of Noble Street. Most of the wall superstructure here is post-medieval. This length ends with the curved SW corner of the former fort with footings of its original square internal tower.

From here the wall went west, making a re-entrant angle with the older wall of the original fort. Almost immediately was Aldersgate, rebuilt in 1617, and repaired in 1670. Then the wall passed round the large precinct of the Franciscan friary, the church of which was the largest of any friary in Britain, and along to New Gate, where the Roman layout of two carriageways flanked by square guard-rooms is known from excavations. Newgate was taller than the other gates, with four storeys. It became notorious as a prison, surviving until 1767. Ludgate was rebuilt in 1215, 1450, and 1586. It was remodelled c1670 and demolished in 1760. It too was a prison, usually for freemen and clergy who had got into debt and were allowed to exercise upon the flat lead roof. Between Aldersgate and a NW corner bastion were three more intermediate bastions. There were two more between Newgate and Ludgate, and another four on the last length of wall as it extended further west round the precinct of the Dominican friary to the river bank. Within this precinct, located at the original SW corner of the Roman walled city stood Montfichet Tower, a fortress which existed by the 1130s but was probably dismantled just before or after the Dominicans took possession of the site in the 1270s.

There was no proper wall along the river bank, which in Roman times lay further north along the line of the south side of Thames Street. Documents suggest there was provision for wooden hoarding on the wharves and that there were watergates with some sort of defences between high-walled properties facing the river, including many warehouses. The Mermaid Theatre south of the cathedral stands on the site of Baynard's Castle, a late medieval palace on the site of an 11th century fortress.

Corner bastion near St Giles' Church in London

LUDLOW   Shropshire

This is a classic example of a planned town, laid out beside the stone castle of the de Lacys on a virgin site which formed part of the manor of Stanton Lacy at the time of Domesday. However it has been suggested that the castle outer bailey is a late 12th century addition which took over part of the original town. The layout is a rectangle of 400m by 300m with slopes down to the River Teme on the west and south sides, whilst the north side faces where the River Corve 400m away flows west to join the Teme. The castle fills the NW corner where the natural fall of the ground is steepest, and the large parish church lies near the north side. Several houses around the churchyard area have medieval stone basements. Two friaries lay outside the walls, the Carmelites to the north and the Augustinians to the east. Murage was first granted in 1233 and the walls are generally assumed to have been completed by the early 14th century. In 1459 the Duke of York fled from his base at Ludlow after the marshal of his forces deserted to the approaching Lancastrians, who then plundered the town and castle. In 1472 York's son Edward IV set up the Council of the Marches based at Ludlow which survived until 1689, when the castle was abandoned. Here in 1501 died Prince Arthur, eldest son of Henry VII, sent here as a figurehead for the Council of the Marches. No attempt was made to hold the town in the 1640s, but Royalists in the castle held out until July 1646.

Much of the town wall still survives although some sections have been rebuilt and others are no longer very high. Most of it was a retaining wall rather than free-standing. A late 12th century chapel of St Thomas Becket lies near where a minor fragment of the Dinham Gate survives facing west, to the south of the castle. A section of low wall hidden away in private gardens leads around the curved SW corner and past one D-shaped tower to the site of Mill Street Gate. Further east is Broad Gate, a structure with two D-shaped towers 6.2m wide flanking a passage with a portcullis groove and a ceiling with beams which are ancient but probably re-used from elsewhere. The two upper storeys and embattled northern side are mostly 18th century work. A wing of that period totally obscures the western tower, but the second and third levels of the eastern tower still each have one original loop facing south through the rendering. This gate faces down towards the 15th century Ludford bridge, near which are remains of St John's Hospital.

Broad Gate at Ludlow

Wall below the churchyard at Ludlow

Site of Dinham Gate at Ludlow

East of Broad Gate there is a section where the outer face of the wall is accessible to the public, although it is much reduced and rebuilt and has later arches in front of part of it. Old Gate was another twin-towered gateway, the eastern tower of which survived until the 1820s. The wall then went round a corner and headed NW. Initially the only relic of it is a much altered three storey rectangular tower incorporated into a house hidden away in a new estate. East of here lay the Augustinian friary. Further north walling can be glimpsed through a gateway just south of the site of Galdeford Gate. The wall then rounded a corner to arrive at a gate across Corve Street. Beyond there lay the Carmelite friary. The northern walls still rise 4.5m to a level top. They pass the churchyard and also can be glimpsed from a narrow lane below them. The section west of the site of Linney Gate has been repaired recently and the top is accessible since it forms the boundary of a large public car-park. Parts of it are built upon low rock outcrops. The gap just NE of the castle outer bailey is the likely site of a former postern.

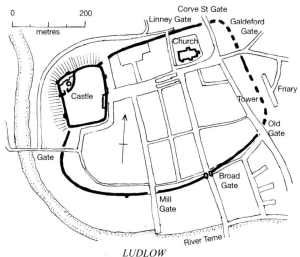

LUDLOW

Tower altered into a house at Ludlow

LYDFORD   Devon

Lying on the west side of Dartmoor, Lydford is a rare instance of a Saxon burgh which has neither been entirely abandoned nor overdeveloped in later times. Some of the side-streets are still unsurfaced. The village lies on a promontory about 320m long by 220m wide with steep drops to the gorge of the River Lyd on the south side and to a tributary stream on the west and north sides. Here lay a Saxon town defended on the naturally weak NE side by a rampart which was later given an external stone revetment. Excavations have shown the Saxon bank originally continued around the whole perimeter of the promontory. Lydford had a royal mint by the late 10th century and was recorded as one of five towns in Devon in Domesday Book in 1086. It remained a royal borough until transferred to the earldom of Cornwall in 1239. Earl Richard obtained a market and fair for the town in 1267, but it must have rapidly declined in the 14th century. By 1795 there were only "wretched remains" and "a few hovels" of the former town buildings.

At the west end of the village is an 11th century ringwork. East of it lies the parish church. Further east still is a keep-like building built in the mid 13th century on a basement of 1195 later buried in a mound. It contained the courtroom and prison of the Stannary Court which administered the tin-mining districts of Devon until abandoned in the late 17th century. Ramparts and ditches enclosed a bailey between the courthouse and the town perimeter.

LYNG   Somerset

Beside the church of this small village set on a low ridge by the Somerset Levels are traces of the western rampart and ditch of a burgh mentioned in the 9th century Anglo-Saxon Chronicle and in the Burghal Hidage. The other three sides were defended by natural scarps up to 2.5m high above marshland across which was a causeway to Athelney to the east.

0   200
metres

SP - Stannary Prison

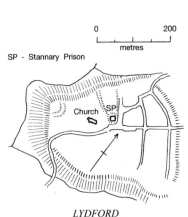

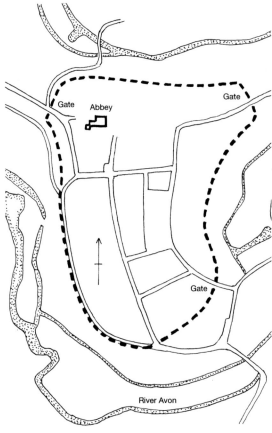

LYDFORD   *MALMESBURY*

MALMESBURY   Wiltshire

The system for responsibility of maintenance of the Saxon defences was recorded in the 13th century. Domesday Book records Malmesbury as a royal borough in 1086. Steep slopes to the River Avon protected the west and south sides of the town and a tributary flows round the north and east sides, leaving the NW corner as the only approach not across water. Here, within the precinct of the great Benedictine abbey founded in the 7th century, lay the motte erected by Bishop Roger of Sarum in defiance of King Stephen, who attacked the town in 1139. Bishop Roger is thought to have also enlarged the area of the town defences. At least some of the new work was a stone wall which survives as footings and rebuilt portions, mainly in Nun's walk on the east side, where part of the NE gateway remains. A garden wall by Abbey House overlies the north wall base. A street on the SW side is called King's Wall. Other gates faced the bridge to the SE and NW beside the abbey, whose church remains partly in use. Neither of two other churches of medieval origin remains in use and just one arch remains of the hospital of St John by the river. The town centre has a fine market cross of c1500.

MANCHESTER

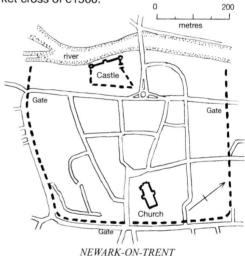

The Hanging Ditch connecting the River Irk and River Irwell may be part of the defences of a 10th century burgh lying south of the former Roman fort which was rebuilt with stone walls c200. A medieval bridge crossing the ditch (ie it was still in use then) has been excavated and is now on display in the cathedral visitor centre. The cathedral was a collegiate church when built in the 15th and 16th centuries when Manchester was prosperous from the wool trade. The town had an annual fair by 1223 and a Saturday market. It was granted a charter in 1301.

NEWARK-ON-TRENT

NEWARK-ON-TRENT   Nottinghamshire

There are remains of outer defences and sconces of 1645 and an impressive riverside wall of the castle of the bishops of Lincoln in which King John died in 1216, but the medieval town defences remain elusive. It is thought that Saxon ramparts enclosed an area 500m by 380m going east around Lombard Street from the river, then north along Carter Street to the East Gate, which stood until 1762. The rampart then followed Appletongate and headed west to where the North Gate stood at the point where Bargate Street becomes North Gate Street, and thence back to the river, here called the Devon, but an alternative course of the Trent. A low wall is said to have supplemented at least part of the rampart in the early 14th century, but no murage grants are recorded. It has been suggested that at that time a larger eastern area including Barnbygate and Balderton Gate was included within an outer ditch and rampart. A house of Observant Franciscan friars stood beyond North Gate. A brass in the single huge parish church of St Mary Magdalene on east side hints at the wealth of the local wool merchants, whose guild of the Holy Trinity existed in the 13th century. Domesday Book records 56 burgesses at Newark in 1086. During the Civil War the town resisted several Parliamentary assaults, remaining a Royalist stronghold until surrendered on Charles I's order in 1646.

NEWCASTLE-UPON-TYNE   Tyne & Wear

Hadrian's Wall once passed through the district probably on the alignment of Westgate Street. By the late 2nd century there was a fort here, named Pons Aelius since it guarded a wooden bridge on stone piers forming the lowest crossing-point of the River Tyne, but it was of far less importance than the fort at Corbridge. Although the bridge is assumed to have remained in use during the Saxon period there is no evidence of a major settlement. The town sprung up around a royal castle built in 1080 following considerable and effective resistance by the Northumbrians to Norman rule, both an earl of Northumberland and a bishop of Durham having been successively killed. Henry II rebuilt the castle in stone in the 1170s and granted the town a charter. By 1216 it was important enough to have a mayor and it was granted separate county status in 1400 with its own sheriff. The numerous houses of friars are evidence of prosperity, the Augustinians, Carmelites, Dominicans, Franciscans and Friars of the Sack all having houses within the walls by the end of the 13th century. The Trinitarians arrived in the 14th century, after the Friars of the Sack had been suppressed. There was also a small Benedictine nunnery.

It is likely that a town ditch and rampart existed by the early 12th century. The re-entrant angle of the later western defences now filled by the railway station suggests that the Clayton Street, Grainger Street and Market Street parts of the town represent a later extension beyond an original defensive line roughly following Pudding Chare, High Bridge and Broad Chare, which would have enclosed a D-shaped area 600m by 400m with the castle isolated on the straight south side. This would have included the parish churches of St Nicholas (now a cathedral) and All Saints. The area eventually walled includes the churches of St John and St Andrew and was double the suggested possible original size, being 150 acres with a perimeter of two miles. Lengths and fragments of wall totalling about 500m still remain, plus eight D-shaped towers out of seventeen, but none of the six main gates have survived. Murage was granted almost continuously from 1265 until 1384 after which funds for maintaining the walls seem to have come from other sources. It appears that the basic circuit was completed c1315-8, ie just in time to secure the town from Scottish raids after their victory at Bannockburn in 1314.

The base of the Ever Tower at Newcastle

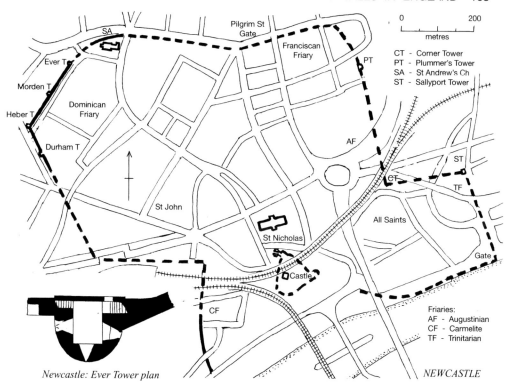

Newcastle: Ever Tower plan   *NEWCASTLE*

The defences of Newcastle were notoriously strong, John Leland being most impressed with them. No invading Scottish army ever captured the town until the Civil War period. In the autumn of 1644 a force under the Earl of Leven finally stormed the defences, which had been broken by undermining and cannonfire during three months of siege. The Royalists had been quick to secure the town at the start of the war because of its value as a port, and especially the coal exporting trade, which was first recorded here c1250 and licensed by the crown a hundred years later. See pages 13 & 15.

The castle is now sadly bisected by a railway viaduct. The wall actually started further east at Sandhill near the head of the medieval bridge which seems to have had a gate-tower on the second free-standing pier from this end. The wall along Quayside appears on the Buck brothers' print of 1745 but seems to have gone by the time of Ralph Beilby's map of 1788 showing the rest of the circuit then still complete. There was an east facing gate at the end of Quayside. From here the wall climbed up the slope, passing west of Milk Market. Remains are first encountered in the form of the Wallknoll or Sallyport Tower which was mostly rebuilt in 1716 to provide a meeting hall for the Ships' Carpenters Company. The wall then dropped down westwards to cross the valley of the Pandon Burn. The Pandon district to the east of the burn, which included premises originally used by Carmelite friars but later used by the Trinitarians, was only taken into the walled area c1300 as an afterthought. This resulted in the next surviving feature, the Corner Tower, where the wall made a re-entrant angle. It is not a true tower as such, just a turret slightly corbelled out, allowing the wall-walk to go through it as a vaulted passageway. Turrets of this type were a common feature of the town walls at Newcastle. Adjoining the angle is a south facing buttress, proved by excavation in 1978 not to be a former continuation of the intended original line of the wall as was once thought.

The turret known as the Corner Tower at Newcastle

Beyond the Corner Tower the wall headed NNW past a tower which existed by 1300 near the Augustinian friary and across the line of the railway and motorway to the Plummer Tower. This tower was rebuilt in 1740 as the meeting place of another trade guild, this time the Company of Masons, but retaining an original double-chamfered plinth like that of the wall itself. The map of 1788 shows this area of the town as open ground both inside and outside the wall. It continued to a corner at the Carliol Tower, which was replaced by the 19th century Central Library. The wall then passed along the south side of New Bridge Street and the site of the Franciscan friary to Pilgrim Street Gate. This building, demolished in 1810, was a square structure with two 18th century windows in the single upper room. The parapet retained one original crossloop with oillets.

There were two towers on the 300m section of wall following the south side of Blackett Street from Pilgrim Street to New Gate. The cutting of a ditch in front of this section is mentioned in 1297. New Gate was a huge block of a building three storeys high which served as the town gaol from 1400 until it was demolished in 1823. Not far west of New Gate Street the north side of St Andrew's churchyard has a section of wall with the back of the Andrew Tower, the rest of which was destroyed c1830. The west end of this section has a corbelled turret backed against a building. Heading SW from across the road west of the churchyard a long section of 2m thick wall standing mostly to wall-walk height begins with the lower part of the Ever Tower. This is the only tower that can be easily inspected internally. A rectangular room 3m wide has a thin back wall projecting slightly from the inner face of the wall. Stairs lead up onto the wall-walk on either side.

The Heber Tower at Newcastle

The three outer sides each have a wide embrasure for a firing loop in the round outer face towards the former ditch. Next comes the Morden Tower with a top storey of c1700 added by the company of Plumbers, Glaziers and Pewterers. Like all the towers along here it is ashlar-faced but not bonded to the main wall, possibly because it was built first. There are three storeys. Beyond lies the best-preserved example of the intermediate turrets still having a stair up from the main wall-walk to the platform over the walkway. There is evidence of rebuilding here, perhaps the result of a grant in 1407. Stepped merlons protect the wall-walk as it rises to pass through the turret in a passage. Behind an outer firing loop is a recess in the back wall to give a bowman enough draw-space.

West wall of Newcastle looking north to Morden Tower

The postern may be that which the Dominican friars were allowed to cut through the wall to access their garden. In 1312 they were licensed to provide a swing-bridge over the newly-cut ditch along this section. At the corner is the Heber Tower, which retains corbels for hoarding externally, good crossloops, a projecting latrine, a double chamfered plinth and a pointed barrel-vault inside. A large window was inserted in 1770-1 by the Company of Armourers, Curriers and Feltmakers. The wall then runs SE to the Durham Tower, with another barrel-vault carried on three arches, and corbels for hoarding. Next came West Gate, another large block of a building which was strengthened in the 1330s when a large barbican with corner turrets was added, resulting in a structure like the gateway at Tynmouth Priory. Within the barbican was a turning bridge mentioned in 1587. Prisoners were kept here in the 16th and 17th centuries and the House Carpenters' Company used it in the 18th century. It was blocked up in 1745, and a footway to one side was only opened up in 1782. The building was demolished c1811-12.

Beyond the West Gate the site of Gunner Tower can be seen in Pink Lane. Coins of Edward I were found under footings of the tower. The wall then went diagonally across where Central Station now is and then headed south. The station stands on the site of the hospital of St Mary, the brethren of which were in 1290 allowed to make a postern in a section of wall then under construction across their land. A long section of wall stands to parapet height beyond Forth Street and parallel with Orchard Street. At the end of this section stood the White Friar Tower, named after a friary here originally used by Friars of the Sack but latterly by the Carmelites or White Friars. This was a very unusual tower, with a circular upper storey on a polygonal base. From here the wall descended steeply (hence the name Breakneck Stairs) to the Close Gate. Footings of another short section of wall from there to a corner tower and then a short length of wall beside the river bank still exist under the piling supporting a new development at this corner. The rest of the river bank back to Sandhill does not seem to have been walled. Invaders landing here would have been trapped and overlooked by the castle and high ground to the west of it. Several late medieval timber-framed merchants houses still survive in The Close.

NORTHAMPTON   Northamptonshire

Excavations east of St Peter's Church have revealed traces of a fine late 7th century hall replaced by one of stone in the 8th century which have been interpreted as evidence of Northampton being a seat of authority at that time. It also seems to have been a major administrative centre under Danish rule in the 10th century and probably became what we would regard as a town at that time. The main intersecting streets would have been Gold Street and Marefair running east-west and Horseshoe Street and Horsemarket running north south. The River Nene would have protected the west and SW sides and defences are assumed to have run north of properties in Bath Street and Silver Street, east of College Street and some way south of Woolmonger Street to enclose an area about 550m by 500m, although excavation evidence for this supposed layout has not been forthcoming. In addition to St Peter's, ranked as a minster in the 11th century, this area also included churches of St Gregory and St Mary, whilst the church of All Saints served an area further east which later became the main market and trading area.

A large castle built by the de Senlis family in the western part of the town was taken over by the Crown in the 1150s. Royal visits were frequent until a fire in 1318 destroyed the apartments, after which it served only the usual shire-town castle functions of court-house and gaol. Parliaments were frequently held in Northampton because of its central position and it was here that Henry II fell out with Archbishop Thomas Becket. The town expanded rapidly mainly it seems from the production of cloth and it had a guildhall in the centre by the mid 12th century. Northampton's taxation value rose from a modest £30 in 1086, when it had about 300 burgesses, to £100 in 1130, and £120 by 1184. By John's reign only Dunwich, Lincoln, London and Winchester had a greater taxation value than Northampton. Royal charters were granted in 1189 and 1200 and a mayor and town council existed by 1215. Five friaries provide further evidence of prosperity, the Dominicans having their modest house squeezed in to the original Saxon town centre. There was also a large Jewish population whose synagogue lay in Silver Street.

Murage was first granted in 1224. The walls may have been insufficiently complete to be held by Simon de Montfort against the royal forces in 1264. The area eventually walled was more than four times larger than the Saxon borough, measuring 1200m from east to west by 900m wide and only exceeded in size by London and Norwich. About a tenth of the area of the new enclosure was filled by the walled precinct of the Cluniac priory of St Andrew in the NW corner, and three of the friaries took up quite a lot of space. Much land within the walls was in fact never occupied by houses or industrial premises during the walls' lifetime. Northampton may have had population of over 5,000 in the 12th century when the larger defensive line was stablished by ditches and maybe some sections of walling, but it declined to about 3,000 by the late 13th century.

Northampton was staunchly Parliamentarian in the Civil War and in 1662 Charles II ordered the defences to be slighted. Most of the south and east sections of the wall are marked as still standing on a map of 1746, while part of the south wall east of the Bridge Gate survived into the 19th century. Today nothing remains visible of the town wall and the only tiny remnant of the castle has been re-erected on a different site.

John Speed's map of 1610 shows no wall between the castle and the priory pre-cinct, the river and marshland presumably being regarded as a sufficient barrier. The North Gate lay immediately east of the priory precinct, the west and NE boundaries of which ran along St Andrews Road and St George's Street. Passing Holy Sepulchre Church (with its unusual late 12th century circular nave) and then the large precinct of the Carmelite friary (to the south of which lay the Franciscan friary) the town wall headed SE along the line of Campbell Street and The Mounts to a gate facing St Edmund's End. This was probably the East Gate which existed in some form before 1166.

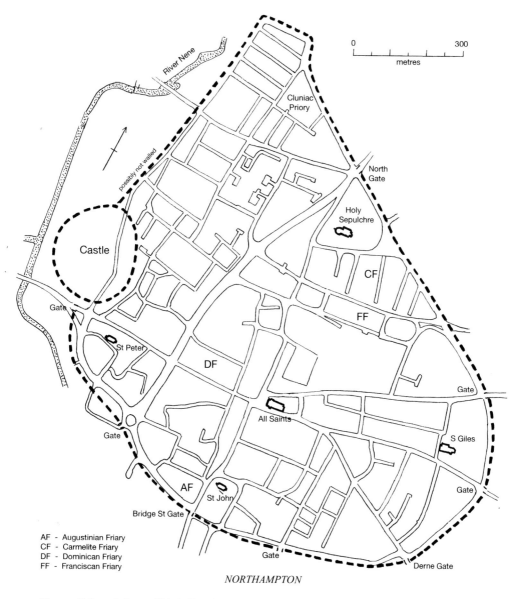

NORTHAMPTON

AF - Augustinian Friary
CF - Carmelite Friary
DF - Dominican Friary
FF - Franciscan Friary

The wall then followed York Road past the church of St Giles to another gate, and then down Cheyne Walk to the Derne Gate. Speed shows a kink in the line of the wall halfway along Victoria Promenade and then two towers on the wall from there to Bridge Street Gate, north of which lay the church of St John. Speed has another tower west of the gate and then the wall (passing the site of the Augustinian friary) as only going about half as far as a mill on the north bank of the Nene. Speed also depicts a short section of wall connecting the south side of the castle with a gateway facing the Hermitage. In 1986 an excavation in Green Street revealed traces of a timber revetted clay rampart of the 10th century. The rampart had been refaced in stone later and a gateway provided which was blocked up in the 12th century. The ditch here was recut in the Civil War period.

NORWICH   Norfolk

Norwich was already a major trading centre by 924-39, when it had a royal mint. It soon recovered from a Danish attack in 1004 and Domesday Book records it with over 1300 burgesses, making it second in size only to London. Domesday Book also recorded the destruction of almost a hundred houses to make way for a new royal castle, originally of wood, but given a large stone keep by Henry I in the 1120s. The bishops also had a tower as part of their palace on the north side of the new cathedral-priory begun in 1096 after the see was moved here from Thetford. The Music House is evidence that by the 1170s the Jews and other wealthy traders were building themselves substantial stone houses in the city. Royal charters were granted to the city in 1158 and 1194 and Edward III made Norwich a county in its own right in addition to being county town of Norfolk, which in medieval times was England's wealthiest and most densely populated county. Of Norfolk's 650 surviving medieval churches over 30 of them are within the walled area of Norwich, although few now serve their original purpose for Christian worship. A new guildhall was begun after Henry IV granted Norwich a charter of incorporation in 1404. North of the castle is an unusually complete Dominican friary. The Augustinians and Pied Friars had friaries SE of the castle, the Franciscans a house east of the castle and the Carmelites a house over the river between St James Church and Pockthorpe Gate.

There is uncertainty about how the city developed before the building of the Norman castle and cathedral and there is no evidence of any Saxon defences. A single reference to a new ditch cut in the 1130s is also the only evidence of Norman defences possibly enclosing a smaller area than the 13th century walls. Six of the churches form a group west of the cathedral precinct (which swallowed up the sites of two more). Seven more form another group further west, both these groups being in the division of the city called Westwyk. Other churches were scattered more sparsely around the divisions of Mancroft to the SW of the castle and Conesford to the south, SE and east of the castle. A further nine churches lie in Ultra Aquam, ie to the north beyond the River Wensum. The former name of one church, St Peter per Mountergate, SE of the castle suggests that it might have originated as a chapel over a Saxon or Early Norman gateway, which would presumably have faced south down King Street.

Boom tower beside the River Wensum at Norwich

Corner tower in Bull Close at Norwich

Section of Norwich city wall with a tower in Queen's Road

It appears that the construction of a rampart and ditch on the existing defensive line was licensed in 1253. The chosen line caused a certain amount of controversy as court records testify. For instance the Benedictine monks complained that the ditch effectively put the city authorities in control of lands claimed by the cathedral-priory. Several of the gates are first mentioned in the late 13th century. Although there may have been earlier grants, the first record of murage is in 1297 for seven years and it appears that grant marked the start of a fairly intensive campaign of wall-building lasting fifty years. Murage for five years was granted in 1305, and other grants were made in 1317, 1337 and 1343, the latter specifically for making a ditch in front of the walls. In 1378 the city bailiffs were ordered to clean out the ditches, repair the walls and towers, and rebuild the paling on the river-bank. Land in mortmain worth a hundred pounds was donated in 1392 towards work on the walls and in 1410 there was a grant of ulnage for seven years for the same purpose. Probably the long arc of walls SW of the city were built first and documents suggest the central section between the St Giles and St Stephen gates may have been built in the 1250s. North of the river the eastern section between the Magdalen and Pockthorpe gates seems to have existed by 1331, whilst the western part was built in the 1340s by Richard Spynko, who also supervised the rebuilding of several of the gateways. At that time the city possessed 28 espringalds (giant crossbows) for its defence, whilst in 1385 there were 40 guns available for defending the walls.

The palisade intended to defend the east part of the city facing the river seems to have been missing or out of repair at least around the Bishop's Bridge area in July 1549 when the city was captured by a large force of rebels under Robert Kett who swam the river to gain entry. The rebels made no attempt to hold onto the city and swam the river a second time to overwhelm a force led by the Marquess of Northampton sent to suppress them. During a running fight with a larger force under the Earl of Warwick at the end of August the rebels breached the walls with cannonfire between the Magdalen and Pockthorpe gates. They were eventually forced to retire and then defeated on the open ground north of the city, Kett later being hanged from the walls of Norwich castle.

The defences were patched up and strengthened by the Parliamentarians in the 1640s but the strength of their forces and support in East Anglia was such that the walls at Norwich were never put to the test. Fragments and longer lengths totalling 700m remain out of the 5km of walls of flint rubble with brick dressings that once existed. Half of the two dozen circular towers remain at least in part but all the gates were removed c1780-1820. The castle lies isolated in the middle, far from any part of the circuit.

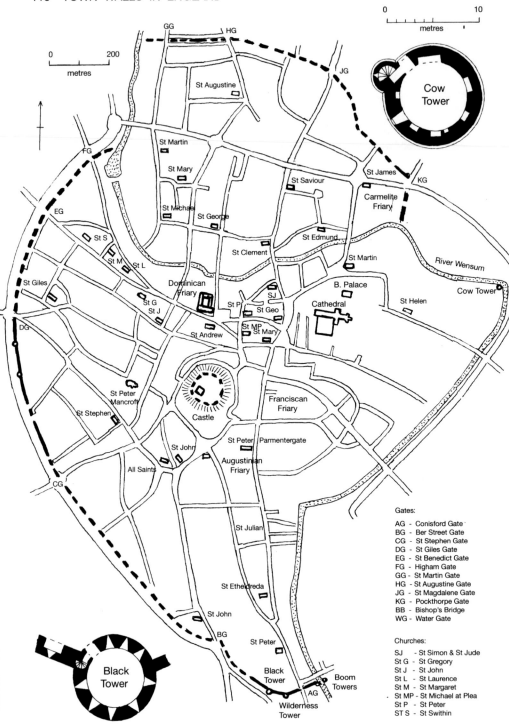

0   10
metres

Cow
Tower

0   200
metres

GG   HG
JG

St Augustine

St Martin
FG
St Mary
St Saviour   St James   KG
St Michael   St George   Carmelite
EG   Friary
St Clement   St Edmund   River Wensum
St S   St Martin
St M St L
St Giles   Dominican   B. Palace   Cow Tower
                    Friary   SJ
St G   St P St Geo   Cathedral   St Helen
DG St J   St MP
          St Andrew   St Mary

St Peter   Franciscan
Mancroft   Friary
St Stephen
          Castle
          St John
All Saints   St Peter Parmentergate
CG   Augustinian
                Friary

St Julian

St Etheldreda

St John

BG   St Peter

Black   Black   Boom
Tower   Tower   Towers
                        AG
                Wilderness
                Tower

Gates:

AG - Conisford Gate
BG - Ber Street Gate
CG - St Stephen Gate
DG - St Giles Gate
EG - St Benedict Gate
FG - Higham Gate
GG - St Martin Gate
HG - St Augustine Gate
JG - St Magdalene Gate
KG - Pockthorpe Gate
BB - Bishop's Bridge
WG - Water Gate

Churches:

SJ   - St Simon & St Jude
St G - St Gregory
St J - St John
St L - St Laurence
St M - St Margaret
St MP - St Michael at Plea
St P - St Peter
ST S - St Swithin

NORWICH

Two towers each about 6m in external diameter stand either side of the River Wensum at the SE corner of the city. They formed part of Richard Speke's works on the walls in the 1340s and were used for the suspension of an iron chain across the river both for defence and to allow toll collection. Both have slightly battered bases and stand up to 7.5m high. The east tower stood isolated from the main defences and is very ruinous. The western one still has three brick loops on the second storey. From it a short length of wall runs to the site of the Conisford Gate across the south end of King Street. A gate here existed by 1186, although not necessarily of stone. Pierced by loops well above ground level, the wall then rises WSW to the Wilderness Tower, which also measures 6m in external diameter over walls 1.5m thick and is 9m high on the SE side. A doorway with brick quoins and a moulded lintel leads into a room with four loops, one of which faces the city and the other three face outside the main wall. An upper room with four more loops can only have been reached by a ladder and trapdoor as there is no staircase.

A 50m long section of wall 1.5m thick and up to 4.5m high then climbs steeply to the Black Tower. At intervals of 6 to 9m apart are loops with internal embrasures. Only two can be reached from ground level and it appears that the others were reached by means of scaffolded timber platforms. The Black Tower stands 11m high and measures 9m in diameter over walls 1.5m thick. Eight firing loops in the vaulted lower storey cover every direction. The second storey has a fireplace and some loops and also brick windows inserted later, probably in the 18th century, when the tower housed a snuff mill. Access to the upper levels and to the main wall-walk was by a stair with brick used both for the treads and lining.

The section of wall heading west from the Black Tower has arcading formed from a continuous series of piers 1.8m wide dividing embrasures each 2.6m high, 1.4m wide and 0.8m deep and equipped with a firing loop. The arches are of brick although the rest of the 1.4m thick wall is of flint. The wall-walk is 3.5m above ground. The parapet survives by the tower. After twenty-five arches there is a break in the wall allowing access to Wildnerness House and then another short section of six. The base of a tower is said to survive in the garden of 11 Bracondale Road. Just short of the site of the Ber Street gate in a re-entrant angle is a short section of wall standing complete with the parapet, the long merlon being pierced by a loop of brick. Ber Street Gate had two round towers but only the southern tower survived long enough to appear on old prints. It had three levels with cross-loops for handguns on the upper two. The main block of the gateway had its inner part rebuilt in the early 18th century but it was demolished in 1807.

Section of Norwich city wall near site of Conisford Gate

The Black Tower and arcaded wall at Norwich

From Ber Street Gate the wall followed the northern edge of Queen's Road, the first part skirting the churchyard of St John de Sepulchre. Nothing remains of the 530m section round as far as the Swinemarket Gate, latterly known as Brazen Doors, which was a narrow postern just for pedestrian traffic. About 150m further along is an arcaded section of wall from which a D-shaped tower projects 4.5m. The wall-walk passed through the second storey, which lies over a brick vault. St Stephen's Gate, demolished in 1793, faced the road to London and was an impressive structure with twin round towers with gunloops. In August 1549 the Earl of Warwick's forces attacking the rebels under Robert Kett broke down the portcullis of this gate with cannonfire and breached the adjoining walls.

The 650m section of wall along Chapelfields Road to St Giles Gate had six towers. First there are two long sections each about 5m high and with a tower in the middle, the second tower being polygonal towards the city but round towards the former ditch. The third tower is assumed to have gone in the late 18th century. Further along is another long section of wall and the fourth tower standing 5.5m high and projecting 3.6m from the wall. Cobbles mark the site of the fifth tower, a much rebuilt structure which survived until the adjacent drill hall was demolished in the 1970s. The St Giles or Newport Gate is mentioned in 1288 but was rebuilt in the 1340s and was demolished in 1792. Over a passage with a four-centred arch with a buttress adjoining the south corner was an upper room with three cross-loops commanding the approach.

An arcaded section of wall beyond St Giles leads to a small square tower, probably a 16th century addition. There were two other towers between here and the St Benedict Gate. A 35m long section of much defaced 1.8m thick wall 4.5m high leads towards the St Benedict or Westwyk Gate which was rebuilt in the 14th century and differed from the other gates in having a projecting stair-turret. It was demolished in 1793 but the south side survived as part of a building until destroyed by bombing in 1942. The next section of wall has been much defaced by houses (now removed) being built against the ditch side of it in the 19th century. Excavations in 1947 found the 7m diameter base of one of two towers along this section. The Heigham or Black Gate is said to have fallen down c1800 despite being repaired in 1742. It had two upper rooms over the gate passage. From it a short length of wall led to a round tower on the bank of the River.

The defences continued on the other bank of the river 400m further north. The lower part 2.5m high remains of a round tower 6.2m in diameter originally on the bank of the river (now 40m away) before the river was made deeper and narrower. Just 15m east of here was the Porte de Coslayn as it was called in 1285 and c1461, but known in the 17th century as the St Martin's Gate. There are crossloops in the 20m long and 4.5m high remaining section of the 200m of wall with two towers going east to St Augustine's Gate, demolished in 1794. Dating from the 1340s it had three shields on the outer face over a four-centred arch. The next section of wall along Magpie Lane originally had four or five towers, of which just the first one now remains with a 18m long section of arcaded wall. This section ends with another 17m long section of arcaded wall 5.3m high. Excavations have shown that the ditch beyond the wall along this section was 17 to 20m wide.

Old print of Ber Street Gate at Norwich

Exterior of the Cow Tower at Norwich (see also page 19)

The Magdalen Gate demolished in 1808 was named after a leper hospital that stood just outside it. Also called the Brigate, it was rebuilt in 1339. Of the section of wall along Bull Close with six towers built in the 1320s just one 45m section remains at the east end with a corner tower 8m high with polygonal facing to the north and east. The south side has collapsed along with the lower storey vault but part of the ribbed vault of the second storey still survives. Just south of this tower stood the Pockthorpe Gate, which probably existed by 1272 but was rebuilt in 1338 and again after damage sustained during Kett's Rebellion of 1549. It was demolished in 1792. Hidden away in the grounds of Jarrolds printing works is about half of the 100m length of wall between the gate and the riverbank. Mostly rebuilt, it is 4.5m high, 0.8m thick and has much deeper footings than the rest of the walls because of the soft ground here.

Old print of St Stephen's Gate, Norwich

A 2km long section of the east side of the city facing the river was only ever closed by a palisade. At a bend of the river stands the late 14th century Cow Tower, a 15m high donjon 10.5m in diameter over brick-faced walls 1.6m thick above a plinth. Beside the ground level entrance facing SW is a circular turret containing a spiral stair connecting all three levels and the wall-walk which still retains most of the parapet. The features are mostly of stone and include a fireplace and many crossloops for guns on the upper levels. South of the Cow Tower is the Bishop Bridge, the only medieval bridge over the river to survive. Until it was dismantled in 1791 because its weight was endangering the bridge, there was a gateway with corner turrets perched on the westernmost pier.

NOTTINGHAM   Nottinghamshire

Nottingham was a place of great strategic importance lying on the north bank of the River Trent, which was regarded as the divide between southern and northern England. The castle founded by William Peveril on the orders of William I in 1068 grew to become one of the largest and strongest in England and was much used by Henry II, John and Henry III, medieval parliaments often meeting at Nottingham. The castle was also the main seat of Richard III during his short reign but was a ruin by August 1642, when Charles I raised his standard here. The town, however, supported the Parliamentary cause and was only captured by the Royalists after several attempts in January 1644.

Nottingham was originally a Danish fortress which was captured and then strengthened by King Edward the Elder. He added a second burgh on the south side of the river to help protect the bridge over the river. St Mary's church lay just north of the centre of the south side of the Danish burgh which long retained its own distinct identity and had its south side by Cliff Road and its north side between Woolpack Lane and Goosegate. The NW corner lay in the vicinity of Bottle Lane and the NE corner probably east of Belward Street, giving an enclosure about 500m long east-west by 400m wide.

The town later expanded westwards towards the royal castle 650m away and also northwards. It was burned by the Earl of Gloucester during his campaign of 1140 against King Stephen. The later extension has a centrally located church of St Peter to the north of which is the Old Market Square. A third church, of St Nicholas, near the castle, was rebuilt in 1678. A new line of defences eventually went north from the castle past the site of a postern ordered to be made in 1271 and round where the General Hospital now lies, then NE along Park Row to a twin-round towered gateway at Chapel Bar which survived until 1743. Near here two low fragments have been briefly uncovered by excavations, one of them with diagonal tooling and a stepped plinth probably of late 12th century date. Another fragment beside Maid Marion Way is now visible behind a glass screen.

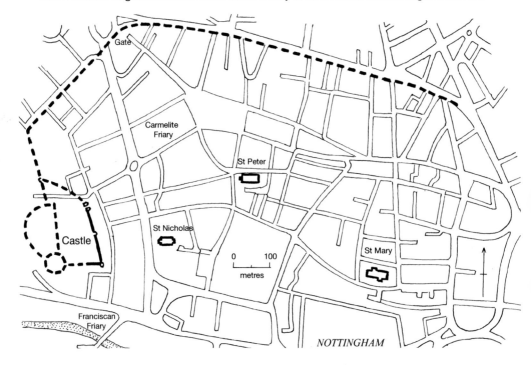

The northern walls ran along Upper Parliament Street and Lower Parliament Street. These sections are thought to have mostly been built during the seventy years following a first murage grant in 1267. A fragment was revealed in 1866 at the top end of Market Street. No traces have ever been found of the east walls, which do not appear on John Speed's map of 1609 and may never have actually been built.

Old print of Chapel Bar at Nottingham

OAKHAM   Rutland

The street grid-plan and the rampart in Cutts Close are thought to be 10th century. An excavation in 2005 of the ditch depicted on John Speed's map of 1611 showed it had been recut after the medieval period but filled in by the 18th century. There were late medieval gates here.

Old print of Beatrice Gate at Oswestry

OSWESTRY   Shropshire

Granted a market by its Fitz-Alan lords in 1190, Oswestry was burned by King John in 1216 and by Llywelyn ap Iorwerth in 1230. Murage for walling the town was first granted in 1257 but work seems to have only started in earnest after a second grant in 1277 coinciding with the start of Edward I's campaigns against Llywelyn ap Gruffydd and the eventual construction of new royal castles and fortified towns in North Wales. A Welsh raid in March 1282 caused the loss of £470 worth of goods, and another raid in September that year was even more costly. The walls are thought to have been finally completed in 1304. The town had 127 burgesses in 1301 and 163 in 1393 and prospered from trading in cloth. In 1398 Richard II adjourned a parliament from Shrewsbury to Oswestry, which was burned at the start of Owain Glyndwr's revolt in 1400. Accidental fires in 1542, 1544 and 1567 destroyed nearly all of the town's medieval buildings. Materials were probably taken from the walls for rebuilding the houses but most of the defences survived until dismantled in the 1650s by order of Parliament although the gates remained in use as toll barriers. Leland's account suggests there were no other towers but there were an effective set of water-filled ditches.

From the castle at the north end the walls went down Chapel Street to a gate across Willow Street which was reported to be in a dangerous condition in 1738. It seems to have collapsed a few years later but parts of it survived until 1782. The walls then passed down the SE side of Welsh Walls and then went behind Broad Walk to New Gate set across Church Street. Projecting entirely within the walls, New Gate had guard rooms on either side of the passage and other rooms above, making it suitable for use as a prison. It was rebuilt in 1570 and removed in 1782. The church of St Oswald with its huge 13th century tower was left isolated outside the town walls, although the original scheme of the 1250s probably envisaged its inclusion. From New Gate the wall went a short way eastwards and then headed NE along English Walls to where the Black Gate stood across the junction of Leg Street and Salop Road. This was the first of the gateways to be removed, in 1771. The walls continued up Coney Green, went round a corner and along King Street to reach a gateway across Beatrice Street. This building also had guard rooms flanking a central passage and lay entirely within the walls. Beyond here the wall line is uncertain but it probably went up Powis Place to the castle. Of the latter only the motte remains. The shape and size of the bailey remains uncertain.

OXFORD   Oxfordshire

Almost half of the town wall still stands but most of it is hidden away in private places so that few people would be conscious of Oxford as a walled town. Only recently has the precinct of the royal castle with its motte and tower at the west end of the town been made accessible to visitors after two centuries of use as a prison. The NE quadrant of the wall in the grounds of New College with its original wall-walk and crenellated parapets and several D-shaped bastions is the finest section of 13th century town wall now left in England, and quite the equal of anything to be seen at Caernarfon, Conwy and Tenby. Along the north side of the town bastions were fairly evenly spaced at intervals of 55 to 65m, a more regular arrangement than was common in England. In the 1290s a long-lost low outer wall 1m thick with its own bastions was built out into the ditch around the NE corner, giving concentric lines of defence 10m apart, unique amongst town walls in Britain, but recalling the double line of walls at Carcassonne in France.

Set on the east bank of the River Thames, Oxford was a Saxon burgh, mentioned in the Burghal Hidage as having 1500 hides allocated for maintaining its defences. The layout of Queen Street, Cornmarket Street, High Street and St Aldate's Street meeting at a crossroads by Carfax Tower must date from then. With Catte Street marking the eastern line, the Saxon town would have been a rectangle of about 600m long from east to west by 420m wide, but with the SW corner cambered off. The eastern part of the town, which extends 40m further north and contains a wider but gently bending section of the High Street, is thought to be an extension of the early 10th century, when Oxford was prosperous but proving vulnerable to attacks by the Danes. This part of the town contained mural mansions belonging to the owners of rural manors elsewhere, these properties being charged with the cost of wall maintenance. The church of St Peter in the East here (now a college library) is known to be of 10th century origin. Other ancient parish churches are St Mary's, a large building set at the junction of Catte Street and High Street, All Saints further west along the High Street, St Michael's by Cornmarket Street, and St Adate's and St Ebbs each to the west of the streets named after them. Carfax Tower itself is a relic of the former church of St Martin demolished in 1898.

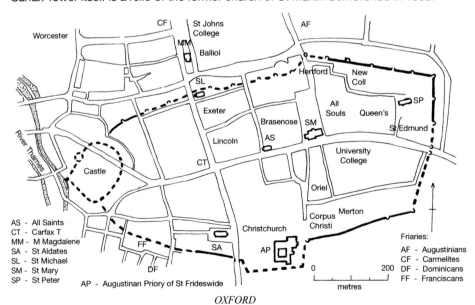

AS - All Saints
CT - Carfax T
MM - M Magdalene
SA - St Aldates
SL - St Michael
SM - St Mary
SP - St Peter

AP - Augustinan Priory of St Frideswide

Friaries:

AF - Augustinians
CF - Carmelites
DF - Dominicans
FF - Franciscans

OXFORD

Section of Oxford town wall in New College Garden

In the 12th century Oxford not only gained a royal palace (Beaumont) outside the north walls but gradually became established as a university or gathering of those licensed to teach by virtue of holding degrees. As such the town attracted large numbers of friars. By the 1240s the Dominicans and Franciscans were settled by the SW section of the walls, the latter house straddling the original defensive line. By the 1260s Augustinian friars were settled on the NE side where Wadham College now is. The Carmelites also arrived in the mid 13th century, eventually being given a site in Beaumont Street on the west side of a northern suburb which was served by the churches of St Mary Magdalen and St Giles. There were also two other rather more short-lived friaries.

Students not attached to friaries originally lived in halls which were basically any premises rented by a magister or lecturer. Larger colleges came later, from the 1280s onwards, and there were still only ten of them by the 15th century as opposed to about seventy halls. Currently eighteen colleges claim to be pre-Reformation foundations. Balliol, St John's and Trinity colleges lie on the east side of the northern suburb, Worcester College lies further west at the end of Beaumont Street and Magdalen College lies beyond the eastern walls. The others take up almost all of the space within the eastern half of the walled town. All Souls, Brasenose, Exeter, Hertford, Lincoln, New, Queen's and St Edmund's colleges lie to the north of the High Street, and Christchurch, Corpus Christi, Merton, Oriel and University Colleges lie to the south.

The Saxon defences may have included a stone wall and this seems to have been maintained during the Norman period since the priory of St Frideswide was allowed to make a postern through it in the 1140s. Work on the existing town wall began c1226, when murage was granted by Henry III. In 1227 thirty-four major landowners in the town were ordered to contribute to the works and several of the mural mansions were later confiscated by the Crown when their owners failed to contribute. The wall eventually may have had up to thirty D-shaped flanking bastions, a third of which remain, and six gateways, none of which have survived, apart from several minor posterns. The walls were surrounded by ditches wide enough to be a formidable barrier on the north side. By 1371 the ditch was full of rubbish but Richard II ordered it to be cleared out in 1378. A proposal to widen the ditch was forestalled by protests from Merton College, whose tenants had already hampered the clearing operations after their road was obstructed.

By the 1640s the medieval defences were considered woefully inadequate. Royalist forces constructed new outer earthwork defences, those who failed to help being expelled. These new works were slighted after Parliamentary forces took Oxford in 1647.

New Road on the west side of Oxford cuts across the northern part of the castle bailey and gives a clear view of the 18m high castle mound on the bailey NW side. Beyond the castle ditch a postern was made through the wall at the end of Bulwark's Lane c1460. It was later known as the Turl from the turnstile there that kept animals out of the town. A new arch was built in 1614 but demolished in 1722. A low section of the wall with one bastion remains to the north of the Methodist Church in New Inn Hall Street. Bits of wall lie hidden behind buildings along the north side of St Michael's Street. There were once two bastions on this section. Across the north end of Cornmarket Street was the North Gate, demolished in 1772. This building had two round flanking towers and a portcullis is mentioned in 1325. It was later extended to serve as a prison, resulting in the vaulted 3.6m wide gateway passage attaining a length of 21m, but was demolished in 1771. East of here the wall projected out to pass round the north side of St Michael's Church with its early 11th century tower. Two bastions remain hidden in the yards of buildings on the north side of Ship street. The wall then continued east with its line coinciding with the south facade of the Sheldonian Theatre. Beyond the third of three lost bastions on this section the wall headed diagonally NE to the Smyth Gate, a simple arch across the north end of Catte Street widened in the 1630s and removed in the 1660s. Beside it was an octagonal corner tower containing a Lady Chapel.

The wall re-appears along the north side of the cloister of New College, this being the start of a continuous and very well preserved section 450m long and 7.5m high to the top of the parapet. One bastion NW of the cloister has gone and another was replaced in the late 14th century by the square Bell Tower forming part of the college. The wall continues beyond the north range of the Great Quad of New College with one bastion. The next bastion along has lost its outer end so as to make an entrance into the garden further east. The wall bounds the north and east sides of this garden with one more north facing bastion, a diagonally projecting NE corner bastion, and two more along the east side. The wall has two blocked-up posterns, one which must be that me

that mentioned in 1378, a year before these lands were leased to New College. Flights of steps bring the narrow main wall-walk up and round the summit of each bastion, and there are loops further down in each bastion.

Oxford: bastion on the south side near Merton College   *Last remnant of the town wall at Poole*

Now missing is 150m of the central section of the east wall with two bastions and the East Gate across High Street just east of where Merton Street joins it. Rebuilt with a new round outer archway in 1711, and having the Holy Trinity Chapel in an upper room, the gateway was demolished in 1772. There is uncertainty as to whether the flanking towers were square or round. The wall next reappears around the garden of Merton College. The SE corner bastion is missing but the next one to the west survives. There is along here a 290m long section of continuous walling ending in another bastion and the south face of most of this part is publicly accessible, but not so impressive, being much patched and nowhere more than 3.5m high. A missing section of wall projected south beyond here to enclose the precinct of the Augustinian priory of St Frideswide suppressed in the 1520s by Cardinal Wolsey for the creation of Christchurch College. The 12th century priory church became a cathedral in the 1540s.

The South Gate across St Aldate's Street by the SW corner of Christchurch College fell down in 1617 perhaps as a result of part of it being removed for building the college. To the west buildings of Pembroke College founded in 1624 lie over parts of the wall up to 4.5m high along the north side of Brewer Street. Beyond was Little Gate, with a large upper room usually leased to scholars above a pedestrian arch which survived until 1798 and a wider arch for carts which was in a dangerous state by the early 17th century. From there up to the side of the West Gate across Castle Street demolished in the early 17th century only minor fragments of the wall remain, all of them hidden away in backyards. The locations of any bastions along these sections are not known but there is a record of two bastions near the South Gate being leased to a burgess.

The Folly Bridge 400m south of South Gate once carried the New Gate, a hexagonal tower probably built in the late 13th century, heightened c1615 and demolished in 1779. In the 1560s it was leased out as the Berkshire archdeaconry court. See also page 17.

PLYMOUTH   Devon

Murage granted in 1378, licences to crenellate issued in 1404 and 1439, and royal grants in 1463 and 1485 all suggest that the town had some sort of wall by the late 15th century. It was then wealthy and important enough to have at its east end three friaries, of the Dominicans, Franciscans and Carmelites. A new section of wall was said to be under construction by order of the Bishop of Exeter in 1530 and the blockhouse on Devil's Point and another by the shore to the NE may also be of that period. The medieval wall extended from the former castle north of the citadel of the 1660s to the south end of Castle Dyke Lane, where the Little Low Gate was made through it in 1593 as part of a new scheme of works encompassing a larger area. This new wall excluded the precinct of the Carmelite friary, the tower of which was ordered to be demolished so as to not overlook the new defences. At some point their former precinct was itself fortified. Further works were constructed in 1643 but were mostly demolished by the 1760s.

POOLE   Dorset

Poole took over Wareham's sea-trading by the 1290s. A yard near the shore behind the SW side of Thames Street has a section of walling about 12m long with steps leading up to a wall-walk and corbelled parapet over a small postern doorway. This appears to be the only relic of the wall for which licences to crenellate were issued in 1433 and 1462. Nothing is known of the line of any other portions of walling but the main landward-facing gateway was in Towngate Street, suggesting an enclosure about 500m long by 300m wide with the parish church near the seaward SW end. The defences were improved by Parliamentary forces in 1643 and demolished in the 1660s by order of Charles II.

PORTCHESTER   Hampshire

Set on a tip of a promontory by Portsmouth Harbour stands one of a series of Roman forts built in the late 3rd century to defend the south and east coasts from Saxon invaders. Nothing remains of any internal buildings of the Roman era but the walls surrounding an area about 180m square are the most complete of any Roman fort or city in Britain. Of twenty original U-shaped flanking bastions rising slightly higher than the main wall fourteen still remain, those at the SW and NE corners plus three each on the north and west sides, four on the south and two on the east. The walls rise 5.5m to the wall-walk and were 3m thick until most of them were cut back and refaced internally in the medieval period. There are internally projecting 12th century gatehouses facing east and west and posterns in the centres of the north and south sides. See page 5.

When the Saxons finally settled in England a township grew up within the old Roman walls. It later became a possession of the bishops of Winchester until 904, when King Edward the Elder enforced an exchange of lands to enable Portchester to be refortified as a burgh. However the township failed long before the Domesday survey of 1086. In the 1120s the fort became the outer bailey of a new royal castle built in the NW corner, with a tall tower keep taking the place of the original corner bastion. Several English kings used the harbour as a point of embarkation for campaigns in France. The church remains of an Augustinian priory established in the SE corner in 1133. Most of the canons transferred to Southwick c1150 leaving only a small cell at Portchester.

PORTSMOUTH   Hampshire

Murage was first granted in 1342 after a French raid on the port. The townsmen asked for it to be cancelled two years later, claiming the tax was hampering trade and had in any case raised very little money towards any fortifications. In 1378-9 the fee farm to the king was suspended for ten years to make funds available for defences and in 1386 a commission was appointed to arrange for the defence of the port. Although it looks like one of Henry VIII's blockhouses and has eight seaward facing gunports of his period in the lowest level, the Round Tower by the shore is thought to have originally been built by Henry V in 1415. It was connected by a chain to a vanished tower on the Gosport side of the harbour. The upper levels may be late 17th century when the adjacent Eighteen Gun Battery was built, but were remodelled later. The Square Tower beyond the King James' Gate of 1687 some 160m to the SE was built by Henry VII in 1490s, when the royal port was also provided with a timber-framed dry-dock. The Square Tower became the governor's residence but was later cut down to form a magazine. Refacing and remodelling in 1827 and 1847-50 has buried most of the medieval work in this tower.

In c1540 John Leland described the landward defences as a "mud wall armed with timber having a ditch without it". Shortly afterwards Henry VIII built a new gateway called the Landport on the NE side of the town, 460m away from the Square Tower's location by the SW shore. The new gatehouse replaced a medieval gateway recently blocked up by building a large new bastion in front of it. In the late 1560s Queen Elizabeth added a bastion in the middle of the SE side and replaced the round corner bastions by others of the improved arrow-head shape like those at Berwick. The moat was also widened and the quay on the NW side of the town was cut off by a new stone wall. By Charles II's reign Portsmouth was England's premier naval base and the defences were then remodelled with new outworks including ravelins and a glacis. All that remains of these later works is the seaward facing rampart connecting the saluting platform near the Square Tower with the King's Bastion at the south corner. Footings of the Spur Redoubt of the 1680s facing the sea here were revealed in front of this rampart in the 1980s.

RICHARD'S CASTLE   Herefordshire

Beside the motte and bailey castle with fragments of stone walls are traces of a former township with an enclosing bank in which was found 11th and 12th century pottery. In the 13th century the bank was linked to the castle bailey by a stone wall. Traces of a dovecote, originally probably intended as a turret on the wall, were found further east. Further south is the church with a detached tower of c1300 overlooking the approach rather than at the west end where it would have hindered defence of the castle. An enquiry of 1364 on the death of Hugh Mortimer shows that the town then had 103 burgages, a market and fair having been granted to it by King John in 1216. Being too close to Ludlow, which had greater natural advantages, Richard's Castle subsequently declined. In c1540 John Leland recorded only two farms (which both still remain) and three cottages as still occupying the hilltop site.

RICHMOND   North Yorkshire

Scottish raids in the early 14th century stimulated the building of a wall around the back yards of the properties facing the large market place adjoining the castle. The archbishop of York ordered the Warden of the Franciscan friary to preach against the Scots and encourage the townsfolk to resist them, and grants for murage were made in 1313, 1337, 1341 and 1400. The total walled area was just 18 acres, of which the castle set above a cliff above the River Swale on the south side accounted for a fifth. The main remnant of the wall is the cobble-floored Bargate, a narrow pointed-headed arch with a segmental rere-arch set in a section of wall 6m high and 2.5m thick on the SW side of the town. A postern also remains in Friars' Wynd on the north side. Removed in 1773 were other gates across Finkle Street facing west, French Gate on the north, and Mill Gate facing SE. The parish church lies well outside the walled area but there was a chapel-of-ease within the market place.

The Friars' Wynd postern at Richmond

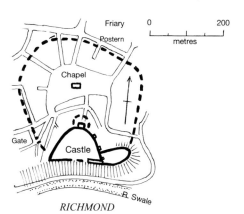

RICHMOND

The Bargate at Richmond

ROCHESTER   Kent

One of the smaller towns of Roman Britain, Durobrivae guarded a vital crossing of the River Medway by a bridge carrying Watling Street from Canterbury to London. It was surrounded by a rampart and ditch late in the 2nd century, and about thirty years later the outer face of the rampart was reinforced with a thick stone wall. The round-cornered enclosure was unusually irregularly shaped for a Roman site, being up to 470m long by up to 270m wide near the west end but with the east end just 140m wide. A see of Rochester was established in 604 with a small cathedral almost centrally placed in the part of the city to the SW of the High Street forming a NW to SE spine road. Aethelred of Mercia destroyed Rochester in 676 and left the see ravaged and impoverished. In 842 the city was sacked by a Danish force but in 884 the defences proved adequate to keep another Danish force at bay until King Alfred arrived to relieve it.

After the rebellious Odo, Bishop of Bayeux was captured in 1088 at Pevensey he was brought to Rochester by his nephew William II in an attempt to induce the garrison there to surrender. However the garrison sallied out and carried Odo back to the city walls, which proved strong enough to resist the royal army for several weeks. The next bishop, Gundulph, began a new cathedral priory further east from the Saxon one and filled the SW corner of the city with a large new castle of stone. The tall keep was added after the castle was handed over to the Archbishop of Canterbury in 1127. The castle suffered devastating sieges in 1215 (when part of the keep was destroyed by King John's miners) and in 1264 when the suburbs outside the walls were burned by Henry III's garrison. The city was also attacked during the Peasants' Revolt of 1381.

Rochester was one of the centres of the Royalist uprising of 1648 but the only damage sustained on that occasion was the burning of the drawbridge midway along Rochester Bridge as they retreated. This drawbridge between the 6th and 7th piers formed part of a new stone bridge 170m long built in 1382. It lasted until 1857 and stood closer to the castle than the existing bridges. It replaced a 12th century bridge destroyed by ice the previous year but which had previously lain broken for 24 weeks back in 1339. The Saxon bridge was probably a wooden structure set on the piers of the Roman bridge on the same alignment as the present one continuing the line of the High Street.

A section of the southern walls at Rochester

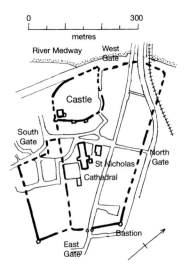

ROCHESTER

Bastion at the east corner of the walls at Rochester

Two small defaced fragments are reported to survive (but are not easily visible) at the riverside end and centre of the NE (usually described as north) side of the walled city. Along here lay the North Gate. Visible standing remnants of the walls are mostly clustered around the SE (or east) end. The High street was closed by the East Gate, a gatehouse composed of parallel walls with a D-shaped turret facing along the walls on each side. It may have resembled the Black Gate of the castle at Newastle. East of here a section of crenellated wall facing a carpark stands 7.5m high and runs for 50m to a rounded corner from which projects a bastion also 7.5m high with three lancet windows lighting its upper storey. The lost gateway and most of what stands were built in the late 14th century, Roman work only surviving as footings. On the other side of the High Street a lower section of wall survives as far as the original rounded Roman corner.

The Roman wall along the SW side of the city as far as the former South Gate was removed to make more space for the claustral buildings of the cathedral priory, the south range containing the refectory and the bishop's palace further west both being placed outside the line of the Roman wall. By the mid 14th century a new SW wall 36m in front of the old one stood in line with the still surviving Prior's Gate, but it appears there may have been an earlier medieval wall and/or ditch not so far out. Anyway, by the end of the 14th century the boundary had been moved still further out another 70m up the gently rising slope. A pair of 90m long sections of fairly thin and low wall still enclose the Deanery Garden and meet at a round corner bastion and a further section survives in front of the old grammar school further to the NW. Beyond the site of the South Gate the SW side of the castle keep stands on the line of the Roman wall.

The medieval west gate probably lay beside the Bridge Chapel just north of the castle. Parochial services took place in the nave of the cathedral-priory until the parish church of St Nicholas was built between it and the High Street in the 15th century. On the north side of the cathedral is the lower part of a large 11th century tower shown in old drawings as originally having a machicolated top probably of c1380-1400.

RYE   East Sussex

Rye has a natural defensive site, a sandstone plateau rising 15m above what was once a flourishing port. It joined the Cinque Ports confederation in the late 12th century when its neighbour Hastings had difficulties in fulfilling obligations of ship-service to the Crown. The south coast became vulnerable to French raiders after the loss of Normandy during John's reign and in 1249 Peter of Savoy, Constable of the Cinque ports was ordered to build a castle at Rye. What was actually built, near the SE corner of the town, was a small 12m high two storey stronghouse, 7.5m square over walls 1.5m thick with round corner turrets 3.8m in diameter containing small rooms at each corner. It was originally calling Baddings Tower but later gained the name Ypres Tower from a later owner. From 1491 until 1891 it was used as a local prison and it is now a museum. It has seen a lot of alterations owing to continuous usage and bomb-damage in 1942 but quite a number of the narrow windows are original. Adjoining wall stubs are the only evidence that a town wall around the steep south and east sides either existed or was planned.

Fortification of the rest of the town began in the 1330s but was insufficient to prevent the French doing serious damage at Rye in 1339 and again in 1377. At the NE corner of the town stands the Land Gate built c1340. It was given a new top storey following murage being granted in 1369 and 1377 and a commission being set up to improve the fortifications in 1385. A pair of round towers 6.4m in diameter over walls 1.4m thick above moulded plinths flank a pointed arch with a portcullis groove, above which are two narrow and low levels of rooms. The upper room (now without a floor or roof) has a fireplace on the south side and access to a latrine contained in the top of the SE corner buttress, the twin SW buttress of which has been removed. Above, on the north side, are corbels for a machicolated parapet. Each tower has a lower chamber with several loops reached from the main passage, and the western tower has a spiral staircase. This tower had a basement below ground level. The eastern tower contains a staircase of later date following the curve of the inner wall.

Bastion projecting from the wall at Rye

Rye: close up of arch of Landgate

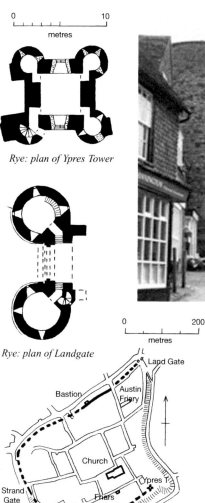

0   10
metres

Rye: plan of Ypres Tower

Rye: plan of Landgate

The Land Gate at Rye

0   200
metres

RYE

From the Land Gate the wall headed SW down the NW side of Tower Lane. Higher up to the south of this section, which was removed in 1763, there survives the church of the Augustinian friars reached from Conduit Street, where there was a postern. The next section of about 70m survives as a retaining wall at the back of a car park on the south side of Ports Street. The projection here may be a later bastion. There was probably another postern at the bottom of Market Road. At the NW corner of the town about twenty properties are built against the outside face of the wall and the only place where it can be seen easily is in a shop just south of the site of Strand Gate at the end of Mermaid Street. A house on the corner has a shield with the arms of the Cinque Ports from the Strand Gate, which was destroyed in 1766, although something of it remained until c1820. There are no remains of a wall around the south and east sides of the town where there are precipitous slopes beyond the back-gardens of the houses. One building near the middle of the south side, opposite the SW corner of the churchyard, belonged to a second friary, that of the Friars of the Sack. The terrace below the Ypres Tower is named Gun Garden and at the SE corner a natural outcrop provides what looks like a projecting artillery bastion.

SAFFRON WALDEN   Essex

In the 12th century the town gravitated up the hill to surround the castle, but in the 13th century the Saxon earthwork defences seem to have been put back into use, at least for part of their length.

SALISBURY & OLD SARUM   Wiltshire

Old Sarum is a superb Iron Age fortress with an oval natural plateau 425m long by 340m wide with slopes descending 15m or more on all sides to a deep ditch with an outer bank. During King Alfred's conflicts with Danish forces it was re-occupied and to Old Sarum was transferred a mint which operated at the nearby town of Wilton at a river junction 4km to the west until in 1003 that town was sacked and burned by Danes under Sweyne. In 1075 the see of Sherborne was moved to Old Sarum and by the 1080s a new cathedral was under construction in the NW quadrant of the site, whilst the centre was raised up to form a royal castle. New palaces each for the bishop and Henry I were built here in the early 12th century and the keep added to the castle formed an important royal treasury, although Henry II preferred to stay and hunt at Clarendon Palace 6km to the SE and the royal mint here was then closed. The east gate of the town had a chapel of Holy Cross above it, and a church of St Peter lay nearby. There was also a leper hospital (St John's) surviving in the 16th century, likely footings of it being excavated in 1931.

Space was at a premium on the crowded and windswept hilltop of Old Sarum making expansion of the cathedral and clergy houses difficult. There was also a lack of water despite the presence of several wells. In 1194 Richard I approved a plan to build a new cathedral on the flatter ground by the River Avon 3km to the south. Some of the townsfolk had already transferred there. The clergy finally followed them after they found themselves locked out of the city walls by the royal garrison during the 1217-8 crisis when much of the country was occupied by French invaders. Bishop Richard Poore obtained a licence for a market at the new town of Salisbury in 1219 and began the existing cathedral in 1220. Work proceeded quickly and much of it was complete by 1250.

The transfer of tombs of three previous bishops in 1226 marked the abandonment of the cathedral of Old Sarum and in 1236 the bishop's palace there was demolished for its materials. The final straw was the opening in 1244 of a new bridge over the Avon allowing traffic to bypass the older trading centres of Wilton and Old Sarum. Much of the fabric of the old cathedral still stood until the 1330s but by 1377 Old Sarum only had ten poll-tax payers compared with 326 in Salisbury. Old Sarum retained a mayor until 1422 but most of the site except for the castle was then derelict. Despite having no houses left at all by 1540, two members represented Old Sarum in Parliament from 1295 until "rotten boroughs" (of which Old Sarum was regarded as a classic example) were finally abolished by the 1832 Reform Act.

The new town of Salisbury eventually covered an area ten times the size of Old Sarum. A grid system was laid out with water channels between the squares. By 1225 it had a charter as a free city, the main trade being in fleeces and finished cloth. It seems to have initially only possessed a boundary ditch. Work on ditches in 1310 was followed by a licence to crenellate in 1328. Another licence for crenellation was issued in 1372 and in 1378 this was followed by a grant of timber from a royal forest. Earth ramparts and probably palisades were then erected around the east and north sides of the town, leaving the river and marshland as a sufficient barrier on the other sides. A will of 1455 left £20 towards "making bars about the said city for its defence and safety".

From a point east of the cathedral and north of the Franciscan friary the rampart followed the line of St Ann Street where there was a gate to the NE. Rampart Way and Greencroft mark the eastern boundary, with the site of the Winchester Gate near the north end. The north rampart extended between St Edmund's College and a gate across Castle Street lying near the river, beyond which was the Dominican friary. Near the east bank of the river is the church of St Thomas, whilst that of St Martin lay outside the SE corner. John Speed's map of c1600 shows an embattled close wall all around the cathedral in the SW corner, parts of which remain, but no town defences.

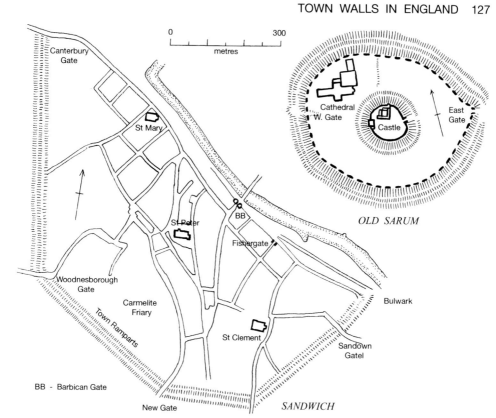

0 300
metres

Canterbury Gate

St Mary

St Peter

BB

Fishergate

Woodnesborough Gate

Carmelite Friary

St Clement

BB - Barbican Gate

Town Ramparts

New Gate

SANDWICH

Bulwark

Sandown Gatel

OLD SARUM

Cathedral W. Gate

Castle

East Gate

Gate known as The Barbican at Sandwich

SANDWICH   Kent

One of the original Cinque Ports, Sandwich did a considerable trade in wool until the River Wansum began to silt up in the 15th and 16th centuries, after which town life was kept going by immigrant cloth workers from Holland and France. The town has never outgrown the wedge-shaped enclosure 900m long by 450m wide on the SW side of the river, defined on the landward sides by a substantial rampart rising up to 7.5m above a wide ditch probably at least partly water-filled. In 1891 the number of houses here was barely double the number recorded in Domesday Book. See plan & photo, page 127.

Fortifications are first mentioned in 1274-5 when the Crown ordered the earthworks to be levelled and the timberwork including a "barbican" taken off to Dover Castle. The town was granted murage for seven years in 1321 and in 1339 those who had left to avoid being taxed for fortifications were ordered to return. When Sir Simon Burley, Constable of Dover, summoned some of the townsfolk to speedily erect fortifications in 1385 it was claimed that plagues and other problems had postponed the previous works. A land tax, a two year grant from customs and murage for two years from 1387 were to help pay for the work. Murage for seven years was granted again in 1405 and renewed in 1412. Cleaning out of the ditches was ordered in 1436. The building in 1451 of a two-storey gun battery known as the Bulwark guarding the seaward approach at the SE end of the town only delayed rather than prevented the sacking of Sandwich by French raiders in 1457. Other devastating attacks had been in 1400 and 1438.

Further works and repairs to the Bulwark were paid for by debt collecting and taxing properties in 1458, when a second gun battery of brick was ordered to be built outside Fishergate. Edward IV made annual grants of £100 for works from 1461 until 1465, when the town was exempted from certain customs duties, this privilege being renewed in 1477 and in 1483. Accounts from this period mention great quantities of stone and the purchase of 15 sets of stones cut ready to make crenels in a parapet. This makes it likely that there was a stone wall closing off the town from the riverside quays, but there is no evidence of the landward ramparts having anything other than a palisade.

At the SE end of the town was the Sandown Gate, a brick building with two D-shaped turrets projecting slightly towards the outside. Newgate on the south side was under construction in the 1450s. Beside the SW ramparts lay the Carmelite friary. Beyond, facing west, was the Woodnesborough Gate, with two turrets flanking a pointed archway. Facing west at the northern corner was the Canterbury Gate. In 1929 half of the base of the northern one of a pair of 4m diameter flanking turrets was uncovered. The riverside rampart then headed SE past the church of St Mary down to the Barbican, a gateway now with a wooden superstructure over a lower stage with flush-work on two D-shaped towers flanking an arch with a portcullis groove. In the middle of the town west of it lies the church of St Peter. A third church, of St Clement, lies further SE. Not far SE of the Barbican is Fishergate, a square 15th century structure with one original room over a passage with a portcullis groove, and a gabled third storey probably added in 1571.

The SW side of the Fishergate at Sandwich

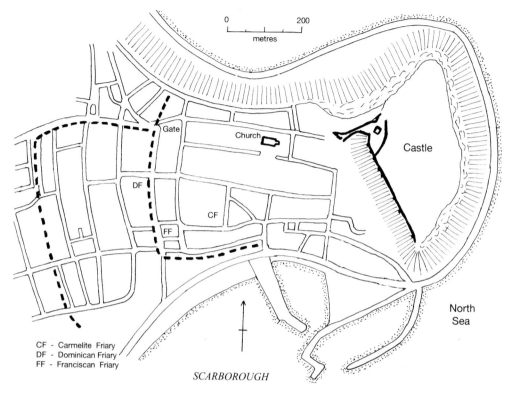

CF - Carmelite Friary
DF - Dominican Friary
FF - Franciscan Friary

SCARBOROUGH

SCARBOROUGH   North Yorkshire

The town lies on an isthmus high above two bays separated by a considerably higher headland occupied by the huge royal castle and thus only needed defences on the west side. Leland described Scarborough as walled "a little in stone, but mostly with ditches and walls of earth". Murage, along with forty oaks from a royal forest, was first granted in 1225 and again at intervals during the 13th and 14th centuries but the town is said to have had defences by King John's reign. The old burgh (Awburgh) measured about 600m east to west by 420m wide within 13th century walls running along the line of Awburgh Street and Cross Street to King Street and then east along the south side of Merchants Row, now called Eastborough. The large parish church of St Mary originally held by the Cistercians lies on the north side and the Carmelite and Franciscan friaries were in the SW corner where there is a street called Friargate. Bases of towers on either side of the Awburgh Gate were found in 1812.

The western suburb of Newborough was later walled along the line of Huntriss Row to St Thomas's Hospital and then (route uncertain) across to Awburgh Gate, adding 300m to the length of enclosed area. The new outer wall made the old wall south of the Awburgh Gate redundant and in 1284 the Dominican friars, whose house lay on the west side of it, asked if they could remove part and use the materials for their buildings, but this was refused. This section of wall may have become derelict soon afterwards. The 200 foot long section that was collapsing in 1304 and which John Pychford was allowed to repair and then build houses against must have been part of it. There is a mention in 1312 of Robert Uttred as having a house within a 100 foot long gap probably in the same wall. An unlocated northern portion of wall is said to have been built by Richard III.

SHREWSBURY   Shopshire

The town lies within a loop of the River Severn with the inner bailey of the royal castle occupying the eastern third of the isthmus at the north end. The town was burned during a Welsh attack on the castle in 1069. Domesday Book records the recent destruction of about a hundred houses to make way for extensions and outworks of the castle. The 12th century town just occupied the highest part of the site, with walls along the north side of Castle Street and Pride Hill and the SW side of High Street, enclosing an area 300m long beyond the vanished southern outer bailey of the castle and about the same in width. This area contains the churches of St Alkmund, St Julian, St Mary and Old St Chads, all presumably founded during the era when Shrewsbury was a Saxon burgh.

With the stimulus of Welsh attacks on Shrewsbury in 1215 and 1234 Henry III had the town refortified. Murage was first granted in 1220 and then continuously until the mid 15th century. The donation of some surplus stone to the Dominicans in 1242 marked the end of a campaign of new wall building in which the enclosed area was greatly extended to the SW by taking in a D-shaped area 700m in diameter and 300m wide. From Pride Hill the new wall went NW down Roushill, where footings of a short portion 1.4m thick with steps in its plinth were discovered in 1959. The wall then followed the river-bank to the Welsh Bridge. The Mardol Gate lay on a pier of the bridge and had two round turrets on the NW side. In 1575 the drawbridge in front was replaced and the upper part of the SE side rebuilt. At the far end of the bridge lay the Welsh Gate, the upper room of which remained in use as a guard room almost until it was demolished in 1773.

From Welsh Bridge the wall curved round the outside of Claremont Bank, where there were several towers and the Augustinian friary lay outside. Flat parkland known as The Quarry separates the line of the wall from the river, which is eventually 290m away. Posterns lay at the bottom of each of St John's Hill and Swan Hill. A small embattled tower 5m square with separate entrance doorways to upper and lower chambers stands on the south side of the street called Town Walls. The tower is a National Trust property and is very occasionally opened to the public. Further along to the east are remains in the form of a sandstone retaining wall externally rising 3m to the level of the wall-walk forming the pavement for pedestrians. It has a chamfered plinth and irregular buttressing.

Buttressed section of the walls of Shrewsbury

Tower on the walls at Shrewsbury

NG - North Gate
EB - English Bridge
WB - Welsh Bridge
WG - Water Gate
AF - Augustinian Friary
DF - Dominican Friary
FF - Franciscan Friary
SA - St Alkmund's
SC - Old St Chad's
SJ - St Julian's
SM - St Mary's

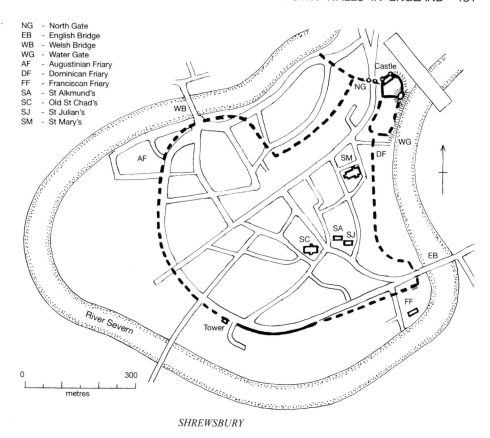

SHREWSBURY

The wall continued east along Beeches Lane to the Stone Gate facing the English Bridge. Floods in 1542 caused the collapse of this gateway and the survival of a prisoner shackled up within it was regarded as miraculous and he was set free. This gate had two square turrets facing the bridge, beyond the other side of which are remains of the Benedictine Abbey. Outside the wall, by the river near this gate lie remains of the Franciscan Friary. From the gate the walls went back diagonally to the NW to regain the higher ground. Near the castle outer bailey was a gate leading to a long flight of steps down to a still-surviving water-gate by the river. South of here, between the wall and the river, lay the precinct of the Dominican friary.

West of the castle inner bailey was a twin towered gatehouse, probably 13th century, although the survival until the early 19th century of remains including a reset stone with arms of Henry VII suggests some later adornment or rebuilding. The passage here is thought to have had two portcullises. In later times the western tower here was a prison, with the gaolers using the other tower. By the late 13th cenrtury a new outer wall was built out to the river, where Grewald's Tower stood at a corner, and Gilbert's Tower stood further along the bank.This made the older wall higher up redundant and merchants soon starting building houses over it. The rest of the riverside wall as far as the Welsh Bridge was only completed in 1644-51. Work begun by the Royalists on the very decayed defences of both castle and town were continued after the latter was captured in a surprise night attack early in 1645 by Parliamentary forces. They exploited a weakness in the defences and persuaded the castle garrison to surrender the following day.

SOUTHAMPTON   Hampshire

The county of Hampshire takes its name from Hamtun, which is first mentioned in the 8th century and may have been on (or just north of) the present site by the confluence of the rivers Itchen and Test. There was an older settlement called Hamwic around St Mary's church at Northam further to the NE on the west bank of the Itchen, and a Roman one at Bitterne on the east side of that river. The five parish churches within the medieval town were all originally subservient to St Mary's. Only St Michael's beside Castle Way remains in use, St John in French Street being lost in the 18th century, All Saints and St Lawrence were later rebuilt and then destroyed in the 20th century, whilst Holy Cross on the east side of High Street remains a gutted shell following wartime bombing.

The bombing has had one good result from an antiquarian's point of view in that since 1945 many later buildings have been removed so there are now clearer views of the remains of the walls, which total about half of the original circuit of just over a mile. There are remains of four impressive gateways out of seven, and of thirteen of the original twenty-nine towers and bastions. The complete circuit as shown on Philip Brannon's 19th century painting of the arrival of Queen Mary's future husband King Philip of Spain in 1554 looks magnificent, with the seaward west and south sides in the foreground being particularly ornate and varied in outline. These two sides meet in a curve, distorting the regularity of a rectangle established by the meeting at a right-angle of almost straight north and east sides, which are respectively 280m and 700m long. The position of the royal castle on the west side is unusual, neither projecting forwards to command the landward approach from the north nor keeping a town's length away from it. The probability is that the castle bailey once projected beyond the northern defensive line of the 11th century town like that at Totnes and that in the 12th century a new line of town defences was made further out to include a northern suburb. See photos on page 23.

In 1202 and 1203 King John granted Southampton £100 towards work on defences. Bar Gate and East Gate existed in stone by then but the rest of the works were of earth and wood. Murage grants from 1260 until the 1290s probably paid for building the north walls and towers on either side of the Bar Gate and perhaps a fair amount of the east wall with its D-shaped towers. A second series of murage grants started in 1321 and there are references to a quay and adjacent walling being under construction in 1327.

The south side of Bar Gate at Southampton

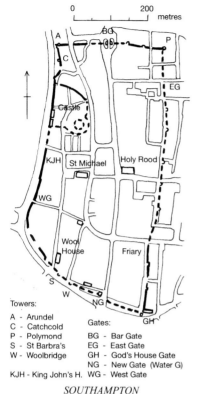

0   200
              metres

Towers:

A - Arundel
C - Catchcold
P - Polymond
S - St Barbra's
W - Woolbridge
KJH - King John's H.

Gates:

BG - Bar Gate
EG - East Gate
GH - God's House Gate
NG - New Gate (Water G)
WG - West Gate

SOUTHAMPTON

Southampton: plan of Bar Gate

An inquisition into the spending of funds on defences was set up by Edward III after a mixed force of sailors from France, Genoa and Monaco attacked the seaward side of the town in 1338, found it weakly defended and ransacked it. The king had lost a lot of supplies, especially of wine, and he was furious. Eventually one of the customs officials was very heavily fined. Further grants of murage then followed in the 1340s and 50s, but serious work only seems to have begun after a three-jury inquisition was held in 1363. A property tax in 1369 raised more funds and in 1374 the mayor and bailiffs were ordered to find twenty masons for work on the walls. Remission of the town's fee-farm was granted in 1376, 1379, 1382 and again in 1400 when the mayor was licensed to take stone from the Isle of Wight. During these years expenditure greatly exceeded revenues. In 1460 the town officials were ordered to fortify and defend it against the Yorkists.

Now isolated within a big open space, Bar Gate is a good starting point for a tour of the walls. At the heart of it is a round arch 3.5m wide of the late 12th century. It is flanked by two U-shaped towers 5.8m wide. At ground level each tower has two firing loops, one commanding the archway and the other the adjoining walls of which short stubs remain. The plan-form suggests the towers and wall are coeval, both probably of c1270-85. The nearly square inner chambers behind the towers may be of the same period, resulting in a plan similar to that of late 13th century castle gatehouses at Tonbridge, Caerphilly and Harlech, but on a smaller scale. The south facade was much restored in 1864. Part of the central arch is original. Those flanking it are Victorian remodellings of 18th century openings. Above is a regular row of four south-facing two-light windows of the guildhall above. This is reached by a straight flight of steps within a modern porch on the north side up to a doorway with a cinquefoiled arch. Between the middle windows a niche contains a statue of George III which has replaced one of Queen Anne, itself likely to have succeeded an effigy of one of the first three King Edwards. On the north side of the guildhall is an original fireplace. In order to free the guildhall of portcullis winding machinery (although no slot for one remains), a north addition of c1400 with canted sides to the NE and NW provided an extra upper room with gunloops. This lies over an extension of the gate passage on each side of which are now pedestrian openings, but which may have once been embrasures for gunloops. The painted shields in panels above the string course are 18th century. At the summit buttresses facing north and stepped corbels carry an ornate machicolated parapet around three sides of the extension.

An old photograph of the arcades on the west side of Southampton

The walls adjoining Bar Gate survived complete although much obscured by other buildings until the 1930s. About 50m west of Bar Gate lay a tower. From here as far as the Arundel Tower the wall retains its wall-walk which is now fully accessible, a modern bridge now spanning a wide gap made in 1960 to take Castle Way. The late 13th century Arundel Tower is a three-quarter round 6.8m in diameter and 17m high to the top of a corbelled parapet probably added c1375-80. A modern steel staircase allows visitors to descend to the hexagonal middle level of the tower with three loops facing the field (there is an infilled bottom level below), and then go out through a doorway on the west side of the tower onto a 7m long spur wall, the western part of which has a polygonal corbelled top looking down the western walls (see page 19). This was needed to flank this side since a change of plan meant that the Arundel Tower was not far enough west to flank the western side of the defences as must have originally been intended. South of here a late 14th century retaining wall runs south to the 9m high Catchcold Tower, a semi-circular 15th century addition with a low vaulted upper room with three gunloops and a boldly projecting corbelled parapet. The Forty Steps against the outside of the wall beyond were added in 1850 after the land outside was reclaimed from the estuary of the River Test. The wall then turns SW to meet the late 12th century castle bailey wall which provides the next part of the circuit for 110m and has a 19th century parapet.

The castle Watergate is a deeply recessed 14th century opening now blocked up. The next portion of the castle wall adjoined the main hall set over an undercroft and has gunloops. Council housing now lies on the site of a missing section of wall between the castle SW corner and the site of the Biddel Gate at the end of Simnel Street. South of here the wall takes the dramatic form of an arcade carrying the parapet over a series of buttresses built in front of older walls of merchants' houses, the seaward openings of which were mostly blocked up as recommended by the royal commission of 1363. The Blue Anchor Postern lies in one of the recesses, which were commanded by machico-lations. South of here King John's House, a rare survival from c1160-75, is one of the merchant's houses incorporated in the town wall. In the blocking of its openings are two keyhole-shaped gunloops. If these are of c1365-75 they would be the earliest of their type in Britain. Set against the house north wall is a chimney stack of c1200 moved here in 1953 from a property in High Street destroyed by wartime bombing.

The next features are the small rectangular Nicholls Tower (beside which further 12th century houses were excavated in the 1960s) and the West Gate giving access to the town quay. Originally a mid 14th century tower 6m wide by 5m deep with a portcullis groove in the passage, it was extended westwards by another 4m with a new outer portcullis in the late 14th century. The upper rooms have 16th century gunloops. The so-called guard room adjoining to the south is more likely to have been a 17th century merchant's store. Footings of more merchants' houses used to be visible on the south side of Westgate Street nearby.

The wall projects slightly beyond West Gate and arrives at a section with five more arcade arches. The first three arches are only of 1899, replacing a Georgian House where the wall had been breached. Between site of the Bugle Tower and footings of the Square Tower only fragments of footing remain. The next section with the St Barbara and Woolbridge has vanished. In streets behind this section lie a fine 14th century two-storey warehouse called the Wool House and a ruined 12th century merchant's house called Canute's Palace. Southampton has more remains of medieval traders' houses publicly on show than any other English town.

The late 14th century Watergate (originally Newgate) on the south side of Southampton retains one three storey D-shaped tower adjoining a later block added outside the main wall. This part has a recessed south front with machicolations between buttresses, one of which contains latrines on each level. The lowest level was originally vaulted. Part of another extension on the north side of the D-shaped tower also survives.

East of here the wall swung southwards to the Watchbell Tower and then east to the early 14th century God's House Gate at the SE corner, a tower 9m by 7m named after the nearby hospital of St Julian. The outermost of the two portcullis grooves in the vaulted passage and the angled south side of the room above with its several trefoil-headed lancet windows are probably the result of later 14th century remodelling or completion of incomplete work. Adjoining the gateway a two storey range with two-light upper windows runs out eastward for 17m to connect with the 9m square God's House Tower built c1400-20 to control the sluice of the east ditch. This tower is diagonally buttressed and rises through three storeys to about 17m. There are more two-light windows here, the second storey ones flanked by keyhole-shaped gunloops. The connecting range retains an original upper fireplace and a concrete floor has replaced a former vault. This very impressive ensemble housed a museum from 1963 until 2011.

The irregularly angled west wall of the God's House Tower link block is earlier, forming a unit with a well preserved 13th century section of the east wall complete with the wall-walk and parapet. It runs for 50m to a D-shaped tower 7m in diameter with several original loops. The open back of the tower must have had a plank bridge to continue the line of the main wall-walk. There is then a gap followed by a ruinous section with two shallowly projecting rectangular bastions 6.7m and 9m wide respectively and possibly dating from the early 13th century. Just west of here remains of the Franciscan friary survived until the 1940s. There is then quite a long gap, originally with five D-shaped towers, before a very ruinous section south of the site of the East Gate demolished in 1775. Like the Bar Gate it had a pair of round towers added in front of a round arch of c1200. An upper room served as a chapel of St Mary in the 1380s. A missing section with one more tower then led up to where it made a straight joint with the late 13th century Polymond or St Denys Tower 8.5m in diameter at the NE corner. Excavations on the south side showed that a wall just 0.8m thick was set into an earlier bank and that it was then thickened internally later on. This may be the section of wall where in an inquisition of 1353 a parapet made of boards upon earthworks was reported to have collapsed. The topmost of the three storeys of the tower was removed in 1828. There are two more D-shaped towers on the section of wall leading west back towards Bar Gate.

STAFFORD   Staffordshire

Stafford is mentioned as a walled town in Domesday Book. There was a royal grant of timber for defences in 1215 and in 1224 the sheriff was ordered to spend 20s on them. A long series of murage grants began in 1233, when the townsfolk were given sixty oaks from Cannock forest to repair three gaps in the walls. The defences of that period may have enclosed a larger area than that enclosed in 913 by Ethelfleda, being about 500m across each way. The western half was nearly rectangular but the eastern half was closer to a triangle in shape. Friaries of the Augustinians and Franciscans well beyond the south and north walls attest to the wealth generated by the wool and cloth trading of the medieval town. Within the walls are two medieval churches, the largest of which, St Mary's, was collegiate and replaced a Saxon church of St Bertelin. The castle is a separate entity, set on an eminence 2km to the SW, whilst the Augustinian priory, an early instance of a dedication to Thomas Becket, lies far out to the east of the town.

A map of c1620 shows a full defensive circuit with half of it stone walled but with palisaded sections on the west and NE sides. The defences were strengthened by Parliamentary forces after they captured Stafford in 1643, and an observer in 1660 commented on the strength of the combined natural and man-made water defences. The North Gate was also known as Gaol Gate, being used as the county prison in the 17th century. First mentioned in 1170, it had two flanking towers and a barbican and drawbridge in front of it. In 1617 the passage through this gate was widened ready for a visit by James I. Buttresses on the wall east of this gate are mentioned in 1599.

North Walls marks the line of the defences down to East Gate, most of which was demolished c1800. Beside a traffic island is a reconstructed fragment with a portcullis groove of the north wall of this early 15th century building, moved in 1938 from its original position. The wall then went down South Walls to the Green or South Gate facing down towards Bridge Street. A pedestrianway to the west of it was created in 1723, but it was removed in 1777. From here walls followed the bank of the River Soar back towards North Gate via Mill Bank (where a small wall fragment was located in 1928), Tenterbanks and Chell Road. John Speed and Celia Fiennes both suggest that there was a west gate facing a bridge over the river but it may have been removed by the 1620s.

Corner tower at Stamford

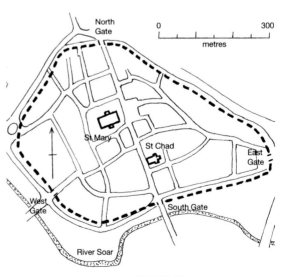

STAFFORD

STAMFORD   Lincolnshire

Stamford was captured from the Danes by King Edward in 912 and he built another burgh on the south bank where St Martin's church is. This suburb also had a church of All Saints and a hospital of St Thomas by the bridge over the River Welland, plus a leper hospital further south. By the late 10th century Stamford was one of the five main towns of the Danelaw, with a market and mint. There was iron-working and a pottery producing some of the first glazed pots made in England since Roman times. The town withstood two attacks during Stephen's reign before being finally being captured in a third attack.

Of 14 churches here by c1500 (4 are mentioned in 1086), there remain All Saints and St John's on either side of Red Lion Square, Great St Michael's by the High Street, and St Mary's and St George's on the south side. Clustered beyond the east end were friaries of Carmelites, Dominicans and Franciscans, enough of an enclave of learned men for an abortive attempt in the 1330s to found a university. Their precincts were huge, that of the Dominicans extending down to the river taking up ten acres (as large as Totnes walled town). Further SE lay the Benedictine priory of St Leonard, and to the south of the town lay the St Michael's nunnery, also Benedictine. Stamford lost some wool and cloth trade to East Anglia later on and was sacked and burnt in 1461 by the Lancastrians. The founding Brown's Hospital in Broad Street by one of the merchants in 1475 demonstrates that there was still prosperity in the town in the years afterwards.

Royal timber was donated for defences in 1218 but the stone walls seem to have been built later on, with a murage grant in 1261 and others through the first half of the 14th century. They enclosed an irregularly shaped area of 75 acres some 1000m long from NE to SW by up to 360m wide. The castle was awkwardly perched on a slope near the west end of the south side. From the west side of the castle bailey, near which stood a church of St Peter, the wall ran west along the south side of Austin Street, named after the friary of the Augustinians to the SW, where they replaced the suppressed Friars of the Sack. The wall then headed NW firstly to the site of a gate across St Peter's Street and then to where a small and much rebuilt round corner tower still stands.

From the tower the walls ran along West Street to Scotsgate, passing a former church of St Clement. The next section along North Street and East Street passed churches of St Augustine, St Andrew and St Paul. Opposite the gate across St Paul's Street lay the church of Holy Trinity and St Stephen and the Carmelite friary. From halfway down Brazenose Lane the wall headed SW down to a gate across St Leonard's Street, on the north site of which lay the church of St Michael Cornstall. The wall then went down the NW side of Wharf Road to reach Bridge Gate. A section of wall near the river bank then linked up with the castle.

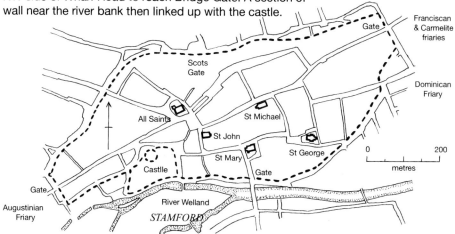

STOCKPORT   Greater Manchester

The town is not mentioned in Domesday Book, although the name appears to be of Saxon origin. Later buildings partly obscure the natural strength of the sandstone plateau site with cliffs facing the River Mersey on the north, the River Goyt on the NE and the Hemsham Brook on the SW, leaving only the SE side open. Stockport became a free borough in 1260 with a weekly market and an annual fair. A bridge replacing the old ford over the Mersey is mentioned in 1377. Little is known about either the castle or possible town walls. Fragments of old walls discovered in the past have variously been described as parts of either the castle or town walls, or simply as remains of houses needing substantial retaining walls below them on the steep slopes. A row of such houses could form an effective barrier. One fragment of old walling in Great Underhill is said to have a medieval type buttress and gargoyle. Stockport is included on a list of places in Cheshire which were to be demilitarised as part of a 1642 pacification agreement.

SWAVESEY   Cambridgeshire

Traces remain around the village of ditches cut c1200 and maintained until c1500 as shown by excavation on the NW. The name Turnbridge suggests a former drawbridge.

TAMWORTH   Staffordshire

Offa, King of Mercia from 757 to 796 had a palace at Tamworth by 781 and is said to have surrounded the town with a rampart and ditch. It remained the capital of Mercia until destroyed by Danish forces in 874, and then lay derelict until restored in 913 by Ethelfleda. She governed Mercia as a province of the kingdom of her brother Edward the Elder. Excavations in Brewery Lane confirmed that the boundary of the medieval town originated with Ethelfleda's new defences, comprising a walled rampart and wide ditch. They were intermittently maintained until the late 14th century. Her nephew King Athelstan (924-40) made Tamworth one of his seats, but the town was again destroyed by Danes in 943 and was never again a royal residence, although a royal mint survived until the 12th century. Unusually for a Saxon town, Tamworth had one large medieval parish church of St Editha, of Saxon origin and collegiate. The River Tame defended the south side of an enclosure roughly 450m square with the castle on the river bank near the SW and the church in the middle. The county boundary once bisected the site. The ramparts passed west of Balfour, to the south of Hospital Street and west of Marmion Street.

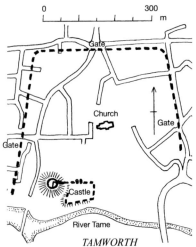

TAMWORTH

TAUNTON   Somerset

A bank and ditch are mentioned in 1158, and in 1216 there is a reference to money spent on digging moats and paying carpenters. Excavations found a ditch 10m wide and 4m deep in front of a 3m high rampart but no trace of any stone walls.

THETFORD   Norfolk

Sacked by the Danes in 1004 and 1010, Thetford was a prosperous settlement in the 11th century with eleven parish churches and a brief tenure of the see of East Anglia. The older part of it south of the river had a ditch 12m wide and 3.3m deep running from St Margaret's churchyard on the London Road to Red Castle on the Brandon Road, where it has been seen in excavations.

TONBRIDGE   Kent

Earthwork defences possibly of the time of a licence in 1259, but perhaps earlier, are thought to have enclosed the town to the north and NE of the castle beside the river. Excavations have failed to reveal any remains of a stone wall. Murage was only granted in 1318, after the last of the de Clare lords of Tonbridge had been killed at Bannockburn.

TOTNES   Devon

Set upon a hill rising 30m above the lowest crossing point of the River Dart, Totnes was important enough by the time of King Edgar (959-75) to have a mint. Domesday Book in 1086 records 95 burgesses here within the borough and another 15 outside it. A deed of c1200 refers to walls here and the bridge is first mentioned about that time. Excavations on the north side have shown the 9th or 10th century rampart to have been 9m wide and fronted by a ditch 10m wide and 5m deep. The area enclosed by the later stone wall was unusually small for an English town, being just 290m long by 170m wide. Inevitably a suburb soon extended for 350m down Fore Street from the East Gate to the bridge. The NW corner is filled by the lofty castle mound, with a bailey projecting well beyond the town walls, and traces of a possible outer bailey beyond that. Murage was granted in 1264 and again in 1355, although the latter was surrendered because no work was actually being done. John Leland described the town walls as "clene down" in 1538 although the town still remained prosperous. Excavations did confirm that the ditches were largely infilled by then but a quarter or more of the actual wall may still stand even if much obscured, reduced in height and/or rebuilt. See extra picture on page 223.

East of the castle is the North Gate, a simple round arch standing high above a roadway that has probably been lowered. From here the wall went east along North Street and Guildhall Yard. Some remains of the wall are probably obscured by houses built over or against it around the NE corner, where there is a "rampart walk" outside the churchyard. The church also served a Benedictine priory, probably no more than a small cell. East Gate has been much rebuilt over the years, most recently c1835. Originally it may have had two round towers. South of the gate houses preserve the wall line into South Street. Here there is a long section of retaining wall dividing upper and lower roads which must be a relic of the wall, even if much rebuilt. Along this side is a small semicircular turret containing rooms just 1.8m across set beside Tower Cottage. The West Gate, demolished in 1810, actually stood at the SW corner next to the last remaining conduit of the town's 16th century water supply.

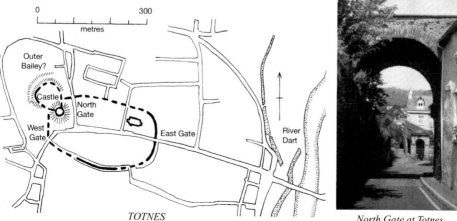

TOTNES

North Gate at Totnes

WALLINGFORD   Oxfordshire

The Saxon defences around a space 770m long north-south by 600m wide here are unusually well preserved, although there are no traces of the stone wall said to have sur-mounted the rampart now standing up to 7.5m high above a 6m wide ditch. The River Thames provided sufficient protection on the east side and a large castle replaced the town defences at the NE corner. The defences were repaired in the early 13th century but there are no records of murage being granted. A new north gate provided c1250 was swallowed up by extensions to the castle c1275-1300. The town had a merchant guild before the 1150s when it was the scene of a peace treaty made between Stephen and his eventual successor Henry II, who gave Wallingford a charter. Of eleven churches existing in the 12th century, there were four in the 15th century of which three survive.

By the central crossroads stood the church of St Martin. Just east of here lay St Mary the Less and towards the castle was All Hallows. Near the bridgehead still stands St Peter's, with the site of St John's south of it. St Michael's lay between here and the surviving church of St Leonard in the SE corner. Another surviving church is St Mary le More by the Market Place. To the SW was St Rumbold's, and near the west gate was another church of St Peter. Most of the NW quadrant is still an open space called Bullcroft and there is a nar-rower open space called Kinecroft on the west side of the SW quadrant.

Bridge Gate at Warkworth

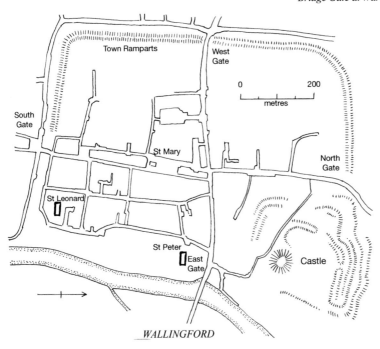

WALLINGFORD

WAREHAM   Dorset

The grid-plan of the streets and the ramparts up to 17m wide and 5m high were probably laid out by King Alfred in 878-9 but archaeological finds indicate Iron-Age and Romano-British occupation of the site. The Burghal Hidage allocates 1600 hides to the maintenance of the defences. Danish forces attacked here in 876, 998 and 1015, after which King Cnut probably had removed a stone wall added to the ramparts c890. The ramparts enclose an area 600m square with the NE corner canted off and the SW corner by a bend of the River Frome. Here lay the 12th century castle, with Trinity Lane probably marking the outer edge of the bailey ditch. On the north side of the town is the River Piddle and together with their associated marshes the two rivers offered good natural defences. On the south side is St Mary's church, originally an important Saxon minster and royal burial place, later serving a Benedictine cell. The former church of Holy Trinity lies by the south of the south gate. Just south of the site of the north gate is a second Saxon church, that of St Martin. By 1290s Wareham had lost its maritime trade to Poole. The town was captured by Parliamentary forces in 1644. See page 6.

WARKWORTH   Northumberland

The town is almost entirely surrounded by a loop of the River Coquet around an area 300m wide from east to west by 500m from the late 14th century old bridge to the south front of the castle occupying more than half of the width of the isthmus. At the south end of the bridge is a plain ruined gatehouse measuring 8.3m by 5.5m. An upper room with one window facing north and two facing south is reached by a staircase lighted by three loops opening off the east side of a vaulted passage once closed at the north end by a two leaved door. On the other side is a small guard room with loops at each end. A similar gatehouse by the castle and a short length of wall would have been sufficient to defend the town but there is no evidence that such were ever actually built.

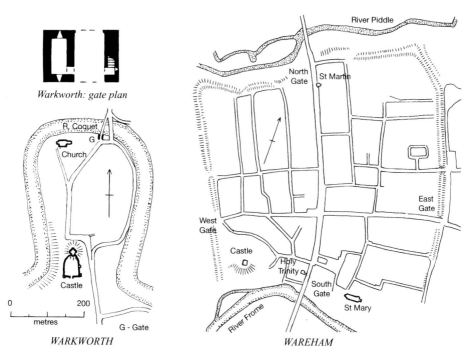

Warkworth: gate plan

0   200
metres

G - Gate

WARKWORTH

WAREHAM

WARWICK   Warwickshire

Warwick protected a crossing of the River Avon by the Fosse Way and was one of King Edward's burghs of 914 but no traces of defences of that period have been found. Murage grants were received in 1305 and 1317 and eventually a wall enclosed an oval area 500m from NW to SE by 400m from SW to NE on the north bank of the river. Since the 17th century the SE third of this space has been walled off as a private park around the castle. A very large collegiate church of St Mary lies within the northern half of the walled area and the church of St Nicholas (later rebuilt) served a suburb beyond the East Gate, whilst to the west of the walled area lay a Dominican friary. Possibly never completed, the walls decayed early on, Leland only seeing sections of them adjoining the gates.

The West Gate is first mentioned in 1129 and already had a chapel associated with it. The building is now an impressive structure 25.5m long with the first 6.5m of it formed by a tall embattled 15th century west tower of the chapel of St James lying over the gateway passage. The tower has diagonal buttresses at all four corners and a tierceron-star-vault. The next section 12m long and probably 13th century, is partly made from the natural sandstone with semi-octagonal wall-shafts and a tunnel-vault with slightly chamfered transverse arches. Bending very slightly to the south, the 7m long eastern part carries the chancel and continues with the vault and transverse arches of the passage. No security or barrier arrangements appear anywhere along the passage.

Passageway at the West Gate at Warwick

A short section of retaining wall survives north of the West Gate. The line of it as briefly seen in excavations lies through properties east of Bowling Green Street and Theatre Street and north of Barrack Street to a gateway across Northgate Street first mentioned in 1272 and said to have been demolished in the early 16th century. The wall then passed down through properties on the NE side of The Butts, where one bastion still remains, to reach the East Gate. This is another substantial building with a tunnel-vaulted passage 13m long and 3.6m wide between walls 2.6m thick. The outside was all refaced when the original chapel of St Peter above it, already ruinous by 1576, was replaced by the existing structure of 1788. Apart from a possible drawbar slot on the south side security arrangements are again curiously absent for such a large and massive gatehouse. It is uncertain if the pedestrian passage north of the main passage perpetuates a medieval feature.

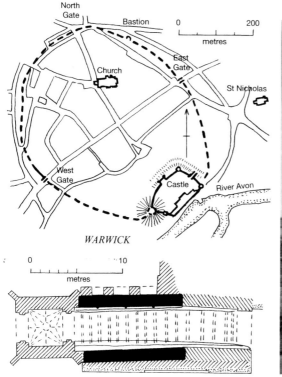

Plan of the West Gate at Warwick (see also page 20)

The East Gate at Warwick

From the East Gate the walls cut across to where Mill street ends below Caesar's Tower of Warwick Castle. Here lay the medieval bridge, first mentioned in 1208. There was no south gateway as such according to Leland, although reports of one pier of the bridge being bigger than the others suggest some sort of barrier at that point. The existing bridge 200m further upstream is late 18th century.

WEM   Shropshire

There are no references to any defences having existed but Noble Street, Leek Street and Bramwell Lane form a likely line of a 12th century town ditch to the north, east and SE of the castle mound. Bars or gates are thought to have existed in Mill Street, by the grammar school in Lowe Hill Road, and perhaps by the Pinfold in Aston Street.

WHITCHURCH   Shropshire

A ditch on the west side of the town is thought to be a 12th century work out of use by the late 13th or 14th century. Possible locations for gates are the end of the High Street, the junction of Sherry Mill Hill and Newton and west of Bargate.

WILTON   Wiltshire

Once important enough as a Saxon town to give its name to Wiltshire, Wilton had a palace of the Kings of Wessex in the 9th century and is mentioned in the Burghal Hidage. The mint was transferred to Old Sarum after an attack by Sweyn Forkbeard in 1003 but there was a merchant guild here by 1121, and originally as many as eight churches.

WINCHELSEA   East Sussex

In 1280 Edward I obtained the manor of Iham on the west side of the River Rother for the founding of a new town of Winchelsea for the purpose of trading in Gascon wine. It was to replace the original settlement on low ground to the east which was subject to flooding in 1252 and 1288, and had been wrecked during the de Montfort wars of the 1260s. A roughly triangular plateau of 150 acres was laid out with a regular grid of new roads at the north end. The defences extended further south than the population was ever likely to occupy so as to command the harbour to the SE. This silted up in the 16th century. Earthwork defences were provided on the west, the only naturally weak side, but funds became diverted to the king's wars and building projects in North Wales and the intended castle on the west probably never proceeded beyond the digging of ditches. In 1295 murage was granted for five years but the town never developed as intended, and is really only a village today. Numerous medieval wine cellars still survive, but only the eastern part of a huge cruciform parish church of St Thomas stands complete.

The inner face of New Gate at Winchelsea

Winchelsea was burned by the French in 1359 and after another attack in 1380 a commission was set up to look at the fortification of the town. A second commission in 1414 examined proposals to halve the size of the enclosed area with a new wall around the landward sides of the twenty grid squares in the NW corner. Compensation would be offered to landowners affected by the works, although the king still held much of the land. Most of the royal grant of 200 marks for each of three years from customs duties in neighbouring ports seems not to have been received but certainly ditches were dug and in the spring of 1415 masons were working on a tower "near the canons in the town", probably in the NW corner. The SW corner of this inner enclosure contained a second parish church, that of St Giles, plus a Dominican friary. The choir of a Franciscan friary church lies in the SE corner. A third parish church, of St Leonard, lay to the west and there were also three medieval hospitals.

The inner face of the Pipewell or Land Gate at Winchelsea

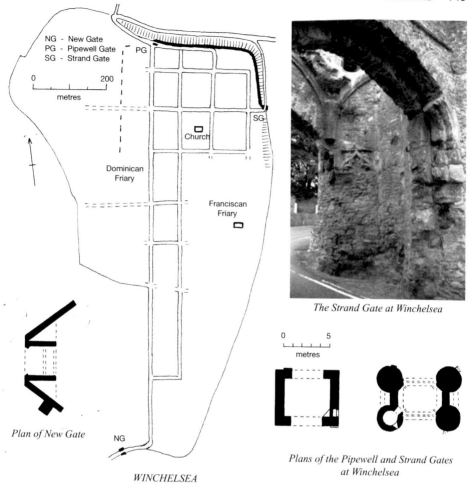

NG - New Gate
PG - Pipewell Gate
SG - Strand Gate

0   200
metres

PG

SG

Church

Dominican
Friary

Franciscan
Friary

Plan of New Gate   NG

WINCHELSEA

The Strand Gate at Winchelsea

0   5
metres

*Plans of the Pipewell and Strand Gates
at Winchelsea*

The Pipewell or Land Gate on the north side is a rectangle of 7m by 6m with the lower parts of one upper room over a passage, once vaulted, closed by two-leaved doors. Over a weathered shield on the outer archway (facing west) there is said to have been inscribed the name of John Helde, mayor here in 1404-5. An older gate here was wrecked in the attack of 1380. Walls extended from the SW and NE corners of this gate. The latter wall still exists, as a 2m high and 0.6m thick retaining breastwork extending round the precipitous NE corner of the town as far as the NW corner of the Strand Gate.

Strand Gate also probably dates from the early 15th century and is a rectangle 6.4m by 4.4m over walls 0.8m thick with round turrets 2.8m in diameter at each corner. The passage has springings for a rib-vault and portcullis grooves at each end. The turrets contained rooms at the upper level and the NE turret also has a porter's lodge at ground level. A stub of the next portion of wall 3.6m high adjoins the SE turret. See page 22.

New Gate lies isolated far from any houses at the south of the original intended enclosure. It takes an unusual form, having a thinly walled but lofty passageway 3m wide and 3.4m deep covered with a ribbed vault and set diagonally though a sharp angle of the defences marked by short lengths of thin walls. On the inside the arch is flanked by side-arches into triangular spaces now walled off.

WINCHESTER   HAMPSHIRE

The walls of the Roman town of Venta Belgarum extended in a very gentle slope up westwards for 1000m from the rather irregular line of the east wall following the west bank of the River Itchen. The enclosure was 900m wide and contained 138 acres. Winchester was the capital of Wessex from the time of King Egbert in 829, and in King Alfred's time 2400 hides were assigned for the maintenance of its defences. No Saxon work is detectable in the remaining parts of the defences but footings of two successive Saxon cathedrals have been found to the north of the Norman cathedral, which in medieval times was the longest in Europe, and had one of the richest sees. Here King Cnut was buried in 1035 and William I was crowned for a second time in 1066. All the Norman kings were frequent visitors and kept their treasure in the royal castle which straddled the line of the southern half of the west wall of the Roman town. In 1141 the city was the scene of a battle between King Stephen and the Empress Matilda.

The presence of four friaries attests to wealth here even though the royal mint moved away. Few of the medieval churches within the walls now survive. St Lawrence by the High Street remains in use, but St Thomas's has gone and St Maurice's is just a tower.

The four main gates are mentioned in 1110 and 1148. Royal timber was donated to Winchester in 1217 for the making of towers and "alures", an unusually specific reference. Murage grants began in 1228 and covered most of the years to 1244. Murage was granted again in 1264 and in 1271, followed by other grants in the 1280s and 90s. A royal commission was ordered in 1339 to investigate the condition of the walls, the inhabitants being commanded to pay for repairs. Nothing was done until after another commission in 1369 and grants and subsidies were provided for the work in the 1390s. The town accounts frequently note expenditure on the walls during the 15th century with funds raised though local taxation and a fifty year alnage subsidy but details are rarely recorded. Part of the SE section of walls was repaired in 1473-4.

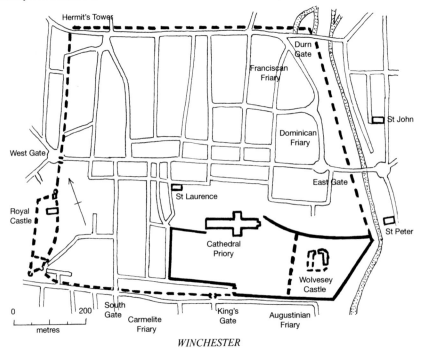

WINCHESTER

Close up of the shields and machicolations on the West Gate at Winchester

Cleared of encroaching houses in 1940, West Gate is an interesting composite structure. The lower parts built of flint with ashlar quoins are 13th century. The western arch with its portcullis groove is later, and so are the upper parts bearing shields with the royal and city arms. A machicolated parapet is carried on a row of four stepped corbels between the buttresses. Richard II's badge of a white hart couchant (adopted in 1390) is said to have appeared on the lower string course. The two gunloops and the machicolated top may well be a response to the crisis period of 1392-4 when a French invasion was expected. Flints show where the main wall went off to the north.

Much of the 320m of wall southwards to the SW corner was actually provided by the castle, of which Henry III's hall is the main remnant. The street name Constables Gate refers to a castle entrance. The wall then headed east for 200m to the South Gate, destroyed in 1771 but commemorated by the name Southgate Street. Along the 250m long next section of the wall two minor fragments remain between Canon Street and St Swithun Street. This section was provided with new battlements following riots by the townsfolk in 1264 which resulted in the destruction of King's Gate. The present structure there is late medieval and lacks defensive features (see picture on page 12). Three arches support an upper room forming a chapel. From the gate a complete section up to 6m high runs east beside College Street and then goes round the episcopal palace of Wolvesey Castle and heads as far NE as a bend in the river. Part of it is still crenellated and has an earth bank 2m high and up to 9m wide behind it. Work of the Roman period and the 13th and 14th centuries can be detected. South of here the Augustinian friary lay outside the walls, the Carmelite friary being further west.

Excavations in land adjoining Colebrook Street, just south of the East Gate, showed that the Roman wall was reduced to a low core by the 12th century. A new wall was built in front in the 13th century and this was repaired in the 14th century. Beyond East Gate, which was surmounted by a chapel, the line of the wall is uncertain and probably had an irregular course. The street called Durngate perpetuates the name of what was probably a newly created postern in the 13th century and was blocked up in 1377. The presence of a second gateway in this area shown on Speed's map is not backed up by any references to it. This area once contained the Franciscan and Dominican friaries.

Little remains of the wall along the northern side of North Walls. Excavations showed the 13th century wall built on top of the Roman core in some places but to the south of it in others. North Gate was destroyed in 1771. The Hermit's Tower at the NW is a modern structure on the site of a 13th century drum-tower. Speed shows two more towers on the missing section of wall back to the West Gate. Robber trenches at the site of one of them indicated it to have been 6m wide over walls 1.5m thick. The outer part was too disturbed for its shape to be clearly made out and there was no dating evidence.

WORCESTER   Worcestershire

Set beside the River Severn, and commanding an important crossing, Worcester is not mentioned amongst the towns fortified either by King Alfred or King Edward and his sister Ethelfleda, but it is said to have been fortified in 899 against the Danes by Aethelred, Earl of Mercia. The city was devastated by a fire in 1113 which also destroyed the castle and it received a royal charter in 1189. The cathedral is the burial place of King John, who had demanded £100 from the citizens for the right to keep their fortifications. After his time land taken in the 11th century for the northern bailey of the castle was returned to the cathedral priory. The rest of the castle, which projected beyond the south end of the defences, was then abandoned. This remained a weak point through which Robert Ferrers, Earl of Derby, entered and captured the city in 1263 for Simon de Montfort.

Much of the city wall was built with the aid of a series of 13th century murage grants starting in 1224. There were more intermittant grants in the 14th century. Parish churches within the walls were All Saints in the NW quadrant, St Nicholas, St Martin and St Swithun (all rebuilt) in the NE quadrant, and St Andrew, St Alban and St Helen in the centre. St Mary's by the cathedral, and St Peter's in the SE corner, have vanished.

Foregate Street is a natural starting point for a tour, which is aided by plaques near the site of each of the seven gates. Road widening in the 1890s revealed traces of the flanking towers of Fore Gate. From it the walls went east down Sansome Street to the site of Trinity Gate. The dual-carriageway City Walls Road arcing round all the eastern side of the city has taken the place of the wide water-filled ditch on this side. Creation of the road has resulted in the permanent exposure of a formerly hidden long section of sandstone walling up to 2m thick and 2.5m high. It extends south from near the site of the St Martin Gate, passing the base of a 5m diameter solid round turret with a good splayed plinth. After the Battle of Worcester in 1651 Charles II escaped from the city by the St Martin Gate, which was demolished in 1777.

Turret base at Worcester

*Cathedral precinct Water Gate
at Worcester*

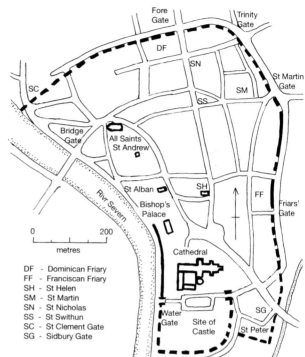

DF - Dominican Friary
FF - Franciscan Friary
SH - St Helen
SM - St Martin
SN - St Nicholas
SS - St Swithun
SC - St Clement Gate
SG - Sidbury Gate

WORCESTER

The wall base with a battered plinth survives in patches down to Friar's Gate, which allowed the Franciscans access between their friary within the wall and their burial ground outside them. The Sidbury Gate at the SE end of the city was demolished in 1768. The storming of this gate by Parliamentary forces in 1651 cost the lives of 1000 of Charles II's defending Scottish troops. An excavation against a section of the wall near here found it to have a thick foundation 1.2m deep set into an earlier rampart.

To the west the wall followed the former line of the castle bailey, passing the site of Frog Gate and forming the cathedral close. The huge Edgar Gate of the close survives, along with the Water Gate and much of the west wall facing the river. The Water Gate is late medieval, with four-centred arches and a portcullis groove. A house surmounts it. Here a ferry used to operate across the river. Another gate faced the medieval bridge to the north of the present bridge of 1932. There was also the St Clement Gate facing north. From it the wall followed the line of The Butts back to Fore Gate.

East walls at Worcester

YORK   North Yorkshire

The Roman settlement at York comprised a 50 acre fort founded in AD71 as the base of the Ninth Legion, with suburbs to the south and west of it and a town or colonia on the opposite SW bank of the River Ouse. As rebuilt by Constantius I c300 the fort had stone walls 1.5m thick and about 6m high enclosing an area 480m from SW to NE by 410m wide. Bootham Bar, St Helen's Square, and King's Square mark the positions of three of the gates and a fourth lay on the NE side, further NW from Monk Bar. There were square towers projecting internally along three sides and at the rounded east and north corners. The SW side towards the river was a show front with large polygonal corner bastions and sets of three polygonal fronted towers between each corner and the gateway.

York formed the royal seat of the Anglian kings of Northumbria but the tower once thought to be of that period is now regarded as Late Roman work. Orientated east-west, the existing cathedral or minster lies diagonally across the old fort just north of its centre and stands on the site of a cathedral founded in 627. Danish forces captured the city in 867 and refortified it, covering three sides of the crumbling Roman wall with an earth rampart which was extended SE to where the River Foss once flowed closer to the old fort so as to protect landing stages on the river banks. The trading settlement on the SW bank of the river was also enclosed by a high bank over its former rampart.

As part of his campaigns to bring the North under his control William I had a pair of motte and bailey fortresses built opposite each other on either side of the Ouse. King William had the Foss dammed just below the eastern castle (which proved to be the longest lasting), creating considerable expanses of water further upstream. On the NE side the ramparts were pushed out to include St Cuthbert's church and it was probably in this period also that the Walmgate Bar suburb was first given defences. Three of the gates are late 12th century in origin but documentary references to the walls only first occur in 1196 and 1210. Murage was first granted in 1226, but work on the existing stone walls is only likely to have begun after Henry III began rebuilding the castle on the east bank in stone in 1244. Murage grants were in force every year from 1251 until 1267. Another series of grants began in 1284 and with only short breaks continued until in 1449 the right to levy tolls to pay for maintaining the walls was granted in perpetuity.

Twenty medieval parish churches still remain within the defences, two of them being in Walmgate and six of them being in the Micklegate part of the city. There were also friaries of the Augustinians, Carmelites, Dominicans and Franciscans, plus a shorter-lived house of the Friars of the Sack.

See illustrations on pages 10 & 20.

Interior of the Multangular Tower at York

The Red Tower at York

Work on the walls would have still been in progress when Scottish raiders came close to York in 1319 and 1327, prompting some improvements to the defences such as the adding of barbicans and upper rooms with bartizans to the gateways. The late 13th century close wall around the Benedictine abbey of St Mary lying beyond the NW wall was heightened and provided with towers. Work on a new wall around the Walmgate suburb was begun in 1345. In that year a contract was made between the mayor and citizens and the mason Thomas de Staunton for the erection of the section between Fishergate Bar and the bank of the Foss opposite the castle. Henry VII had the rectangular towers at either end of the Walmgate defences added c1486-90 as part of a strengthening of the defences which proved justified in 1489, when rebel forces attacked this quarter, damaging both gateways. The city possessed cannon for its defence as early as 1463 and others were purchased in 1511. York was captured by the rebels during the Pilgrimage of Grace in 1535 and was threatened in 1569 by the rebel northern earls.

In 1644 Royalist forces under the Earl of Newcastle were besieged in York by combined Scottish and Parliamentary forces until Prince Rupert arrived in July to relieve it. He and Newcastle were defeated at Marston Moor soon afterwards and the city was surrendered a fortnight later. Parliament then granted £5000 from the confiscated estates of Royalists to pay for extensive repairs to the walls. The risk of attack from Prince Charles' Jacobite forces in 1745 led to further improvements such as deepening ditches, although it was realised the walls could never stand up to the cannon of that age. The gates and portcullises were also overhauled. In 1807 Skeldergate Postern was demolished as the first stage of an intended removal of the defences. Work ground to a halt after the archbishop sued the council for the loss of tolls collected there and at other gates during the Lammastide Fair. In the end demolition over the next few decades was limited to the removal of several posterns and three of the gateway barbicans. Maintenance of the walls as an ancient monument and public amenity began in the 1860s.

The area within the walls at York is huge, measuring roughly 1100m from SE to NE by a greatest extent of 1280m from NW to SE. Just the Walmgate suburb alone was as big as some other walled towns. About 3.7km of city walls still stand but rivers and lakes and the large precinct of the abbey of St Mary brought the entire defensible perimeter to about 5km. The rivers Ouse and Foss bisect the site and converge in the southern corner, whilst much of the eastern corner was a lake formed by damming the Foss. The city still suffers from occasional flooding on both sides of the Foss. Lakes and water-filled ditches overlooked by high ramparts constituted a major part of the defences and the wall itself is rarely more than 2m high to the wall-walk, with the much rebuilt parapet adding another 2m to the external height. The walls are mostly faced with blocks of white magnesian limestone from quarries near Tadcaster. Projections from the wall are here described as towers on the assumption that they originally had upper storeys at wall-walk level. Most of them currently appear as solid bastions although in fact they do contain chambers, often with original crossloops. Four main gatehouses survive complete with their portcullises (a great rarity) and there are other minor gateways. The Ouse is now crossed by three late 19th century bridges. Only the centrally placed Ouse Bridge had a medieval predecessor, which was replaced in 1564 after part of it collapsed.

Having crossed Lendal Bridge from the station our tour starts with the Lendal Tower on the NE bank of the Ouse, across which a chain was suspended to the Barker Tower opposite to enforce tolls being paid by river traffic. Only the lowest storey has survived rebuilding in the 17th century when the city was supplied with water from this point. From here the wall runs NE to join the line of the original Roman fort (now represented by 13th century walling on the older footings) going NW past the remains of St Leonard's Hospital to the Multangular Tower. This polygonal open bastion formed part of improvements c300 to the 2nd century wall of the Roman fort. Originally called Elrondyng, but renamed by Dr Martin Lister in 1683, the bastion has a diameter of 13.6m and ten facets facing the field, each one with a crossloop in the late 13th century upper part.

The so-called Anglian Tower at York

Beyond the Multangular Tower part of the Danish and Norman earth bank supporting the 13th century wall has been removed to reveal the Roman wall within it. This wall still has sections of the tiled cornice on which stood the parapet, but much of it remains buried. Beyond remains of a Roman internal tower is the Anglian Tower, recently re-interpreted as Late Roman rather than 7th century. It has 0.5m thick walls of oolitic limestone supporting a vault over a room 2m wide and 2.7m long. Long buried in later earthworks, it was discovered by accident in 1839 and fully exposed for visitors to see in 1969. The creation of St Leonard's Place in 1831-35 caused the loss of the next stretch of wall to Bootham Bar, along with one tower.

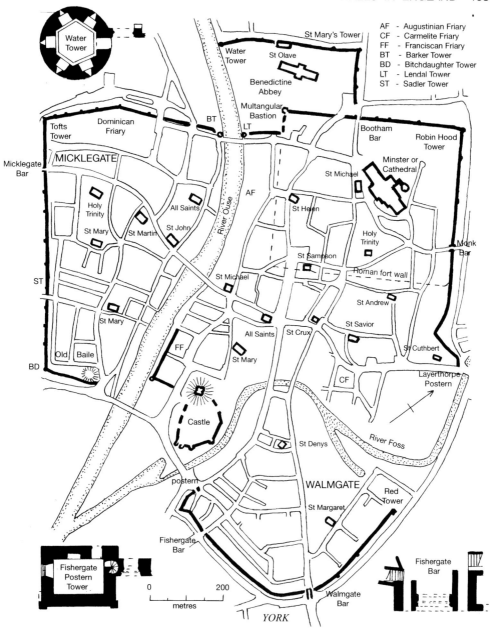

Water Tower

AF - Augustinian Friary
CF - Carmelite Friary
FF - Franciscan Friary
BT - Barker Tower
BD - Bitchdaughter Tower
LT - Lendal Tower
ST - Sadler Tower

St Mary's Tower

Water Tower

St Olave

Benedictine Abbey

Multangular Bastion

BT

LT

Tofts Tower

Dominican Friary

Micklegate Bar

MICKLEGATE

Bootham Bar

Robin Hood Tower

Minster or Cathedral

St Michael

Holy Trinity

All Saints

St Mary

St Martin

St John

River Ouse

AF

St Helen

Holy Trinity

St Sampson

Monk Bar

Roman fort wall

ST

St Michael

St Andrew

St Mary

St Savior

Old Baile

BD

All Saints

St Mary

St Crux

St Cuthbert

FF

Layerthorpe Postern

CF

Castle

St Denys

River Foss

postern

WALMGATE

Red Tower

St Margaret

Fishergate Bar

Fishergate Postern Tower

0   200

metres

Walmgate Bar

Fishergate Bar

YORK

Beyond this section of the city wall lies the walled precinct of the abbey of St Mary founded c1080. The original wall of c1270-80 was heightened 1.8m in 1318. The Water Tower by the river and St Mary's tower of the 1320s are full rounds, the latter partly re-built with old materials after being undermined by Parliamentary forces in 1644, causing the loss of monastic records stored within it. The walls here retain merlons with slots for wooden shutters and six other small turrets, plus the 12th century abbey gatehouse. The gate beside a square tower by Bootham Bar was built in 1497 as a back entrance for the abbot's lodging, later the King's Manor, and seat of the Council of the North.

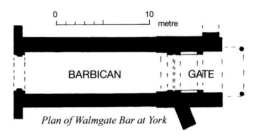

Plan of Walmgate Bar at York

Monk Bar at York

Bootham Bar is a 12th century replacement of one of the Roman gateways. The upper storeys are early 14th century but the bartizans of that period required rebuilding after bombardment in 1644, and the barbican in front of the gate was removed in 1835. The inner face of the gatehouse was rebuilt in 1719 and again in 1835. The next section of wall to Monk Bar and beyond lies on a rampart thrown up over the Roman fort wall. Three of five small towers between the gate and the north corner are semi-hexagons. A 15th century circular gunloop has been inserted into the base of the second one. Of 1887-9 are the parapets on all the towers, the section of main wall-walk on arcading, and the whole of the corner bastion, the original here having gone by 1680.

Monk Bar was created entirely anew c1330 as part of a scheme to keep traffic out of the cathedral close. A depression in the rampart further NW marks the site of the original Roman and Norman gateways. This gatehouse is the only one at York with a medieval stone inner face. It measures 8.2m wide by 9.6m long including the buttresses supporting bartizans to a height of 19m. A straight stair leads up to two levels of vaulted rooms lying over the vaulted passage. The outer arch with a working portcullis is round, but there is a pointed arch supporting an open gallery with a machicolation between the bartizans. Shouldered-lintelled doorways led out onto the sidewalls of the former barbican. The top storey is a 15th century addition and has facing the outside two gunloops in the form of squares with cross-shaped sighting slits above them. As heightened the bartizans have three levels of tiny rooms each with crossloops with end roundels like those in the second and third storey rooms. These chambers now house a museum commemorating Richard III, an able administrator who was very popular in York.

The next section of wall has a wall-walk on arches of the late 15th century. On the outer face of the wall is a buttress containing latrine shutes. The wall passes remains of firstly a Roman interval tower with thin walls enclosing rooms 3m by 3.6m and then the Roman east corner of c200 with a rather larger internal tower. Beyond here there was once a postern. The wall bends slightly to follow the line of Danish ramparts, and then turns through a right angle to follow a Norman rampart. The tower in the angle is described as new in 1380. Like all the towers along here it has a 19th century parapet. The wall passes a rectangular bastion with a stepped base and gunloops and ends at a corner with a turret perched partly on an arch and partly on corbels, possibly the result of reconstruction in the 1660s. Originally the wall continued SE for another 70m to a rectangular tower containing the Layerthorpe Postern demolished in 1829.

Beyond a former lake 410m wide the mid 14th century wall of Walmgate begins with the Red Tower. It lay ruinous from c1735 to c1800 and is a brick structure of 1490 measuring 7.5m by 5.4m set on a limestone base. It has a hipped roof and upper windows of 1858. The local stonemasons resented the tilers or bricklayers being employed here and were accused of murder when a tiler was found dead, although no-one was ever convicted. The upper room has a latrine within a corbelled projection which originally discharged into deep water on the north side. The wall-walk of the next section is carried on arches of c1500 and there are renewed crossloops with tiny canopies in the parapet merlons. Further along are two shallowly projecting rectangular bastions.

Walmgate Bar is of 12th century origin and measures 7.5m by 7.2m. A sag in the walls of the 15.2m long barbican in front is a relic of a mine dug under it by Parliamentary troops in 1644. The mine's presence was betrayed by a prisoner to the garrison before it could be fired. Cannonfire so damaged the gatehouse most of its upper parts with two bartizans had to be rebuilt afterwards. It had previously suffered damage in an attack in 1489. Two columns support the timber-framed late 16th century inner part of the building. The two circular bartizans on the barbican outer corners may be original.

There is one rectangular projection at a corner between Walmgate Bar and Fishergate Bar. The wall has a chamfered plinth and its parapet embrasures have been made into musket loops. Fishergate Bar appears to be early 15th century and has a wide arch with a portcullis groove flanked by narrow pedestrian passages which appear to be original. This gateway was so badly damaged by attacking rebel forces in 1489 that it was blocked up and not re-opened until 1827. It has lost the upper rooms used as a prison. The wall heads west and angles SW to a corner turret measuring 6.6m by 4m formerly closer to the riverbank. The cruciform gunloops are of c1500 and the fireplace and brick vaulting inside are of the 1660s. The wall soon bends again and terminates with a narrow postern with a portcullis groove beside a rectangular tower 8m long by 6.4m wide built c1500. It contains three storeys of habitable rooms linked by a spiral staircase in a turret beside the south end wall. A latrine projects at second storey level. The tower now has a hipped roof above the level of the original flat root and open parapets. Originally there was about 80m width of water between here and the castle bailey walls.

Walmgate Bar at York

Fishergate at York

To the SW of the castle mound lay the Castlegate Postern which was widened in 1699 but demolished in 1826. The wall from here to the bank of the Ouse was always low and appears even more so now as the land outside it has been raised in level. The wall-walk here is just a narrow ledge. A brick summer-house of 1750 lies on top of the Davy Tower on the river-bank. Until it was sold off in 1553 a chain was stretched across the river from here to the lost Crane Tower on the far bank. A section of riverbank upstream from here retains part of the wall of the precinct of the Franciscan friary.

Since the Skeldergate Postern was demolished in 1807 the wall now starts again below the mound of the Old Baile, a second castle originally with a bailey 120m square within the next angle of the walls. This space was latterly used for military exercises and traditional Shrove Tuesday games. The citizens had to persuade the archbishop, then owner of the Old Baile, to replace the palisade with a stone wall as part of the city defences. The south corner tower is probably the Bitchdaughter Tower mentioned in 1451 and again in 1566 when stone from an upper storey was removed to rebuild the Ouse Bridge. The brick vault and fireplace inside are of 1645. The towers along the straight wall to Micklegate Bar are variously semi-circular, rectangular and polygonal. The Victoria Bar of 1838 replaced a long blocked-up postern. Beyond is the Sadler Tower, with a good battered base of 13th century type. The second tower beyond had a vault.

Roman coffins are built into the walls of the 12th century passage of Micklegate Bar. The 14th century upper parts with bartizans and doorways to barbican wall-walks bear the arms of Edward III. The inner face is of 1827. This was the busiest of the city gates and the one where visiting royalty were received. Severed heads once displayed here included those of Hotspur Percy in 1403, Richard, Duke of York in 1460, Lancastrian leaders captured at Towton in 1461, and the 7th Earl of Northumberland in 1572.

The wall out to the west corner has one rectangular bastion and several buttresses. Tofts Tower at the corner was mostly rebuilt of gritstone and with a vault to support cannon after being damaged in 1644. Two of out of three towers on the next section above the station yard are polygonal. There is now only internal access to one of them. A fourth tower has been rebuilt and a fifth removed, as this section has been pierced for 19th century roads and railways, although the wall-walk is still continuous. There was originally a small postern next to the Barker Tower on the river-bank. A 17th century conical roof now covers this building, with windows in the crenels of the original parapet.

Section of arcaded wall-walk near the Red Tower at York

Barker Tower at York   *Turret by Layerthorpe Postern at York*

OTHER REFERENCES TO FORMER TOWN DEFENCES IN ENGLAND

AXBRIDGE, BURPHAM, HALWELL, SHAFTSBURY, SOUTHWARK, WATCHET
    All in the Burghal Hidage record but without any surviving traces of fortfifications.
BOLSOVER, BUNGAY, FRAMLINGHAM, KILPECK, LONGTOWN, ONGAR, PLESHEY,
    SKIPSEA, TUTBURY - examples of village enclosures adjoining Norman castles.
BUCKINGHAM, CHIRBURY, HERTFORD, RUNCORN, THELWALL and WITHAM:
    Burghs of King Edward's campaigns of 909-14 without remains.
BEDFORD - King's Ditch named after Edward's burgh of 915 on south bank of Ouse.
BRIGHTON - Defended from seaward attack by a blockhouse of the 1540s
BROADSTAIRS - 16th century arch with portcullis groove closed off town from beach.
CHESTERFIELD - Medieval ditch found in 1970s assumed to be defensive.
DERBY - The Mercian Register implies fortifications here by 917. No later defences.
EDDISBURY - Excavation evidence of Ethelfleda's refortification of Iron Age fortress.
FOWEY - Leland mentions a wall and gates. 1540s blockhouse at harbour entrance.
GODMANCHESTER - Saxon enclosure traceable to SW of Roman enclosure.
HENLEY-ON-THAMES - Town ditch mentioned 1397 and 1531. May have had a wall.
HEXHAM - Two gates recorded in 1698. Possible minor fragments east & NE of abbey.
HUNTINGDON - Danish burgh. Ditch of 17th century and earlier has been excavated.
ILFRACOMBE - Murage was granted in 1418. There are no remains.
MELCOMBE - Murage granted in 1338. Unsuccessful petition for defences in 1379.
PENRITH - Murage grants of 1346 & 1391 only evidence of intended fortifications.
SOUTHWOLD - Murage and licence to crenellate in 1250. Fort of 1588 also gone.
TEIGNMOUTH - Leland c1538 mentioned an embattled defensive wall here.
TILBURY - Earthworks ordered in 1402 but no evidence of pre-Elizabethan defences.
TOWCESTER - The Saxon burgh is reported to have had a stone wall by 917.
WELLS - Murage was granted in 1341. WOODSTOCK - Murage granted 1322.
Abingdon, Banbury, Bewdley, Droitwich, Henley-in-Arden, Morpeth, Tewkesbury, and
Yarmouth (Isle of Wight) all had gates, probably toll barriers rather than defensive.
Roman walls not used later:Cirencester, Dorchester, Leintwardine, Silchester, Tadcaster.

GAZETTEER OF WALLED TOWNS IN WALES

There were at least twenty-two circuits of medieval town walls of stone in Wales, all built between the 1240s and the 1340s, and mostly by English lords. Of places which became county towns Dolgellau was the only one that remained undefended, although Flint never had walls or gates of stone. None of the four medieval cathedrals (Bangor, Llandaff, St Asaph and St Davids) was directly associated with a walled town. The only Roman walls to remain in later use were those buried under the castle outer bailey rampart at Cardiff, and the tiny Caer Gybi fort at Holyhead retained to enclose a major church. Only at Dryslwyn is there evidence (not currently visible above ground) of a stone-walled settlement beside the castle of a Welsh prince. Other townships beside native Welsh castles at Dolforwyn and Dynevor only had earth and timber defences. The enclosed area at Dryslwyn was tiny, and the walled areas at Carmarthen, Caernarfon Cardigan, Denbigh and Haverfordwest were also very modest in size.

Town walls in Wales have either tended to survive in a remarkably complete state or have almost vanished. The North Wales towns of Conwy and Caernarfon have the best preserved combination of medieval castle and town walls now remaining in the British Isles. Each has walls more continuous and considerably less altered and rebuilt than those at York and Chester. The hilltop town of Denbigh retains three quarters of the circuit of town walls, but the castle there is much more ruinous and a second gate is reduced to footings. In South Wales the landward-facing walls of promontory-towns at Chepstow and Tenby are almost complete each with one original gateway. Pembroke retains the feel of a walled town, although only fragments of actual original wall remain, with four towers. A gateway and wall fragments remain at Kidwelly. Monmouth has the only surviving medieval bridge-gate in Britain but only minor remnants of the town wall itself. Walls with one gate remain at Cowbridge. There are also meagre (and sometimes difficult to see) remains at Abergavenny, Beaumaris, Brecon, Carmarthen, Hay-on-Wye, Monmouth and New Radnor. Nothing remains standing at Newport and Swansea.

ABERGAVENNY Monmouthshire

Hamelin de Ballon established the castle and town c1088 on the site of a Roman fort. Walling of an oval area 350m long by 215m wide with the castle projecting beyond the SW corner may have begun after the marriage of the heiress Ava de Braose to William de Cantilupe c1240 although the castle itself was possibly not rebuilt in stone until fifty years later. A smaller rectangular area was enclosed by the original 11th century palisade. Murage was granted in 1241-6, 1259-64, 1285, and 1314-19. The castle was ordered to be slighted in 1647 and parts of the town wall were probably also dismantled then although it is shown as virtually complete on a map of 1801. Minor and obscured fragments remain behind some of the shops on the north side of Neville Street, behind the market and behind a single house in each of Cross Street and Monmouth Street. The townsfolk used the nave of a Benedictine priory church just outside the walls to the east and this has ensured the church's survival.

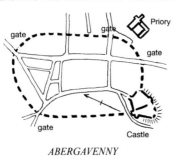

ABERGAVENNY

BEAUMARIS

ABERYSTWYTH   Ceredigion

Edward I began establishing a town and castle here in 1277. Both originally were known under the name Llanbadarn from the older settlement to the SE containing the medieval parish church, although a chapel-of-ease later stood near the castle. Neither the castle or the town were probably fully defensible by the time of the Welsh attack of 1282, when ramparts here were said to have been destroyed. A lack of locks, bolts or bars on the town gates was recorded in 1280, and presumably remedied by subsequent expenditure of £180 on the town defences. The town was burned after being captured by Owain Glyndwr in 1404. Excavations have uncovered lost parts of the castle, from which it appears that it was radically redesigned after the attack of 1282, but little is known about the town defences, which enclosed an area about 400m from SW to NE by 370m from the SE to NW.

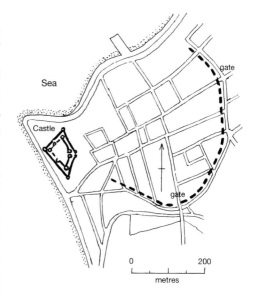

ABERYSTWYTH

What little of the defences that survived a siege by Parliamentary forces in 1645-6 and slighting in 1649 were removed in the 19th century. From the east side of the castle set on a low promontory the walls followed the curved line of South Road (where footings 1.8m thick were found in 1955) and Mill Street round the south side of the town, with a gate facing a bridge over the Rheidol. The walls then followed Chalybeate Street to a gate at the bottom of Great Darkgate Street and then down Baker street to the East Gate (which actually faced NE), and then down Alfred Place towards North Beach.

BEAUMARIS   Anglesey

A flat location by the shore, allowing supplies to be brought in by sea, was chosen for a royal castle begun in 1295 in response to the Welsh uprising of the previous year. A town founded alongside it, and granted a charter in 1296, replaced the original Welsh settlement of Llanfaes inland to the north, where lie slight remains of a Franciscan Friary. The inhabitants of Llanfaes were moved across Anglesey to Newborough. The English townsfolk requested building of a town wall in 1315, as had presumably been the original plan, but it was actually only built in 1407-14 as a response to the Glyndwr rebellion. The walls enclosed an area of about 330m by 300m to the SW of the castle, south of which extends a short length of thick wall footings towards the shore. The seaward side suffered from natural erosion and the southern corner has been entirely lost. From it the wall ran NW to a gate across Castle Street, and then went around the churchyard, which formed the western corner. Traces of the ditch around that part were found in 1975. A section of 2m thick walling 35m long remains in a location parallel to Rating Row between the church and Castle Street. Another section, 25m long and up to 3.3m high runs parallel to Steeple Lane and a third fragment remains on the north side of Castle Street. NE of the church lay a gate across Burgh Street. Between here and the castle the wall was removed in 1669, but other portions were repaired in the early 18th century.

BRECON   Breconshire

Brecon suffered attacks by Llywelyn ap Iorwerth in 1217, 1231 and 1233 and was again captured by the Welsh in 1263 and 1265. The town walls are assumed to have been begun by Humphrey de Bohun after his marriage to the heiress Eleanor de Braose in 1241. Including the castle the walled area was 600m long with a maximum width at the SE end of 300m. One gate faced SW towards a bridge over the River Usk where there are remains of a Dominican friary outside the walls near the south bank. Another gate close by faced a bridge over the Honddu, beyond which are remains of the castle. The Struet Gate faced north towards a Benedictine priory (later the parish church and since 1923 a cathedral) lying 200m further up above the Honddu. The Watton Gate lay at the SE corner near where there is a length of rampart. Above a private garden NE of the site of the Watton Gate are ruins about 4m high of a rectangular tower 6m wide projecting about 3m from a 20m length of retaining wall. Beside the Usk is a square ruined gateway tower from which extends a long section of the south wall, mostly rebuilt above the footings. What is now a parish church of St Mary in the middle of the town ranked only as a chapel-of-ease to the priory church until the 1920s despite its size and tall early 16th century tower added when the Stafford dukes of Buckingham were lords of Brecon.

In 1404 the town bailiff was authorised to spend 100 marks on the gates, walls and ditches. He was later given an annuity as a reward for his "great labour and perils" during the recent rebellion. The 1536 Act of Union made Brecon one of four regional centres in Wales and established county town status which was retained until 1974. The walls are assumed to have been dismantled during or after the Civil War period and an act of Parliament of 1776 allowed the dismantling of the gates.

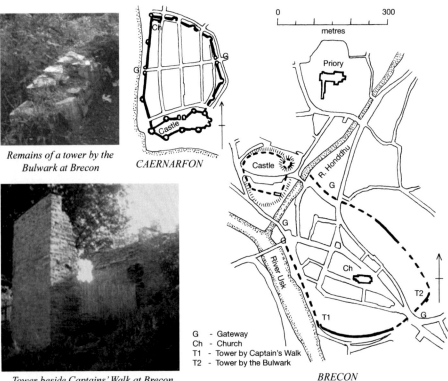

Remains of a tower by the Bulwark at Brecon

CAERNARFON

G   - Gateway
Ch - Church
T1 - Tower by Captain's Walk
T2 - Tower by the Bulwark

Tower beside Captains' Walk at Brecon

BRECON

The Exchequer Gate at Caernarfon   *Caernarfon: first tower of the town wall, and the castle*

CAERNARFON   Gwynedd

Following the defeat and death of Llywelyn ap Gruffydd in 1282 work was begun by Edward I on a huge new castle and an accompanying walled town both as a governmental seat and a display of English might. The banded masonry and polygonal towers of the castle recalled the works of imperial Rome, and there had indeed been a Roman fort here, sited further up the River Seiont. The castle was built on the site of a motte and bailey fortress built by Norman invaders in the late 11th century but not used by the Welsh princes. Most of the town wall seems to have been completed by the autumn of 1284 when the Welsh rose up and captured the place, since the castle was then far from complete. After recapture by the English in 1295 more than £1,000 was spent within twelve months on repairing damage done to the town walls. The castle was finally left close to its present condition as a partially completed shell c1330. By then the castle, town walls and quays had together cost the enormous sum of over £25,000.

Although the layout of streets at Caernarfon is a regular grid-plan the area enclosed by the walls is irregular in shape and quite small at just 250m long by 200m wide. The area within is packed full of buildings, without even a churchyard as an open space. The town walls tend to be overlooked as a monument because of the sheer size and magnificence of the castle, yet the circuit is one of the most complete in Britain. There is public access to the whole of the exterior of the walls, which were cleared in the 1960s of houses built against them since the 18th century and to a section of the wall-walk on the north side. The castle fills the south side, the long western side faces quays and the sea, and there were ditches, of which traces survive, along the more vulnerable east and north sides. Twin-towered gatehouses face east and west and there are eight flanking towers, most of which have open backs probably once with wooden inner walls since each one has an upper row of firing loops which presupposes the existence of an upper floor. The towers extend down the slope of a stone-revetted bank upon which the main wall is built. The lost upper rooms of the east gate housed the Exchequer for North Wales. See pictures on page 22 and on the front cover.

The NE corner tower at Caernarfon

Until the street called Castle Ditch was created in the mid 19th century the town wall adjoined the NE tower of the castle. A thickening of the wall by the first tower to carry a staircase up to the wall-walk and tower upper storey is pierced by a postern called the Green Gate, closed by a portcullis and a door secured by a drawbar. This tower has lost all its internal facework. The second tower lies at a corner and beyond the ditch survives, now a roadway. In 1301-2 a new bridge was built across the ditch to reach the Exchequer Gate, although the innermost arch must be later as there was a draw-bridge in front of the gate until at least the 1520s. Only the lower parts of the towers are original, and there are corbels for an upper storey latrine on the north side. The original upper rooms have gone and the passageway has been widened.

The next tower marks a corner, where the wall heads NW. This next section is well preserved despite being pierced by modern arches for three roads. The two central towers along here both retain the bridges added in 1347 to carry the wall-walk across the open backs, and between these towers original crenellations with firing loops still remain. At the NW corner is a fully circular tower 9m in diameter containing a heatable living room for a priest over a vestry, for this corner is filled with the church of St Mary, which now has 19th century north windows in deep embrasures pierced through the town wall. Built in 1307 as a garrison chapel, this was technically a chapel of ease to the original parish church of St Peblig some distance away beyond the former Roman fort. The chapel had a west doorway through the town wall replacing a former postern.

The wall then heads south down the quayside, passing a much-altered tower now in use as one of the Landmark Trust's holiday homes. The West Gate or Porth-yr-Aur (Golden Gate) has long been occupied by the Royal Welsh Yacht Club, with consequent alterations and rebuilding. The passage retains a portcullis groove and there are corbels for an upper latrine on the north side. A barbican extends out to the water's edge and would block the quay but for doorways in the sidewalls. urther south, the last of the towers sits at another corner and has one surviving original firing loop. The last part of the wall was built only in 1326 after abandoning plans for a watergate beside the castle.

The northern section of the western walls at Caernarfon

CARDIFF   South Glamorgan

In the late 11th century the former Roman fort was made into a castle serving as the caput of the lordship of Glamorgan held in succession by the de Clares, the Despensers and then the Beauchamps. By the 12th century a town had been laid out to the SE. There is uncertainly as to when it was walled in stone but it must have had defences from the beginning. From the West Gate, a rebuild of 1921 on old footings, the walls partly followed Westgate Street and extended 600m from the castle down almost to Custom House Street, the area enclosed being up to 300m wide. The East and West gates were demolished in 1781, the North Gate went in 1786, and the South Gate was lost in 1801. There are traces of the wall where it adjoined the castle east wall. A combined parochial and priory church of St Mary on the west side was eventually undermined by the River Taff and a former chapel-of-ease of St John the Baptist just SE of the castle then took over its parochial functions. A Franciscan friary lay near the walls on the north side and footings of a Dominican friary still exist to the NW of the castle in Cathays Park.

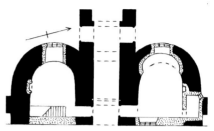

Caernarfon: plan of West Gate

CARDIGAN   Ceredigion

The Norman castle by the bridge over the Teifi was rebuilt by the Lord Rhys, who staged a famous eisteddfod here in 1176. The castle was captured several times in the three decades before it was rebuilt in the 1240s. By then the town contained 130 burgages. It was granted a market in 1227 and had a guild of merchants by 1250. Cardigan became a county town in 1279 and murage for walling it was granted for eight years from 1280 and for another five years from 1299. Speed's map of 1610 is evidence of the line of an area just 250m long by 150m wide straddling High Street north of the castle. Small fragments remain in St Mary's Street and behind business premises in Pwllhai. The parish church of Holy Trinity has gone, the church of the Benedictine priory of St Mary near the river bank 200m east of the site of the East Gate having become the parish church. From the East Gate the wall ran almost due north to a corner tower shown by Speed probably in the vicinity of William Street. Speed shows no gateway closing off the north end of the High Street, but there must have been one in the area of the present guildhall. The wall then ran round a corner and went SSW roughly along the line of Middle Mwldan. There was another gateway at the west end of Quay Street from where the wall ran back to a gateway shown by Speed immediately SW of the castle which led from the High Street to a road leading to the bridge.

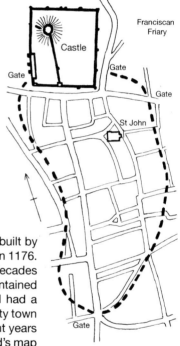

CARDIFF

0   100

metres

CARDIGAN

CARMARTHEN   Carmarthenshire

The castle set high above the northern end of a vitally important bridge over the Tywi was founded in the early 12th century and frequently changed hands over the next hundred years as the Welsh periodically captured it and the Normans took it back. Burgesses from outside SW Wales were brought in during the early 13th century to occupy a kidney-shaped area about 200m from north to south by 140m wide which was probably originally an outer bailey of the castle, the main ward and keep of which were rebuilt in stone about the time of the unsuccessful siege of 1233. In that year the bridge was rebuilt in stone and there was a grant of murage for walling the town. Nott Square was a market place with roads from it extending east, south, SW and NE to gateways and there was a parish church of St Mary which has long since disappeared. Just one tiny fragment remains of the southern part of this wall in Lower Bridge Street. Some of the 112 burgesses named in 1268 were Welsh. The castle was then held by Prince Edmund but in 1279 his brother King Edward obtained it back to serve as the administrative centre of the new county of Carmarthen, thus boosting the importance of the town. Suburbs to the west beyond the Wynveth Brook, including the Franciscan friary and the quays and wharves south of it, were only fortified when enclosed by ramparts and bastions of earth erected in the Civil War period, some parts of the SW end of which still survive.

In 1415 murage was granted for five years for enclosing an area about 200m square containing King Street and Spilman Street extending towards the Roman fort founded c75AD and abandoned about 35 years later. A small fragment of this later wall remains on the south side in Donybank. Beyond this area was a small suburb around the parish church of St Peter occupying the middle of the SW side of the Roman fort area known as Old Carmarthen. This area belonged to an Augustinian priory of St John, with its precinct between the NE side of Old Carmarthen and the north bank of the river.

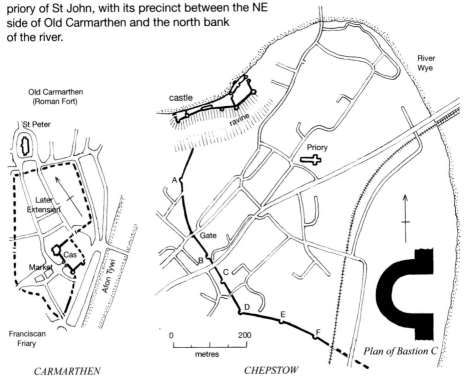

CARMARTHEN   CHEPSTOW

CHEPSTOW   Monmouthshire

Chepstow lies within a loop of the River Wye which is crossed into England by an old bridge facing north. The old parts of the town north of the A48 are 280m wide including the long narrow castle on a ridge on the north side above a cliff to the river. From a street called The Back near the old bridge the town extends 650m uphill towards where it is closed off by the Port Wall probably built in the 1270s when Roger Bigod, Earl of Norfolk was lord of Chepstow (then called Striguill) and new apartments were provided in the castle. About 700m still remains of the Port Wall, which is 2m thick and rises up to 3m from the town side to a wall-walk still retaining sections of its parapet. It survived almost complete until the 20th century. The ditch in front of the wall has mostly silted up. Almost in the middle of the enclosed area is the Benedictine priory church of St Mary.

The exterior of the gateway at Chepstow

An 80m length of the wall runs SSW from a ravine south of the castle to a circular corner bastion 7m in diameter. Just south of here a large breach was made in the 1960s to give access to the town's top car-park. The section from there to the gateway closing off the top of the High Street is obscured by buildings. The gateway is a square structure dating from a rebuilding by the Earl of Worcester in 1524. It lacks defensive features and has modern battlements. The outer face has two heraldic panels supported by angels.

From the gate the wall runs for 100m to a bastion behind the George Hotel. Not far beyond is a gap made in 1971 for the A48 inner relief road. Beyond is a section with two well preserved bastions (C-D on plan). The wall then runs east for 120m to a bastion in a re-entrant angle and then continues for another 80m with one more bastion, this section being best observed from the station. Another 250m of the wall survived intact except for a breach of 1850 for the railway until the shipyards beyond the railway needed to be expanded during the First World War.

Section of crenellated wall at Chepstow (see also page 19)

CONWY   Conwy

Set by the west side of the mouth of the River Conwy, the town of Conwy has no equal amongst walled towns in the British Isles. Enclosing very roughly a triangle with sides each about 400m long, the walls here are very impressive and well preserved. Both the castle and town walls were begun in the spring of 1283 under the personal supervision of King Edward I of England, and to the designs of Master James of St George (from Savoy). The fortifications were substantially completed by the autumn of 1287. The surviving accounts tell us that the vulnerable (and originally gateless) NW side and the short SW side were built first and the other sides added two years later. There is a record of battlements being added to the southern walls and towers in 1286. Minor works continued until 1292, by which time almost £15,000 had been spent upon them. The rapid construction of the castle and town walls, by a workforce up to 1,500 strong in the summer of 1285, is an achievement with few parallels in the medieval world. The walls enclose a space twice the area of that at Caernarfon, and here there is more of an equilibrium between the military might of the castle on a rock by the shore and the town extending up the hillside to the west of it to a corner tower set 35m above sea-level.

The walled towns of Caernarfon and Conwy are unusual in that neither of them had a monastic house within the walls or anywhere nearby outside. Usually walled towns would have at least one friary, but friaries were never common in Wales. At Conwy a Cistercian abbey was removed several miles further up the river to make way for the town. The abbey church in the centre of the walled area was retained for parochial use. The merchants' houses were of stone with timber upper storeys but were all replaced during the 19th century except for the entirely timber-framed Aberconwy House.

Conwy was briefly occupied by Owain Glyndwr's supporters the Tudors in the 1400s. The castle suffered a siege in 1646 but the town survived without being harmed. In 1655 fortifications at Caernarfon and Conwy were ordered to be slighted, but work carried out seems to have been limited to removal of floors, roofs, doors and portcullises. At Conwy greater threats have been posed by modern transport systems. The only serious breaches in the circuit are those for roads beside the castle and the removal of the outer face of a tower on the NW side for another road. An adjacent tower is now badly cracked as a result of tunnelling underneath it for a railway. Conwy, Chepstow, Flint, King's Lynn and London are the only towns in Britain with railway stations within the areas enclosed by their medieval defences.

Latrines on the wall-head at Conwy

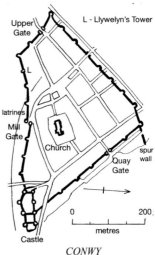

CONWY

Conwy: Llywelyn's Tower lies to the right of this picture

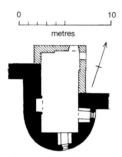

Conwy: Llywelyn's Tower

From the SW tower of the castle round back to a tower on the north side of the castle the town walls extend for 1,250m. They are 1.6m thick and generally rise 8m to where the wall is thickened internally by means of two corbelled courses to carry the wall-walk. Surviving sections of the parapet add another 2m to the height of the outside face. Short sections adjoining the castle walls are thinner and without a wall-walk. There are three twin-towered gatehouses all with portcullis grooves, and twenty-one other towers, most of them D-shaped structures with open backs and generally set with their centres about 48m apart. It has been calculated that manning all the firing loops in the merlons of each section of wall with its tower would have needed about twenty men.

The open backs of the towers were spanned by wooden bridges several of which were replaced (again with timber) as late as the 1520s. The walls and towers all have beam-holes for temporary hoarding. There is public access to the wall-walks of about half of the western part of the circuit, and to the whole of the exterior of the walls, plus most of the interior of the southern walls. The quayside NE walls are internally obscured by buildings and the wallheads on this section are more altered and less complete.

From the castle the wall heads WSW across a road and out to a corner tower. It then goes west for three sections with two intervening towers (with adjoining open staircases) to the Mill Gate (Porth y Felin). This is named after the mill beside the River Gyffin which lies beyond the railway below this section. Instead of facing out to the river the gate faces out along the section of wall just mentioned, thus helping to flank it and with the approach being well covered by the main wall and the adjacent tower. The southern tower is almost a full round but the northern tower is more U-shaped. Both towers retain original battlements with firing slits. Each contained an upper room with a fireplace and a timber-framed room lay over the passageway between the towers. These rooms were used by the Chamberlain of North Wales and were probably reached from an adjoining timber-framed office block set against the town wall west of the gateway. Erected in 1283, and burned by Welsh rebels in 1401, this block housed the staff of an administrative department known as the King's Wardrobe. For the use of the clerks of this office and those of the nearby office of the Master of the King's Works (east of the gateway), a remarkable row of twelve latrines in the form of boxes set upon triple-stepped corbels project out from the top of the adjacent section of the town wall. See pp 3, 21 & 22.

Lower Gate facing the quay at Conwy

Beyond the row of latrines one section of wall between two towers has beeen replaced by an arch and a new wall-walk above the original level to allow the railway to pass underneath. A timber-framed hall possibly older than the town wall (and removed to Caernarfon in 1315) gave a name to Llywelyn's Tower standing beside it. The group of buildings here were intended as a private residence for Prince Edward, son and heir of Edward I after his creation as Prince of Wales. What was originally an open backed D-shaped tower, slightly longer than the others because of a change in alignment of the wall here, was provided in 1302-6 with a stone back and two good upper rooms, the lower one a full rectangle with its own external doorway, a fireplace and two windows with seats in the embrasures. The adjacent section beside the hall itself has three windows with seats in the embrasures. Beyond a corner tower the wall climbs steeply up the hillside past another tower to the Upper Gate (Porth Uchaf).

The original passage between the twin U-shaped towers of the Upper Gate was considerably above the modern road level. There is a portcullis groove and a recess for a raised drawbridge over a rock-cut ditch with a small barbican on the outer edge. Both towers retain their battlements, which are rather oddly set at different levels, so that each tower rises about the same amount above the steeply sloping land outside. A stair around two sides of the southern tower rises to the wall-walk of the adjoining wall and to a series of rooms in the southern tower and over the passageway, the backs having been timber-framed. The accounts refer to their construction in 1286 by Master Laurence of Canterbury. The upper room in the northern tower was quite separate. Beyond it the wall angles out to reach an almost fully circular (but still open-backed) tower at a salient angle at the highest point of the town. The position of this tower allowed it to command the whole length of the ditches along the SW and NW sides of the town.

Apart from a re-entrant angle close to the corner tower the NW side runs straight for over 300m with six intermediate towers before the wall turns through an angle at a seventh tower. All the archways through this section of wall are 19th century openings. The most notable is the remodelling of one tower as a gateway in 1827. On a new alignment the wall then descends to another corner tower by the shore. Towers here with the adjacent bits of wall with staircases up to the wall-walk all display evidence of having been constructed up to a fair height before the rest of the wall itself was added. These two corner towers still retain their original crenellations. Beyond the tower by the shore a spur wall continues out into the sea to close off any possible landward approach to the harbour except via a gate through it (later enlarged) near the landward end. The upper part of this 3.2m thick wall with a parapet on each side was added in the 1320s. It once ended at a round tower standing in the estuary.

The quayside wall is somewhat obscured by buildings, especially on its inner face. It has one tower, then the Lower Gate (Porth Isaf), and then three more towers, all of these features being much altered internally and at the summits. Beside the furthest tower is a postern which was just closed with a door, being covered by the nearby castle.

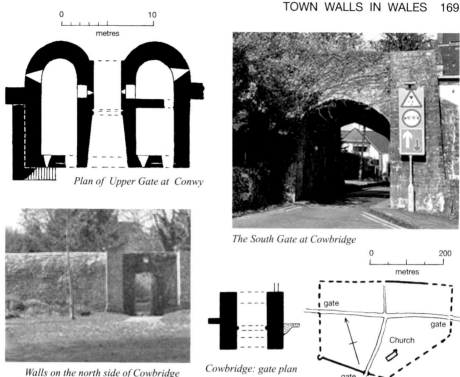

0   10
metres

Plan of Upper Gate at Conwy

The South Gate at Cowbridge

0   200
metres

gate

gate

Church

gate

COWBRIDGE

Walls on the north side of Cowbridge

Cowbridge: gate plan

COWBRIDGE   Mid Glamorgan

By 1300 Cowbridge had a 33 acre walled enclosure straddling the former main road from Cardiff to Swansea. It was granted a charter by Richard de Clare, Lord of Glamorgan in 1256 and the burgage plots were probably laid out about that time. The West Gate was demolished in 1754 and the East Gate about twenty years later. Surviving fragments of the walls include quite a long length on the south side between the SW corner tower and a still surviving gateway which faced towards Llanblethian, where lies the mother church and the castle of the lords of Glamorgan. In the medieval period the church of Holy Cross in the SE quarter of Cowbridge ranked only as a chapel-of-ease to Llanblethian, despite its size. This corner of the wall had a bastion at the bottom of the school grounds. The surviving gateway has a chamfered segmental-arched passageway 3.2m wide through an structure 6.8m wide and 6m deep. The upper storeys have now been lost. A fourth gateway on the north side, where the wall followed the line of North Road down from Eagle Lane was a mere postern facing out to meadows. East of its site more of the wall remains. The town hall lies near the wall NE corner.

CRICKHOWELL   Powys

Crickhowell lies on the road from Brecon to Abergavenny and was too close to these older established walled towns to develop into a major trading centre. Evidence that some attempt was made to wall it is a murage grant of 1281. In Tower Street to the north of the motte and bailey castle rebuilt in stone by the Pauncefoots in the 1290s and 1300s is a tower variously described as a folly and as part of an east-facing gateway, or possibly containing elements of both. Other assumed gateways would have faced NW for the road out to Brecon and SW towards the bridge over the Usk, now a 16th century structure. .The parish church on the NW side was a new foundation of 1303.

DENBIGH   Denbighshireshire

Shortly after being captured from the Welsh in October 1282 Denbigh was given by Edward I to Henry de Lacy, Earl of Lincoln. He is assumed to have built the town walls between then and 1295, when the Welsh briefly recaptured Denbigh. The town was burned in 1402 by Owain Glyndwr's forces and again during the Wars of the Roses. Water supplies were always scarce on the hilltop site and the townsfolk soon migrated down the slope towards the Carmelite friary, leaving the walled area half empty.

Although much broken down in places the circuit is complete except for a 70m long gap on the north. It encloses a small trilobed space 300m from SW to NE by 200m across. The tower of the former church of St Hilary stands in the middle. To the NE of it lie ruins of a large unfinished church begun in the 1570s by the Earl of Leicester probably with the intention of moving the see of St Asaph here. Most of the SW lobe is filled by a castle added by Earl Hugh after the 1295 revolt. The town wall here has five D-shaped towers built in readiness for the intended castle, the townward side of which has much more massive walls with polygonal towers at the corners and around the gateway in a manner similar to those at Caernarfon. Both the castle and town walls were held by Royalist forces against Parliamentary troops in 1646. The order for slighting largely ignored at Caernarfon and Conwy seems to have been more thoroughly carried out here. The parts of the castle formed from the older town wall are particularly ruinous.

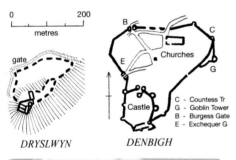

DRYSLWYN   *DENBIGH*

The section of wall between the Red Tower at the NW corner of the castle was thicker than elsewhere to contain a passage linking the castle with the upper storey of the Exchequer Gate within a re-entrant angle on the west side of the town. Footings remain of the southern half and a fragment of the NW corner of a gatehouse 16m wide by 12m deep with chutes for upper storey latrines on either side. A length of wall 150m long (now much obscured by houses) carries round two angles without towers to reach the Burgess Gate facing northwards. This is a fine structure with towers with rounded fronts rising from square bases with spurs, a feature found in a number of late 13th century castles in South Wales. The passage was commanded by firing slits in the towers and by machicolations before and after the portcullis. A large upper room has three windows facing south and doorways out to the walkways on the main wall. The staircase then rose up at the west end to the roof. The upper walls on the north have chequerwork similar to that on the castle gatehouse. The south side has been refaced in limestone at some period, the rest being faced with green sandstone. A long break in the wall starts 30m east of the gate.

The Burgess Gate at Denbigh from the NW

*The NE corner tower
at Denbigh*

0   10

metres

Plan of Goblin Tower at Denbigh

Denbigh: plan and east view of Burgess Gate

After the gap the wall reappears with a section 2m thick and 4.5m wide with a parapet on each side of the wall-walk. It heads east to a round corner tower 9m high with windows having later replaced shooting slits on the upper storey. The wall then goes SE to the Countess Tower, actually a pair of square projections, one containing and the other with larger rooms later built across the back of it. From here back to the castle the wall is thin and low and set upon and against limestone crags. One final tower at the far end was probably originally intended to be part of the adjacent castle. In the 1290s a narrow space on a ledge below the main wall south of the Countess Tower was enclosed by a lofty loopholed wall protecting a passage descending to the lower chamber of the Goblin Tower, a polygonal-fronted structure 11m wide rising 21m above the cliffs outside. From this room the stair zigzags down to a well in the natural rockface. The tower upper storey has a fireplace where the south wall joins the cliff edge. From the tower summit a wall-walk continues along the cliff edge to a bridge-pit and postern.

DRYSLWYN   Carmarthenshire

Undermined and captured by English forces in 1287, the castle formed most of the SE side and south end of a township enclosure. It was 180m long from SW to NE and up to 100m wide and set partly on the hilltop above the Tywi, where several house platforms remain, and partly on land sloping steeply down to slight evidence of a gateway on the west side. The gate was reached over a causeway across the ditch around the west and north sides. The wall that once closed these two sides forms the only certain instance of a settlement being walled in stone by a Welsh prince. There were settlements beside the castles of Dinefwr and Dolforwyn in the 1280s but neither has remains of stone walls around it. By the 1350s a bridge at Dryslwyn had replaced the original ford across the river and there was a small extra-mural suburb in "Briggestrete". The township may not have survived capture of the castle during the Glyndwr revolt of the 1400s.

FLINT   Flintshire

The town still preserves most of the grid-iron layout of streets from when it was laid out in 1277 to accompany Edward I's new castle begun in that year beside the shore at the NE end. The town was allowed a market from 1278 and was given a royal charter in 1284. The whole plan, including the circular keep of the castle, was based on that of the French bastide of Aigues Mortes from where Edward had set out on his crusade. The main coast road from Chester (later paralleled by the railway) bisected the six longitudinal streets, the main one of which was Church Street with the (since rebuilt) parish church on the SE side of it oddly twisted to obtain more of a true easterly orientation. Speed's map of 1610 clearly shows the double rampart and ditch system which enclosed an area 500m by 300m. From Castle Dyke Street by the castle the defences went SW down Evans Street and Earl Street, then turned SE down Coleshill Street. The old layout is more disturbed in the SE corner by modern industrial units with the loss of the two outer original streets. Although the ramparts and ditch were clearly once quite impressive there is some doubt as to whether a palisade ever existed on the rampart.

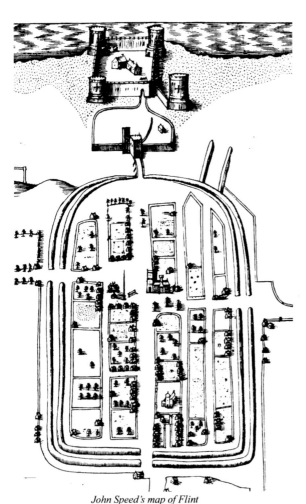

John Speed's map of Flint

HAVERFORDWEST

Pembrokeshire

Not much is known about the former walls here. The town was granted a charter by William Marshal in 1207 and had an original core around the parish church of St Martin to the west of the castle, with gateways facing west, north and NE, the latter towards the old bridge over the Western Cleddau. The single grant of murage for seven years from 1264 was probably for walling this part. Gates in Market Street and High Street seem to have formed part of a later enclosing of suburbs to the south including the parish church of St Mary. It is doubtful if defences ever enclosed either the parish church of St Thomas further to the SE or the Dominican friary on the west bank of the river below the castle. The ruins of an Augustinian priory lie on the river bank 400m to the SE.

HAY-ON-WYE   Powys

The walls at Hay enclosed a triangle with sides about 400m long, with the River Wye on the NW, the Dulas Brook on the NE and the stone castle filling the western half of the south side. The parish church lay 180m beyond the walls, with the motte of the original wooden castle between it and the SW corner of the walled area, within which lies the former guild chapel of St John. Building the walls appears to have been a direct response to the burning of the town by Llywelyn ap Iorwerth in 1231, murage grants being made in 1232 and 1237. At the same time work was done on the curtain wall of the castle, a de Braose possession then in royal hands. Documents of 1454 and 1461 refer to the repair of breaches in the walls and to an annual payment of 15s to the burgesses for the keeping of the three gateways. John Leland described the area within the walls as "wonderfully decayed", attributing this to Owain Glyndwr's activities 130 years ago.

Only the side of the castle within the town is still walled. West of the castle the town wall ran to the Carlesgate or West Gate, near which was a postern. The wall then ran across the site of the cattle market to the steep bank above the river. It is uncertain if that side was in fact walled, and cutting through for the railway has altered the terrain here. The bridge is not of medieval origin and was not faced by a main gateway. Facing NE near the river was the Nyport or Water Gate. Overgrown parts of the NE walls remain, with a 6m long fragment 1m thick and up to 5m high externally and 2.5m high internally near the Nyport, and further south is another section about 20m long and 2.5m high. Otherwise the wall is represented by footings upon which lie modern boundary walls. The Black Lion pub stands near the site of the Lion Gate facing SE, from which the wall ran west to the castle.

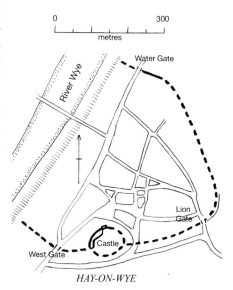

HAY-ON-WYE

KENFIG   Glamorgan

The castle lies in the NW corner of a town enclosure 200m from north to south by 170m east-west, ramparts with ditches remaining at the SW and NE corners. This settlement was over-run by dunes and had moved to Pyle by the late 15th century.

Last remains of the walls at Hay-on-Wye

KIDWELLY   Carmarthenshire

Murage for walling the town was granted in 1281, when Patrick de Chaworth was busy rebuilding the castle which was the caput of a lordship established in the early 12th century by Roger, Bishop of Sarum. It was frequently attacked by the Welsh and the town had been burned by them during the rising of 1257. The main activities of the settlement gradually moved further south beyond the bridge over the Gwendraeth Fach to where there was a suburb with a Benedictine priory forming the parish church. By 1401 the original town was described as "desolate". Kidwelly is now a quiet backwater but until fairly recently all traffic between Swansea and Carmarthen passed over the bridge, and up New Street and Water Street along the NW side of the fortified town and castle, whilst there were busy quays just west of the bridge and many local industries.

A ditch extending NW beyond that of the inner parts of the castle divided two outer baileys to the north from a town enclosure 120m wide extending 160m down a slope to a surviving early 14th century gatehouse. Leland in 1539 describes the then ruinous upper chamber as a court room so this must have been the shirehall burned in 1403 during Glyndwr's rebellion. One of the rooms set either side of the entrance passage served as a prison. These rooms are set in slight projections (not really true towers) with spur-buttressed chamfered corners. The portcullis groove of the outer arch of the gateway was blocked by later alterations. Slight traces of a retaining wall remain to the SE of this gateway whilst on the edge of the ditch separating the town from the castle outer baileys are defaced parts of a wall up to 1.8m thick and 2.3m high containing a gateway arch. It is likely there was a third town gateway on the east side not far south of the main gateway into the castle.

Plans of the main gatehoiuse at Kidwelly

The back gate at Kidwelly

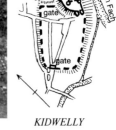

KIDWELLY

Interior of the gatehouse at Kidwelly

Archway of the gatehouse at Kidwelly

KNIGHTON   Powys

Murage grants of 1260 and 1277 are the only evidence of former defences here but the town seems to have been regarded as defensible in 1402 when Edmund Mortimer sent 400 men from Ludlow to hold it against Owain Glyndwr. The lower part of the town has the grid pattern typical of a late 13th century planted town with the church fitting into that pattern. The River Teme encloses the NE side and earthworks of Offa's Dyke would have enclosed the NW side. A large motte called Bryn Castell lies beyond to the SE, but the castle captured in 1262 by Llywelyn ap Gruffydd appears to have been the smaller and probably earlier earthwork in a garden up on higher ground to the SW.

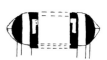

Monmouth: Bridge Gate

LAUGHARNE   Carmarthenshire

Authority for erecting defences was given in 1465. There is no evidence walls existed but it appears there were gates, suggested to have been by the Island House on Wogan Street, at the east end of Victoria Street, and by Mariner's Corner, the latter supposedly removed c1780.

Machicolations on Bridge Gate at Monmouth

MONMOUTH   Monmouthshire

Monmouth has a good defensive site set on the NW bank of the Usk, which is crossed by a bridge. The River Monnow protects the north side and then makes a loop 400m out to the west before joining the Wye further south. The enclosed space was roughly a round-cornered square 360m across with the castle (latterly part of the earldom of Lancaster) filling the space northwards between the western corner and the Monnow. From a west gate near the castle the wall ran SE down the backs of properties on the SW side of Glendower Street towards the Wye, then NE along the river bank past a gate to the bridge. Part of one of the two round towers of the East Gate (which actually faced NE) is incorporated in the Nag's Head pub in St James Street. The wall then ran NW to another gate across Monk Street, named after the Benedictine priory church of St Mary which also served the townsfolk. The wall ran along Priory Street above a sheer drop to the Monnow and back to the NE side of the castle. See illustrations on page 175.

From the site of the west gate Monnow Street, long the principal trading area, runs for 350m down to the only surviving bridge-gate in Britain. It is usually dated to 1272, but c1300-10 seems more likely. The gate is perched on top of a pier of the bridge nearest to the town. It measures 9m by 3.6m with D-shaped ends pierced since the 19th century by narrow pedestrian walkways flanking a main passage 3.5m wide still used for vehicular traffic. The passage is flanked by crossloops and covered by external machicolations and has a groove for an iron portcullis. There are two upper rooms, originally reached by a spiral stair on the north side. The lower room has a tiny projecting latrine. The wall-heads and hipped roof are post-medieval. In 1988 part of earlier timber bridge was found in the river bank below and dated to the 1170s by tree-ring analysis.

The Bridge Gate at Monmouth

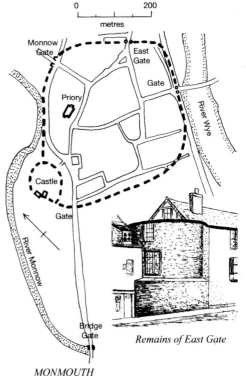

Remains of East Gate

MONMOUTH

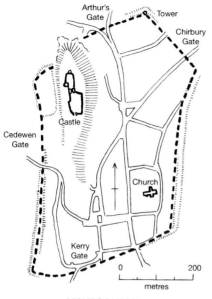

MONTGOMERY

Base of the NE tower at Montgomery

MONTGOMERY   Powys

In 1223 Henry III began building a new castle of stone on a cliff-top site to replace the 11th century earth and timber castle of Hen Domen further north. The king encouraged traders to live below the dangerously exposed frontier castle by offering them the same liberties as those held by the burgesses of Shrewsbury. In 1231 Llywelyn ap Iorwerth burned the township, but neither he, nor his son Dafydd in 1245, was able to capture the castle. Murage for walling the town was granted by Henry III in 1267. The king visited Montgomery that year and there signed a treaty acknowledging Llywelyn ap Gruffydd as Prince of North Wales. In 1279 there is a reference to the palisade around the town being removed for reuse up at the castle, and this is assumed to mark the commencement of stone walls around the town, following on from the recent capture by the English of Llewelyn's rival neighbouring castle and township of Dolforwyn built to defy Edward I. In 1280 the castle constable was paid £60 for work on the town walls and on the castle.

The defences enclosed a large area 600m long from north to south by up to 400m wide. The eastern two thirds is a level platform with the church towards the SE and retail premises and the late town hall in and around Broad Street at the south end, a layout suggesting that the northern end may be a later extension. High ground fills the western third, with the castle at the north end set 75m to the east of the town defences. The Cedewen Gate lay in the middle of the west side. Traces of a ditch and rampart remain on either side of it. Excavations have found the base of the SW corner tower. Towards the west end of the south side lay the Kerry (Ceri) Gate. Traces of the ramparts around the SE corner and along the east side survive, but in a rather cut-up and obscured condition. The Chirbury Gate lay in a section of the defences facing NE. At the northern corner the lower parts remain of a tower about 5m in diameter with a smaller round tower of modern construction built over the western part of them. West of here a well preserved section of rampart and ditch is easily visible for two thirds of the way to the site of Arthur's Gate facing NNW. This gate and the corner tower are shown intact on John Speed's map of 1610 with battlemented walls linking them and the castle rock. He shows the other walls in ruins but none of the other three gates as still standing.

NEWPORT   Monmouthshire

John Leland in the 1530s was undecided whether Newport was ever walled, but he did note three gateways, one facing east to the bridge over the Usk which was guarded by the castle of the earls of Stafford (later Dukes of Buckingham), another in the middle of the High Street, and a third at the west end below the parish church of St Woolos (now a cathedral. The West Gate bore the Stafford arms and was probably built in the time of Earl Hugh. In 1377 he founded the Augustinian friary which stood where the bus station now is and in 1385 he granted the borough a charter. The West Gate provided the town with a clock tower in the 17th century and was later used as a prison. Part of it was incorporated in an hotel in the 1790s and survived along with that building until 1884.

NEW RADNOR   Powys

The village has a regular grid pattern of streets typical of late 13th century planted towns. In 1257 a murage grant was obtained by Roger Mortimer, whose castle, itself a rebuild of an older structure recently destroyed by the Welsh, lay high above the north side of the village. Further murage grants were obtained in 1280, 1283 and 1290. From the castle outer ward a rampart extends almost as far as the Summergil Brook, which probably fed a wet moat on the south side, and then along to the site of the south gate. South of the site of the west gate layers of shale are visible in the bank, which is narrow and may in fact be a collapsed wall rather than an earthwork as such. Less survives of the eastern section of the defences, where there was a third gate, and the NW section with another gate facing the Dingle Brook. The defences were probably never restored after the destruction wrought in 1403, from which the town never recovered. It only attained the status of county town for Radnorshire in the mid 16th century because the gatehouse of the otherwise ruinous castle was being used as a prison, and it soon lost that status to Presteigne. Radnor has never filled more than a third of the twenty-six acres enclosed by the defences depite being ranked as a borough from 1562 to 1833.

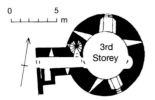

0   5
m

Pembroke: plan of Barnard's Tower

OVERTON   Flintshire

The grid pattern of the streets around St Mary's church suggests a late 13th century planted town and there was a single murage grant in 1300. To the SW is a considerable drop down to meadows beside the River Dee, now 300m further west. The river was never bridged near the village so it was not a place of strategic importance.

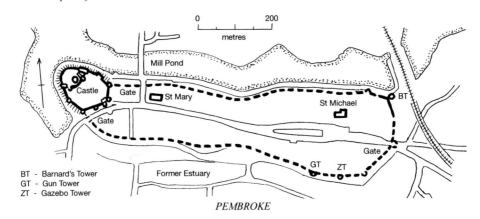

BT - Barnard's Tower
GT - Gun Tower
ZT - Gazebo Tower

PEMBROKE

PEMBROKE   Pembrokeshire

Pembroke has a fine defensive site on a promontory 900m long and up to 200m wide between two tidal creeks, the southern one now dried up and forming parkland. The eastern half with the parish church of St Michael and a main street wide enough for a market represents a later extension to the original late 11th century settlement with the church of St Mary on the north side and the castle set on a rock at the western point of the promontory. Henry I granted the borough a charter in 1102 and in 1138 it became the caput of an earldom which remained semi-autonomous until the 1540s. However by 1400 about a tenth of the two hundred burgages had been abandoned and by 1480 as many as 44 were in decay. In 1543 Pembroke only paid half as much tax as Tenby.

There are no records of work upon the stone walls. They were once considered to be the work of the Marshal family in the first half of the 13th century, but it is unlikely that serious work on walling the town would have commenced before the outer bailey of the castle was fully walled, which was not until c1280. In the summer of 1648 Oliver Cromwell besieged the town for several weeks. Eventually his siege train arrived and after ten days' cannonade the defenders surrendered on favourable terms. Slighting of the east fronts of the castle and town walls seems to have then been immediately effected probably under Cromwell's personal supervision.

Having one long main street without any side-streets, Pembroke still has the feel of a medieval walled town, modern development being well beyond the walled area and particularly concentrated at Pembroke Dock further north. Not much actual town wall itself survives, low lengths of modern retaining walls having replaced sections of it, but five out of the six flanking towers remain at least in part and a jamb of one of the three gateways. Because it was a retaining wall the flanking towers were all entered at an upper level well above ground level outside.

The Northgate Tower of the castle is named after a twin-towered gateway facing the bridge over the river which stood until 1820. Modern walls further downhill have replaced the northern walls, so there are no remains until the first of the towers, a solid structure 6m in diameter, near the eastern end. Barnard's Tower at the NE corner stood out in the ditch protecting the eastern walls so as to command the curving wall-face to the south. It is a full circle 9m in diameter joined only to the main wall by a short spur wall 3m thick carrying a vaulted passage from a doorway with a drawbar slot to another doorway, also with a drawbar slot, into the tower third storey. This is a dome-vaulted apartment for an official of some kind with a fireplace, two windows with seats (one is of two lights) and three loopholes with deeply plunging sills. The passage passes doorways to a corbelled-out latrine and a spiral stair. The latter leads up to the roof and down to another habitable room with four loops and a window with seats and an unlit basement below.

Barnard's Tower at Pembroke

Hidden in private gardens, about 50m of 3m high thin retaining wall remain to the south of Barnard's Tower. In the middle of this side lay the East Gate demolished c1775, which seems to have had a D-shaped open barbican in front like the main gate at nearby Tenby. Leland mentions a portcullis of solid iron here. Near the bottom of Goose's Lane is part of a corner tower with the jamb of a firing loop. This section of the defences was not as well protected by water as that further west and at intervals of 63m there are two other towers each about 7m in diameter and retaining two levels of fully circular rooms connected by spiral staircases and having narrow firing loops. The first one is surmounted by a tall octagonal 18th century gazebo and has its loops blocked up. The other one has modern battlements and once carried a cannon on a vault over its upper level. A sixth tower is known to have existed further west but its location is unknown. Part of the southern jamb and springing of the arch remain of the West Gate, a mere postern leading out towards the Benedictine priory of Monkton on the other side of the tidal creek. The present roadway is far below the level of the medieval one.

Tower with gazebo on top at Pembroke

ST CLEARS   Carmarthenshire

Excavations in 1989-90 revealed part of a town rampart in Foxhole Terrace. The castle and church lie on the east side by the river.

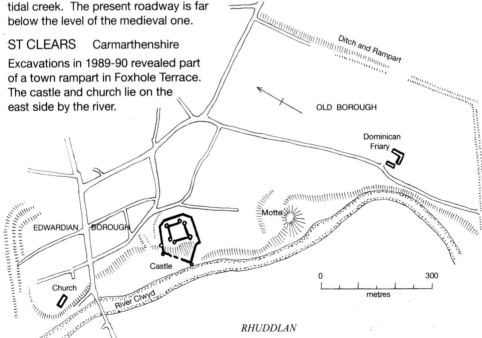

RHUDDLAN

RHUDDLAN   Flintshire

Rhuddlan affords good examples of Norman and Edwardian settlement layouts side by side. Before the draining of coastal marshes and the building of the coastal road and seaside resorts along it Rhuddlan was the lowest crossing place of the River Clwyd. Here lay the palace of Gruffydd ap Llywelyn burned in 1063 by Harold Godwinson. Domesday Book in 1086 records eighteen burgesses here, with a church and mint, in a borough beside Robert de Rhuddlan's motte on the river bank. East of this motte, and with the southern half of it set beside a bend of the river, ditches enclose a huge space 300m wide and possibly 700 long although its northern boundary is no longer clearly defined. The Dominican friary, now a farm, is the only building now within this enclosure.

In 1277 Edward I of England forced Llywelyn ap Gruffydd to submit to him at Rhuddlan. Work there was immediately begun on a fine new concentric castle to the NW of the old motte. The castle was made directly accessible by water from supply points such as Chester by modifying the lower section of the river at the enormous cost of £755, enough to pay about eighty men for three full years' work. The timber bridge over the river must have had a lifting section to give access up to the castle. Later reported in decay, the bridge was rebuilt in stone in 1358 and remodelled in 1595.

North of the castle a platform about 200m wide and 400m long was laid out with a grid of new streets for a new town and surrounded by earthwork defences. The ditch and rampart still survive around the northern quadrant and are much more substantial than the earthworks of the older settlement. The burgesses of the new town, which has a church in its western corner (below which were the town quays), were confirmed in 1278 as having the same rights as those of the old town. In 1281 King Edward proposed to the pope that the see of St Asaph be transferred to Rhuddlan, claiming that it was the finest and most populous town in the diocese and suitably fortified. The castle was complete by 1282, when timber for the town palisade was supplied. However this timber seems to have been taken to Caernarfon in 1283, leaving the town unenclosed, and when North Wales was divided into counties on the English model by a statute issued by the king at Rhuddlan in 1284 it was Flint that became the county town.

SWANSEA   West Glamorgan

Henry de Newburgh, Earl of Warwick established the castle and borough here in the early 12th century as the caput of his lordship of Gower. The 14th century town walls for which murage was granted in 1317 and 1338 had the lost mound of the castle (north of the existing 14th century ruin) in the north corner. Close together on the SW side were the large parish church of St Mary (rebuilt in the 19th century) and the Hospital of St David founded by a Bishop of St Davids (now the Cross Keys Inn). A second medieval church of St John (also rebuilt) lies in a northern continuation of the High Street beyond the town's northern gateway. The River Taff protected the east side, originally coming right up to the road known as The Strand until straightened in the 1840s. The south side faced Swansea Bay. Part of a polygonal tower lies between The Strand and the High Street.

Five Arches barbican gateway at Tenby

TENBY   Pembrokeshire

Set on a promontory between two sandy bays, ideal for its current function as a resort, Tenby was a prosperous port from Viking times until it decayed after suffering sieges in 1644 and 1648. Just one, although the best of its type in Wales, remains of the many good 15th and 16th century stone houses of the merchants, but a number of older vaulted cellars still survive under houses built after tourists began to arrive in the 1780s. Beside the High Street is the largest purely parochial medieval church in Wales. The feeble remains of the castle on the headland between the bays belie its former importance.

As at Pembroke there is uncertainty as to whether the walls were begun before the Marshals died out in the 1240s, or (more likely) they date from the 1280s or 90s onwards under the de Valence tenure of the earldom of Pembroke. An attack on the town in 1260 by Llywelyn ap Gruffydd may have instigated some works. The only record of murage is a seven year grant starting in 1328 and it was probably then that what was originally a low wall built against an older rampart was heightened and strengthened. The gunloops with oillets below sighting slits must all date from a considerable strengthening of the walls undertaken after Jasper Tudor was granted the earldom in 1454. His order of 1457 specified a 6 foot wide walkway was to be added to the inside of the wall.

Remains of medieval retaining walls against the cliffs and steep slopes on the seaward facing north and south sides are difficult to distinguish from 19th century walls there. Part of a D-plan tower remains to the north of the Breckmenchine. Near the approach to the castle is the Whitesands Gate, a brick arch replacing the original gateway demolished in 1797. Beside it is a doorway of the original structure later blocked by a wall projecting towards the harbour. A retaining wall with an original parapet just below the castle headland may actually be part of the town wall.

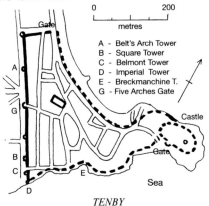

A - Belt's Arch Tower
B - Square Tower
C - Belmont Tower
D - Imperial Tower
E - Breckmanchine T.
G - Five Arches Gate

TENBY

NW corner tower at Tenby   *Embattled parapet below the castle site at Tenby*

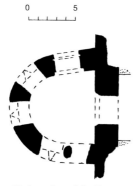

Tenby: plan of the Five Arches barbican gateway

Interior of the barbican at Tenby known as the Five Arches

The walls along the 120m long NW side facing White Lion Street and the 400m long SW side following South Parade stand nearly complete with crenellations, towers and one gateway. The two roads replace ditches filled in by the late 18th century. In Wales only town walls at Caernarfon and Conwy are as complete as the walls beside these two roads. The 7m high wall starts just west of the site of the North Gate demolished in 1782. The lower loops of the next section were originally reached from the earlier rampart, replaced c1457-60 with a new walkway. The circular NW corner tower belongs to the original build of the walls, but the corbelled parapet is a later addition.

South of the corner the wall again has upper and lower firing loops and putlog holes for wooden hoardings. Projecting 6m from the main wall 1.8m thick is Belt's Arch Tower. A pedestrianway through it has been created in 1784 by breaking out loops in embrasures facing along the main wall from the vaulted lowest room. The next section of wall has the mid 15th century walkway carried on arches. Further south is the main gateway. In front of it in the 1330s was added a barbican in the form of a 2m thick wall around an open court 7m across. The outer entrance facing NW has a portcullis groove operated from a loopholed passage round the upper part of the wall and reached from an open stair beside the main inner wall. An upper stair served the barbican wall-walk. Below are three wide embrasures for firing loops that have been broken out to give better access (vehicles still drive through this gateway), resulting in an open space surrounded by five arches, from which the barbican now takes its popular name.

Passing a gunloop inserted into one of the lower firing loops and a datestone recording repairs in the Armada year of 1588, we come to the D-shaped South Pool Tower, added after the heightening of the main wall and retaining several firing loops. Arcading for the wall-walk visible in a garden beyond here has piers 1.2m wide between arches 4.5m high and 2.4m wide. The Square Tower is clearly part of the works initiated in 1457, with two vaulted levels with keyhole shaped gunloops and a latrine on the upper level on the north side. The archway between this tower and the small 13th century circular Belmont Tower is of 1862. The tower parapet and the short wall out to the small square Imperial Tower on the cliff edge are probably of c1457-60. See also pages 18 & 181.

USK   Monmouthshire

Traces of a medieval ditch and rampart have been located west of the cattle-market. The earthwork east of the Gaol was probably a mill-leat. Here also lay a Roman fort later superseded by that at Caerleon. Usk Castle was an important power-base of the de Clares and the parish church in the SE corner originally served a Benedictine nunnery.

TOWN WALLS IN SCOTLAND

Scotland is notably lacking in remnants of town defences of any age. Most of what survives is 16th century: substantial lengths with bastions at Edinburgh and Stirling, a low wall of the 1570s with one turret at Peebles, a gateway at Dundee and a short length of wall hidden away at Dunbar. Little is known about earlier circuits of walls at Perth and Roxburgh. A late 12th century charter to Inverness mentions a ditch to be created by the king and a palisade to be provided by the townsfolk. Aberdeen and Dumfries had only gateways, none of which now remain. Glasgow had only gates, one of which survived until 1755. Selkirk is thought to have had a palisade by the late 16th century. Medieval cathedrals in Scotland were not associated with town walls, although the street layout at Elgin resembles that of an enclosed town. St Andrews has quite a fine ornamental gateway of 1584 but there is no evidence of any ramparts or walls.

ABERDEEEN   Grampian

Medieval Aberdeen had a cluster of streets to the east of the large 12th century church of St Nicholas and a wide open space called Castlegate extended NE from it towards the stone castle built by Alexander III. The present layout bears little resemblance to the old one. The cathedral lay at a separate settlement, Old Aberdeen, 2km to the north. There was no continuous town wall as such but houses and their boundary walls around the perimeter formed a sufficient enclosure at least for customs' purposes. The ravine of the Den Burn (now occupied by the railway and terraced gardens) protected the west side. The burn then looped round marshland (long since drained and built over) and ran along the south side of the city.

Parts of a south-facing gateway in Shiprow survived until Trinity Congregational Church was built in 1876. On the south and north sides of the castle there were gates in Fittie Wynd (now called Castle Terrace) and Justice Street respectively each opening towards the NE end of Castlegate. Heads of executed criminals were displayed on spikes on top of the Justice Gate which was built in 1440. To the east and NE of the church there were gates across the streets known as Nether Kirkgate and Upper Kirkgate. This implies that the church lay outside the enclosed area, again reinforcing the idea that the gates were more to do with money collecting than defence. A sixth gate upon which the royal arms were displayed lay at the far north end of Gallowgate. The town council ordered the gates to be removed in 1769 and no images of them survive. The Upperkirk

The Cowgait Port or Wishart Arch at Dundee

-gate Port survived until 1794. The upper rooms, originally used by the town guard, were accessed from an adjacent house. The parish church is the only medieval building still standing. Marishal College on the north side has replaced the Franciscan friary. The Dominican friary lay to the NW of the parish church and the Carmelite and Trinitarian friaries lay to the south of it. To the SE lay the chapel of St Catherine. The castle probably didn't outlast Robert Bruce's reign. In September 1319 the king stayed in a "palace" built by William the Lion in The Green, between St Nicholas Church and the Carmelite Friary.

DUMFRIES   Dumfries and Galloway

This royal burgh within a loop of the River Nith only required man-made defences on the NE and SE sides. Despite its strategic importance and vulnerability to attack from England no defences are recorded here during the medieval period apart from a 12th century royal castle on the other side of the river which was destroyed in the 14th century. In 1715 whatever then existed in the way of a barrier and ditch was improved enough to dissuade a Jacobite force under Viscount Kenmure from attacking. The Netherport at the junction of Burns Street and St Michael's Street (which was ruinous by 1641) and the Townhead Port at the junction of Catherine Street and Academy Street were then hastily rebuilt. The Lochmaben Gate lay in English Street and a gate on the bridge was transferred there in 1666 from Friars Vennel. Greyfriars Church in the town centre stands on the site of a castle of the Maxwells built in the 1540s near the Franciscan friary in which Robert Bruce killed John Comyn in 1306. Friars Vennel leads towards the old bridge built in the 1430s supposedly on the site of one of the 1260s, and rebuilt in 1620.

DUNBAR   East Lothian

Dunbar lies on a headland with its north and east sides facing the Firth of Forth. There are remains of a castle of the earls of Dunbar at the north end. At the far SE end beyond the walled area a church of 1818-21 has replaced a collegiate church of 1342 which only became the parish church in 1560, presumably replacing a chapel within the walls. On the west side a small plain tower converted into a dovecot remains of the church of the Trinitarian friary lying to the south of the site of the West Port. There was also a gate at the SE end of High Street, and a third gate variously described as either at the north end facing the harbour or along the south side. Both a medical officer in Cumberland's army in 1745 and Daniel Defoe in 1769 mention a high and strong town wall linking the gates but then in a state of decay. One short length of the south facing wall 1m thick and up to 6m high adjoins a 16th century house with vaulted cellars either side of a pend in Bamburgh's Close. It appears that the wall took the form of sections of early to mid 16th century walling linking the gable ends of pre-existing houses rather than a continuous wall with a wall-walk and parapet. Between the Old Harbour and the new Victoria Harbour west of it lies Lamer Island on which is a ruined blockhouse or artillery emplacement built by the Duke of Albany c1520-36. To the SW of the town lay a Carmelite friary.

DUNDEE   Tayside

On the NE side of the town, near where the road to Forfar leaves it, is a short section of 16th century walling containing a loop flanking a round archway known as the Cowgait Port or East Gate. The existing merlons on top are not ancient. It is also sometimes named after George Wishart, who is said to have preached from it in 1544 to plague victims outside the town. The gate narrowly escaped being demolished in the 1830s. A tower or bastion flanking the NW part of the town wall lay in or near Panmure Street. Nothing else is known about the wall but the area assumed to have been enclosed would have had the tower house called Mauchline Tower (which survived until 1812) and the Franciscan friary together almost in the middle and the large 15th century parish church of St Mary towards the SW end. On the SE side was the site of the former royal castle destroyed in the 14th century which lay on a rock above the harbour.

Dundee was frequently the victim of English attacks and was heavily damaged in 1547 by a naval bombardment. It was besieged by Montrose in 1645. The defences were slighted after General Monck captured the town for Cromwell in 1651, two thousand of the people within being slaughtered. The attackers found the town to be full of plunder in the form of valuables sent to it from other Scottish towns for safe keeping.

EDINBURGH   Lothian

The town was well protected on the north side by cliffs above a loch where Princes Street Gardens now are. The castle formed the NW side and the Well Tower of 1362 at the foot of the castle rock on the north covered the gap between it and the loch. The other sides probably had a rampart and ditch by the 1120s when Edinburgh was made a royal burgh by David I. The West Gate mentioned in the 1170s and the South Gate mentioned in 1214 were probably of stone and in 1369 there is the first mention of the Netherbow Port at the east end facing down Canongate towards Holyrood Palace. A stone wall connecting these gateways may have existed by the late 13th century but the first mention of such a wall is in a title deed of 1427 referring to it as a property boundary.

In 1450 James II issued a charter encouraging the provision of a new wall with towers and gates around the town. The wall of that period, known as the King's Wall, enclosed a narrow area 800m long extending east from the castle and having the church of St Giles just east of its centre. A short length of the east side of it remains in Tweeddale Court on the south side of High Street. East of it were found traces of a house which is thought to have been one of several encroaching on the walls which were removed by order of James III in the 1470s. Other parts of the wall may survive within houses. It was still functioning as a barrier in 1635 and parts of it are shown on a map of 1647. Fragments of this wall were found in 1832 and 1842 respectively during construction of the Advocates' Library of the Law Courts and the adjacent Parliament House.

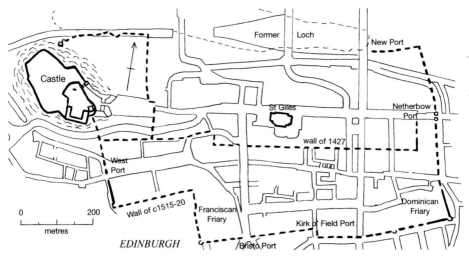

The site of the SE corner bastion at Edinburgh

The Flodden Tower and adjacent walling at Edinburgh, with the castle in the distance behind

Construction of the so-called Flodden Wall 1.2m thick and up to 7.3m high, enclosing a larger area taking in the Grassmarket and Cowgate suburbs, began at the west end in 1514 and continued until 1560. In some sections the wall incorporated parts of the walls of older houses or their gardens. It enclosed 140 acres estimated to have contained a population of 10,000 by the 1560s. The town held out against Regent Morton during a short siege in 1571 but required further strengthening of the defences in the 1650s and at the time of the 1715 and 1745 Jacobite rebellions. Named after the mason in charge of the works, Telfer's Wall was built in 1628-36 to enclose a further ten acres in the SW corner then newly purchased, and now occupied by George Heriot's School.

There are remains of the wall of 1514 on either side of the West Port which closed the west end of the Grassmarket until it was removed in the 1780s. The southern section of wall runs up beside the Vennel to the Flodden Tower, actually a rectangular corner bastion with four cross-loops in it facing north, west and south. A doorway later altered into a window has replaced a second south-facing loop. South of the bastion extends a section of the wall of 1628. Construction of Lauriston Place caused the removal in 1762 of bastions flanking the later wall. Slight traces of both walls survive at the churchyard of Greyfriars, site of the former Franciscan friary. East of here lay the Bristo Port of c1515, and, beyond the Royal Scottish Museum, the Potterow Port which was removed in the 1780s. The wall then continued along the north side of Drummond Street. The SE corner around the former Dominican friary still remains, with a blocked arch which was the entrance to a former corner bastion here. A considerable length of wall then leads north along the west side of the Pleasance towards the site of the Cow Gate.

The 16th century wall then went along the west side of St Mary's Street to the site of Netherbow Port. This gateway was a more ambitious structure than the other gates, with a pair of round flanking turrets with parapets on corbelled coursing like those of Falkland Palace and a tall superstructure over the archway itself (see page 12). A symbol of civic pride, this gateway was threatened with destruction by the government in response to the lynching by the townsfolk of Captain John Porteous in 1736, but it survived until removed in 1764 to ease the flow of traffic up and down the Royal Mile.

HADDINGTON   Lothian

In the spring of 1548 an English force under Lord Grey of Wilton hastily surrounded the town with earthwork defences with corner bastions. The site is a low-lying one west of the River Tyne. Nothing remains of these works and it is uncertain whether the large late-medieval parish church near the river and away from the town centre was within the enclosed area. The town was successfully held against a force of Scots and French troops during July and August but was abandoned in September through lack of supplies.

PERTH   Tayside

Edward I of England had Master Walter of Hereford working on the walls here in 1304 but they may have been begun following floods on the Tay in 1209 which destroyed the castle and bridge. Mill Street is roughly on the site of the north wall, and Canal Street on the site of the south wall. South Methven Street is about on the line of the west wall, in which were two gates opening onto two main streets, High Street on the north, and South Street. The castle was never rebuilt and later kings stayed in monastic guest houses, James I being murdered in 1437 in the Dominican friary on the north side of the town. He was the founder of the Carthusian priory in the middle of the town. There were houses of Carmelite friars to the west, Franciscan friars to the SE and Augustinan nuns to the SW. The only medieval building now remaining is the large cruciform 15th century church of St John in the middle of the town (Perth has never officially been a city).

ROXBURGH   Borders

The burgh of Roxburgh founded in the 12th century at the confluence of the Tweed and the Teviot has almost vanished, having been abandoned during the 16th century in favour of nearby Kelso on higher ground to the NE. Impressive earthworks and a few masonry fragments remain of the large and important royal castle, often in English hands, which guarded the narrow landward approach on the west. There was also a bridge over the Tweed. Excavations by Time Team in 2003 located the stone-faced rampart on the east side and one of the two parish churches. A Franciscan friary lay just outside the defences on the south side.

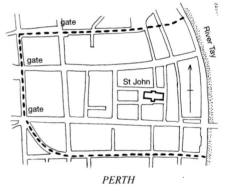

PERTH

0   200
metres

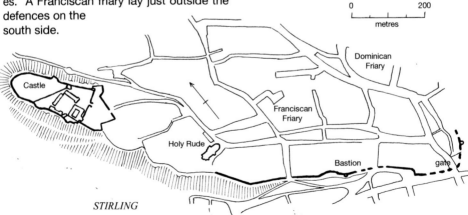

STIRLING

A section of the town wall at Stirling with rectangular gunloops

STIRLING   Central

The old centre of the royal burgh of Stirling, recently made a city, extends SE down a volcanic crag from the castle in which the Scottish monarchs often lived. This is to all intents and purposes the centre of Scotland and the old bridge 700m to the north was until the 20th century the lowest crossing point of the Forth. There is no evidence that the town was enclosed by a wall until one was built hurriedly in the 1540s as an additional protection for the Scottish Court occupying the castle during the period when Henry VIII of England was trying to force a marriage between the infant Queen Mary and his young son Edward. What is now a cemetery between the castle and the large 15th and 16th century church of Holy Rude seems to have been left unenclosed, although it was well defended by nature. Nothing survives of the wall on the NE side of the town, where there were gates at the bottom of St Mary's Wynd and Friars' Street, the latter leading towards the Dominican friary outside the walled area. A friary of Observant Francisans lay in Spittal Street in the centre of the walled area about 500m long by 250m wide. See p17.

Much of the wall built on low crags along the SW side still survives and can be easily seen from an adjacent path called Back Walk made in the 1720s. It appears that the wall may have started near the back of Mar's Wark and ran north of the church and round past Cowane's Hospital. The section behind the former prison appears to have been rebuilt above the foundations but there is a good section from there to Academy Road, and then a long stretch up to 5m high and 1.5m thick extending nearly down to Corn Exchange Road. There is a re-entrant angle on this section, and a round bastion with three gunports opening out of a vaulted room 4m in diameter later altered into a dovecot. SE of the library is an impressive section 6m high and 2m thick on flatter ground. The main gateway known as the Barrisyett was across Port Street. Further round to the NE is one final section embedded into the back of a building in a yard of a former carriage works.

ST ANDREWS   Fife

The West Port with two octagonal turrets with gunloops dates only from 1589. Despite its importance as a cathedral and university town there is no evidence of a circuit of walls although there may have been a palisade and ditch along the west side. See p223.

TOWN WALLS IN IRELAND

The Viking ports of Waterford and Dublin already had stone walls and cathedrals before the Normans took them over in the 1170s. Other Viking ports at Cork and Limerick had cathedrals before the Normans arrived but were only walled in the 13th century, as was the Viking settlement of Wexford. The only other settlements of importance in 12th century Ireland were religious centres such as Armagh, Clonmacnois, Killaloe and Tuam, none of which ever became walled towns, plus Cashel, later walled by an archbishop.

Most of the forty-five walled towns in medieval Ireland were places where English (but originally Norman-French) was spoken, and normally loyal to the English Crown, which from time to time actively encouraged their fortification. A full system of counties was only established in the mid 16th century, and just twelve of the thirty-two places then recognised as county towns already had stone walls. In Ulster only Carrickfergus and Downpatrick appear to have been walled before the early 17th century, from which era date the only standing remains at either of them. West of the River Shannon in Connacht lie Athenry and Rinndown, both with quite long lengths of wall remaining with turrets and single square gateways. Both were spaciously planned and neither prospered later on, Rinndown having now been deserted for centuries. Shorter but impressive fragments survive of a smaller enclosure at Galway and a single gateway remains at Loughrea.

Munster had fourteen towns with medieval walls. None lay in Thomond (Co Clare) or in areas ruled by Gaelic chiefs SW of Cork, Buttevant and Adare. Six lay in Tipperary, with a nearly complete circuit remaining at Fethard, and long sections of some interest at Cashel and Clonmel, plus minor fragments at Carrick-on-Suir. Cashel (like Kells in Meath) was a walled major religious centre that managed to buck the trend of inland towns set away from major rivers not tending to prosper. Low fragments of walling remain at Buttevant, Cork, Kinsale and Limerick, and a gateway and several long but low lengths of walling at Kilmallock. Youghal has a nearly complete circuit of walls on the landward side. There are considerable remains at Waterford with several round towers furnished with gunloops plus the large circular donjon known as Reginald's Tower.

Leinster had no less than twenty five towns with walls. Drogheda has a very impressive gateway plus a second gate and two minor fragments of walling. Several towers and lengths of walling remain at Kilkenny, whilst Dublin, Carlingford, Trim and Wexford each have lengths of walling with one surviving gateway. Fore has two modest gateways and there are also minor remains at Athboy, Castledermot, Kells, and Leighlinbridge. Ardee was laid out on an ambitious scale because the town was used as a mustering point for English armies, whilst in Co Kilkenny the towns of Gowran, Inistioge and Thomastown never fully occupied their modestly sized and poorly defended enclosures.

Many of Ireland's collection of thirty medieval cathedrals were comparatively small buildings in rural locations. Cathedrals at Cashel, Cork and Trim lay outside nearby walled towns, and the cathedral at Kilkenny lay in a suburb only walled at a later date. The towns of Kildare and Limerick seem to have only been fortified after the foundation of the cathedrals within them. Only at the Norse-held coastal towns of Dublin and Waterford were 12th century cathedrals founded within pre-existing circuits of walls.

Towns founded in the 13th century such as Ardee, Athenry, Galway, Kinsale, New Ross and Youghal had just one large parish church. Older towns such as Dublin, Limerick and Waterford had numerous smaller churches within their walls. As in England the presence of mendicant friars in towns gives an idea of their relative prosperity. Most Irish walled towns had at least one friary and/or a house of Augustinian canons close to or within the defences. The two parts of Drogheda between them constituted medieval Ireland's largest walled town and had as many as five friaries. There were three friaries at each of Adare, Galway, Kilkenny and Naas, and two at each of Cashel, Castle Dermot, Cork, Dundalk, New Ross, Trim, Waterford and Youghal. The walled areas at Dundalk and New Ross were nearly as large as that at Drogheda.

ADARE   Co Limerick

Murage grants of 1310 and 1376 are the only evidence of possible former walls. The location and size of the area intended to be walled are unclear since the Earl of Kildare's castle, the parish church and Franciscan friary, all in ruins, lie across the river from the 19th century village, by which are the still-roofed Trinitarian and Augustinian friaries.

ARDEE   Co Louth

Ardee had quite an exposed position on the edge of the English Pale. It was a barony granted to Gilbert Pipard, who built a motte and bailey castle in the 1190s at Castle-guard to the east. The town was destroyed by Edward Bruce in 1315, when the towns-folk took refuge in the church of St Mary, which was then burned by Bruce's men. The line of the town defences around an area about 550m square is shown on maps of 1677 and 1836. The large area thus enclosed was used in the 15th and 16th centuries as a mustering point for occasional campaigns against the Ulster Irish.

    The south side towards the River Dee was left open. The only remains on the other sides are of a 17th century rampart and angled bastion along the northern part of the west side and one side wall of a gate on the east side named after the Cappock family then prominent in the town. One of them was in charge of the funds raised by the earliest of the five murage grants between 1374 and 1416. The other gates were the Head Gate facing north, the Bridge Gate facing south and two other gates in the west wall.

    Some 15th century parts remain in the much altered parish church, to the east of which are ruins of a chantry college of the 1480s. South of the church lies St Leger's Castle, the largest tower house remaining in an Irish town, much altered inside to create a courthouse and prison. A smaller tower built by the Hatch family lies further south and a third tower lies in a farmyard off Jervis Street outside the western line of the walls. All these towers are of c1450-1530. Nothing remains of the hospital of the Crutched Friars in the SE corner of the walls, nor of the Carmelite friary on the south side of the river. There was a northern suburb with its own outer gateway.

ATHBOY   Co Meath

Murage was granted in 1408, the 1420s and 1494. A low portion of the south wall 70m long still remains with the base of one small tower and traces of a ditch to the west of the 18th century parish church of St James, which retains a 15th century tower with a tomb chest beside it. The names of four gateways are known, one of them possibly being an outer east gate serving a suburb beyond the River Athboy on that side. The line of the northern walls is uncertain and may have had a rather irregularly shaped layout. There was a Franciscan friary to the SW, outside the presumed line of the walls.

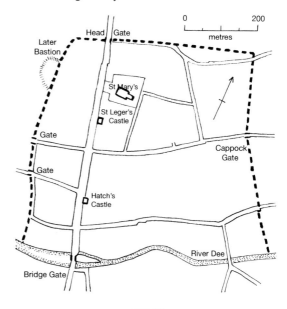

ARDEE

ATHENRY   Co Galway

Athenry was the main seat of the de Birminghams and probably had a rampart on the line of the present walls by the 1230s. Murage was granted in 1310, and there may have been stone walls before 1316, when Richard de Birmingham was one of the commanders of an army that defeated and killed Felim O'Connor outside Athenry. The town never occupied all the generous space within the walls (twice the area of that of Galway) and after it was sacked in 1574 and 1577 by the Earl of Clanricarde's sons a new southern defence line (now vanished) was built to enclose the area actually developed. The town was again sacked in 1596 by Hugh O'Donnell and the castle then left in ruins until the keep was re-roofed as a monument in state care in the 1980s. Most of the walls lying outside the later southern defence line still remain, even if rather reduced in height and overgrown, so that over half of the original circuit still survives.

From the southern corner tower of the castle at the NE corner vanished walls led south to the Brittin Gate and continued south past the east side of the Dominican friary. Standing remains first appear about 125m north of the tall thin circular SE tower. From here the wall runs SW and crosses a stream, just west of which lay the Spittle Gate. It then runs WNW for 350m to the site of Loro gate. Another 50m further on is a circular tower at the west corner. Most of the 420m of wall running NE from there to the site of the Nicholas Gate still remains, with two small towers. About 60m NE of the gate the wall turned through a re-entrant angle for 35m to reach the circular NW corner tower. The 220m of wall running east from there to the castle was pierced by the North Gate which still survives, and the Castle Gate. In 1484 the 13th and 14th century parish church to the south of North Gate was made collegiate by Archbishop O'Murray.

Tower at Athenry

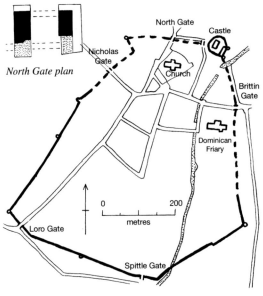

North Gate plan

ATHENRY

North Gate at Athenry

Walls at Athenry

ATHLONE   Co Westmeath

An important bridge over the Shannon here was rebuilt in the 1120s by Turlough O'Connor, King of Connacht and High King of Ireland. The castle on the west bank was built by the Normans to replace Turlough's fort and remained a military base until the 1920s. Henry III allocated 80 merks in 1250 for the enclosing of the vills of Athlone and Rinndown and the repair of their castles. No certain remains survive of the medieval town walls enclosing a D-shaped area 300m long by 200m wide on the east bank of the river. The walls and bastions now surviving around the east side of the town are thought to be of 1618-19 with additional works of the 1650s, but possibly reusing some of the medieval walling as either a foundation or corework. St Mary's Church lies SW of the East Bastion and there was a Franciscan friary at the south end, near the riverbank.

Athlone withstood a 22 week siege by the Confederate Catholics of Connacht in 1641. The new works of the 1650s included enclosing a suburb on the west bank 300m long by 120m wide with corner bastions plus a large bastion on the west side and a west gate protected by a barbican. The town was successfully defended against the forces of William III during the summer of 1690 and only fell a year later after being subjected to a fierce bombardment by General Ginkell.

ATHY   Co Kildare

There are no remains of the walls probably built after the town was burnt by the Irish in 1310 and by Edward Bruce in 1317. The town was held by the Earl of Ormond against the Confederate Catholics in 1642 but was captured by Eoghan O'Neill in 1645, and by Cromwellian troops in 1650. On the east bank of the River Barrow by the bridge is White's Castle built by Sir John Talbot in the early 15th century but enlarged later. A Dominican friary stood on the east bank and a house of Crutched Friars on the west bank. Walls on the east bank appear on a map of 1568 and Preston's Gate, demolished in 1860, is shown in a sketch of 1827.

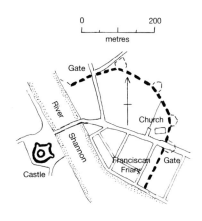

ATHLONE

BUTTEVANT   Co Cork

A recent survey has identified three low fragments of a thin wall probably of 13th century date on the east side of the town facing the Awbeg River. One section lies just below the cliff upon which the castle of the de Barrys is situated above the SE corner of the town. Another extends beyond the east end of the Franciscan friary now assumed to have formed the NE corner of the old town, and the third lies between these two lengths to the SE of the grounds of the Convent of Mercy. David de Barry was allowed a fair and market here in 1234 and murage was granted in 1317 and 1375, a north gate being mentioned on the latter occasion. The enclosed area is now thought to have been about 750m long from north to south by 160m wide. On the west side of the main street lies the surviving south end of a large tower house of the Lombard family. The town walls are mentioned in David Lombard's will of 1479. To the SW of the town are traces of the outer wall or bank mentioned in an 18th century account of the town.

CALLAN   Co Kilkenny

An area as long as 1100m on the south bank of the King's River seems to have been enclosed by a ditch and had gates at either end. It appears that a core area 200m wide and extending 350m south of the bridge had a rampart and either it was actually walled, or it was at least intended to wall it. The 15th century parish church of St Mary lies on the east side of this part, which in 1650 was stoutly defended against Cromwellian troops until Captain Mark McGeoghegan and his men were all killed. There was a suburb on the north bank, where the castle mound lies to the west and the Augustinian friary to the east, but this area does not appear to have been ever enclosed.

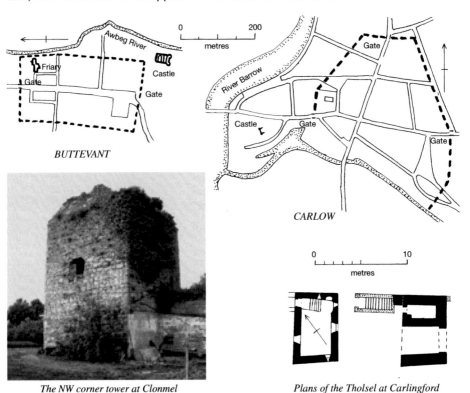

BUTTEVANT

CARLOW

The NW corner tower at Clonmel

Plans of the Tholsel at Carlingford

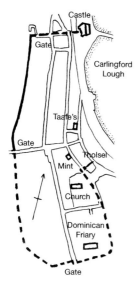

CARLINGFORD

The Tholsel at Carlingford

CARLINGFORD   Co Louth

A railway trackbed divides the rock bearing Henry de Lacy's castle of the 1180s from the NE corner of the town. Although not large, the castle remained important until the 16th century, guarding a vital ferry point, and in 1536 there was a plan to improve or extend the town walls. The railway has removed any evidence of a wall south of the castle past the harbour to Taaffe's Castle, the tower house of a late medieval merchant. Further south lies another merchant's tower known as The Mint, being a 17th century building on the site of the mint of 1467. SE of this tower lies the Tholsel, a gabled building measuring 7.8m by 5m externally containing an upper room with a corner latrine and reached by external steps set over a SE-facing gateway passage flanked on the east side by a small room. South of here lie a section of the wall and the parish church, east of which was a harbour chapel outside the walls. The Dominican friary to the south lay outside the medieval walls and was only taken into what then became an enclosed area 600m long by 200m wide after a late 16th or early 17th century extension with a new south gateway, now lost. Fragments up to 3m high remain of the 1m thick NW wall with four late medieval loops. The Spout Gate lay here but there are no records of other features. The north wall just 120m long contained the north gate just below the castle. Hugh O'Neill tried to capture the castle by surprise in 1596, and there were other attacks by the Ulster Irish in 1642, 1649 and 1650.

CARLOW   Co Carlow

Just half of the 13th century keep remains of the castle of the Marshal family guarding a ferry over the Barrow, and all trace of the town walls and gates set further east had gone by the early 18th century. The moving of the Exchequer here in 1361 by Lionel, Duke of Clarence was a spur to building stone walls. The west gate facing the castle lay just south of the parish church. The Tullow Gate lay 390m to the east of it. Walls extending NE and NW from them formed a nearly triangular shape with the apex cut off by a wall 120m long containing the north or Dublin Gate. Other walls are assumed to have linked the east and west gates with the north bank of the River Burren, which was probably left without a wall. Carlow was attacked by Rory Oge O'More in 1577.

CARRICKFERGUS Co Antrim

Carrickfergus was the chief port of Ulster in the medieval period and the fine castle on a rock by the shore was retained as a government fortress from the late medieval period until 1928. Here William III landed in June 1690 at the start of his campaign against James II in Ireland. A late 16th century sketch shows that a dozen of the wealthier merchants of the town built themselves tower houses like those of Ardglass and Carlingford. None of these survive, nor are there any relics of the medieval town defences which enclosed an elongated pentagon with the parish church of St Nicholas in the NW corner, and the Franciscan friary at the NE end. There is no certain evidence of a stone wall. The landward facing NW side was about 400m long. This side was refortified in the 16th century when the west end was extended by about 50m, with a new gateway, but this work was itself replaced in 1610-25 by a bastioned enclosure extending further to the NW. The north gate of that period still survives, along with parts of a thin wall once backed by an earth rampart and one corner bastion.

CARRICK-ON-SUIR Co Tipperary

Documents of 1324, 1361 and 1362 all refer to a stone wall along the 480m long north side of the town and a wall of stone is mentioned in 1344, when a suspended murage grant was restored. Another grant was made in 1450 after the provost wrote to say only half of the town was then walled and that it had been twice burned in the last fourteen years. Fragments of the north wall remain near the NE corner. The name New Gate suggests the gateway on this side was a later addition. A map of 1657 suggests the northern corners each had towers. The East gate lay just north of the castle of the Butler earls of Ormond in the SE corner beside the River Suir, supposedly founded in 1309 but now a mid 15th century structure with a mid 16th century house added on the north side. There was also a West Gate and a Bridge Gate beside the SW corner where a bridge over the Suir led to a small suburb with a Franciscan friary. There is no certain evidence of a wall facing the river on the south side.

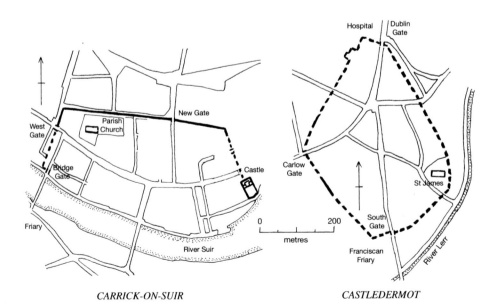

CARRICK-ON-SUIR   *CASTLEDERMOT*

A corner of the walls at Cashel

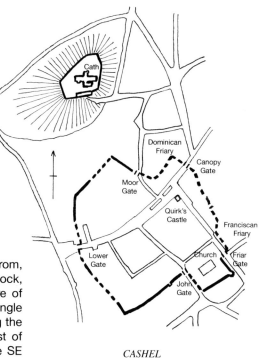

CASHEL

CASHEL   Co Tipperary

To the south of, and quite separate from, the cathedral close on St Patrick's Rock, lay the walled city, roughly a square of about 400m, but with the northern angle cut off by a re-entrant angle excluding the precinct of the Dominican friary. West of this angle lay the Moor Gate. On the SE side the walls projected around the parish church of St John. West of the church lay the John Gate, beyond which have been revealed wall foundations 1.8m thick. On the other side of the churchyard lay the Friar Gate, named after the Franciscan friary beyond it outside the walls. There is a record of the Lower Gate facing west being taken down in 1729 because it was dangerous, and the Canopy Gate facing NE seems to have also been removed about that time. The Archbishop seems to have obtained murage for four years in 1303 to wall in his part of the town, which may have been the 'new vill' mentioned in the 1220s in a dispute with the king, who claimed the lordship of the older settlement immediately to the north. Another murage grant for five years obtained by Archbishop FitzJohn in 1319 specifically mentions a stone wall. Walling with a postern facing the old cathedral has recently been repaired and a section of wall 25m long has been exposed by the new cathedral. Other fragments are currently being restored and in all nearly half of the 1,550m circuit of walling still stands. On the south side of Main Street is a 15th century tower house called Quirk's Castle.

CASTLEDERMOT   Co Kildare

Ruined walls along the 350m long NW side, lower and more fragmentary remains on the SW side also about 350m long, and low modern boundary walls on the SE and NE enclose a diamond-shaped area with the parish church in the east corner where the small River Lerr lies fairly close. At the west corner lay the Carlow Gate, and the Dublin Gate and South Gate each lay just east of the northern and southern corners. Friaries lay just outside these two gateways, with Augustinians to the north, and Franciscans to the south. There are no signs of a castle and a document of 1534, referring to the town as walled and belonging to the Earl of Kildare, calls it Tristledermot.

Arcaded walling in Clonmel churchyard

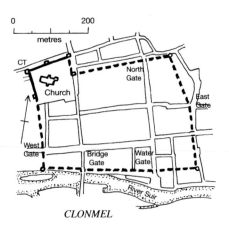

CLONMEL

CLONMEL   Co Tipperary

The de Grandison lord of the town obtained a murage grant in 1298 for ten years and others directly to the town authorities followed throughout the 14th century. Another grant in 1463 specifies work upon the South Gate facing the River Suir and the adjacent bridge. A document of Henry V's reign refers to the town as inhabited by English merchants who have "lately constructed great walls, towers and fortifications".

The west gate survives although it was almost entirely rebuilt in 1831, when it lost its portcullis groove. North of it are remnants of the wall at the backs of houses in Wolfe Tone Street. More impressive are the lengths of walling each over 100m long around the west and north sides of the parish church of St Mary, where the vestry takes a tower-like form. The wall has a series of pointed arches to carry the wall-walk and the lower part of the parapet remains. A tower on the corner (see page 194) takes its name from use as a magazine during the 1798 rebellion and was inhabited by the sexton and his family in the 19th century. It is square and dates from the 15th century, as do two towers further east with round corners. Beyond the third tower the wall made a re-entrant angle as a result of rebuilding in the late 17th century. A round tower remains at the NE corner but the North Gate and the East or Kilsheelan Gate have gone. North of the site of the latter at the junction of Emmet St, Dowd's Lane, Parnell St and Mitchel St are traces of the east wall behind houses in Upper Emmel Street. Parts of the Franciscan friary in the SE corner of the town were incorporated in the Cromwellian fort of the 1650s. West of it lay a sixth gateway. Extensions to the quays led to the demolition of the whole of the 440m long south wall in the late 18th century. An old map suggests several merchants' tower houses once stood on this side.

CLONMINES   Co Wexford

A ditch runs north from the churchyard to cut off the site of the now-deserted medieval town within a bend of the Owenboy River founded by the Marshal earls of Pembroke in the early 13th century. The churchyard contains a ruined church with a western tower and a castellated courthouse probably of just after 1400, when the town was attacked and destroyed. There are also ruins of a 14th century Augustinian friary with a defensive wall adjoining it and a ruined tower house built by the FitzHenry family. A tower house of the Sutton family forms part of a nearby farmhouse. The town decayed after its port silted up c1600 but it continued to send members to the Irish Parliament until 1800.

Clonmel:
NW corner tower plan

CORK   Co Cork

The walls of Cork enclosed two islands totalling 645m long from north to south by 225m wide, the shape being nearly rectangular but with the NE corner curved off. The limestone walls of the southern island were built in the early 13th century. The base of part of the east wall is now displayed in Bishop Lucey Park. None of the other fragments of the walls and their towers and the adjoining quays exposed by excavations are currently exposed to view. NW of the park lay Holy Trinity college founded in 1482 to the east of the southern island's former parish church of St Laurence. North of the college was a water gate straddling the water course dividing the south island from the north island, which had its own parish church of St Peter and was walled using sandstone in the late 13th to early 14th centuries. The walls of the two islands eventually had sixteen mural towers, and there were main gateways towards bridges over the river at either end. Near the Water Gate on the east side lay the two large towers called King's Castle and Queen's Castle which are depicted on the city's shield of arms.

The former medieval cathedral occupied an ancient monastic site well outside the walls to the SW. In 1601 a detached fort was built to the east of it but the existing bastioned structure here, now enclosing a police station, dates from a rebuilding in 1624. North of it, also outside the walls, was the Dominican friary, whilst the Augustinian friary was further out to the SE. The Franciscan friary lay NW of the north gate. There was a suburb there with its own parish church and Shandon Castle, a tower built by the Barrys. It was later occupied by the Carews and was fired upon from the city

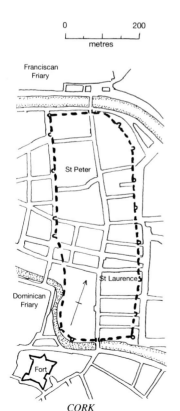

CORK

walls during the accession of James I in 1603, which was unpopular in Cork. Cromwell occupied the castle during Christmas 1649. The castle was damaged by Williamite cannon in the siege of 1690 (when the SE part of the city wall was also breached) and had vanished by 1750. Short Castle Lane nearby is named after a former tower held by the Roche family. Not far south of the north gate stood another tower built on an oak raft foundation in 1445 by John Skiddy, bailiff and later mayor of Cork. It was in use as a powder magazine during the insurrection of 1603 when the citizens broke into it. The lower part was removed in 1892 but footings have been revealed by excavation.

Restored base of Cork city wall in Bishop Lucey Park

DALKEY   Co Dublin

Of seven castellated buildings known to have existed in and around the town three still survive. The former town hall or court house is still used by the council and stands opposite the ruined Archbold's Castle. Bullock's Castle beside the harbour has a turret at one end. An added second turret at the other end stands over an arched gateway which gave access to the port, which was formerly closed off by a wall extending 300m to the east to terminate at another tower.

The Buttergate at Drogheda

DOWNPATRICK   Co Down

There are no visible remains of the wall, which is said to have been destroyed by the O'Neills and enclosed a modest rectangular area extending northwards from the parish church, which retains a tower of the 1560s. South of it lay a stone castle, but the de Courcy motte lies further west. There is a possible reference to murage in 1260 and a short section of wall footings 2.2m wide were found in an excavation in the mid 1960s. Some medieval work remains in the cathedral further to the west.

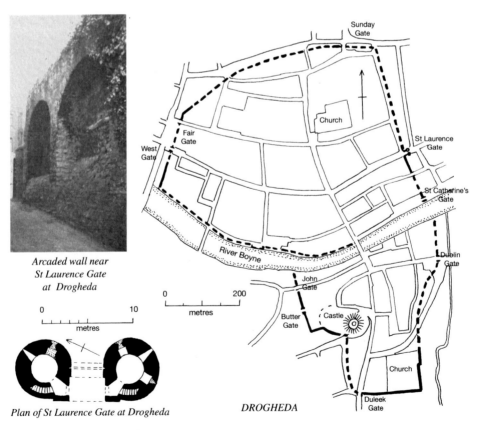

Arcaded wall near
St Laurence Gate
at Drogheda

Plan of St Laurence Gate at Drogheda

DROGHEDA

DROGHEDA   Co Louth

Several murage grants in the 13th century beginning in 1234 and others in the 14th century resulted in an enclosure of 80 acres measuring 700m by 600m on the north bank of the River Boyne, and a separate smaller enclosure of 30 acres on the south bank of the river in Co Meath. Originally these were rival boroughs held respectively by the de Verduns and the de Lacys and were only united as one corporation in 1412. Drogheda hosted six parliaments between 1441 and 1494. It was besieged by Sir Phelim O'Neil in 1641 and in 1649 was the scene of an infamous massacre of the inhabitants when Cromwellian troops broke into the town.

Hugh de Lacy's motte and bailey castle of the 1180s called Mill Mount lies by a re-entrant angle of the southern enclosure, which represents the Norse settlement. Parts of the wall retaining the churchyard of St Mary's in the SE corner have recently been repaired. Here the wall thickness was originally just 0.7m, later increased to 1.6m by adding piers and arcading to carry a wall-walk. There was once also a Carmelite friary here, whilst the Crutched friars had a house outside the West or John Gate. The lower parts of the six-sided Butter Gate, a second western entrance, still survive with evidence of a portcullis groove and a short section of wall running south of it. There was a hospital of St James in the NE corner with the Dublin Gate just south of it. The Duleek Gate lay in the SW corner.

The northern enclosure had numerous towers and gateways. An Augustinian hospital-friary lay near the West Gate, a Dominican friary lay SW of the north-facing Sunday Gate, south of which lay the parish church of St Peter, rebuilt in the 18th century, whilst the Franciscan friary lay by the St Catherine Tower at the SE corner.   A short section of arcaded walling remains on the east side between the site of the Blind Tower and the St Laurence Gate, north of which the wall ran past the Pigeon Tower and the Taylor's Hall Tower to the Tooting Tower at the NE corner.

The St Laurence Gate is the most impressive structure of its kind left in Ireland. It was originally a late 13th century barbican added in front of the actual gateway. It was heightened in the 14th century to where rectangular windows represent former crenels of a parapet, and again c1500 resulting in a structure rising 19m high to double-stepped battlements. Two circular towers 7m in diameter flank a short passage with a groove for a portcullis operated from a wooden platform. The five levels of tower rooms are mostly vaulted and retain several original arrow-loops, plus staircases and latrine shafts.

The St Laurence Gate at Drogheda

DUBLIN   Co Dublin

When the Normans arrived in 1170 Dublin already had a population of over 5,000 and was enclosed by a stone wall 1.5m thick and 3.5m high with seven parish churches inside it and several more outside. Roughly in the middle was the cathedral of Holy Trinity, later known as Christchurch, co-founded by a bishop and a Norse king of Dublin c1030. To the NE of it lay the churches of St John and St Olave. Dublin was the first real town in Ireland and has consistently remained the largest urban area in the country, although several other Irish towns eventually had larger walled enclosures.

The Norse-built stone wall of c1100-30 replaced a rampart and palisade of c1000 which itself superseded a smaller and more lightly defended enclosure of the mid 10th century corresponding to the area between the cathedral and castle. Of the area enclosed by the 12th century stone walls the west end represented the original pre-Norse trading settlement of Ath Cliath beside a man-made ford replaced c1000 by a bridge northwards across the Liffey. The east end had originally been an ecclesiastical community named Duiblinn after a pool on the River Poddle SE of it. On the north bank of the Liffey was a suburb with its own church of St Michan. East of it lay an important Cistercian abbey founded c1140, eventually Ireland's richest monastery. Since the mid 13th century Dublin has had a second cathedral, that of St Patrick, originally a collegiate church lying 200m to the south of the city walls. The Carmelite friary lay east of it. None of the suburbs were ever fully walled but they did have gate-towers. One was added in the 1460s to Crockers' Bars in the west suburb, and about the same time the northern suburb was given two gates, one of which stood in Hammond Lane.

Gateway near St Audeon's Church, Dublin

A large new royal castle of stone with large circular corner towers was begun by King John c1210 in the SE corner of the city, probably on the site of the palace or hall of the Norse rulers. West of it lay the churches of St Martin and St Werburgh. From the castle SW corner the wall ran almost east to the surviving but much altered Stanihurst Tower in Little Ship Street, described in Sir John Perrot's survey of 1586 as a D-shaped structure of three storeys and then on to the Pole Gate. To the south of St Nicholas's church a new section of walling further out than the Norse wall is thought to have been built in the 1190s. A section of it remains in an underground chamber at Ross Road. In this area lay Geneval's Tower, from which the wall went SW to the St Nicholas Gate. Just west of the gate the wall headed NW past several towers to what in 1177 was referred to as the "new west gate".

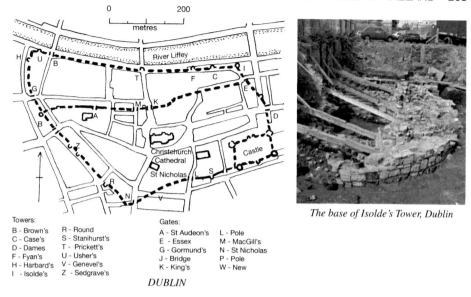

The base of Isolde's Tower, Dublin

Towers:		Gates:	
B - Brown's	R - Round	A - St Audeon's	L - Pole
C - Case's	S - Stanihurst's	E - Essex	M - MacGill's
D - Dames	T - Prickett's	G - Gormund's	N - St Nicholas
F - Fyan's	U - Usher's	J - Bridge	P - Pole
H - Harbard's	V - Genevel's	K - King's	W - New
I - Isolde's	Z - Sedgrave's		

DUBLIN

The next tower beyond the New Gate, Brown's, marked the NW corner of the Norse city, part of the north wall of which with a gateway can be seen beside St Audeon's, the only parish church within the walls now retaining medieval fabric. The gateway was an insertion of the 13th century when a new wall was built 100m further north on the bank of the Liffey. The new area thus enclosed, funded by murage grants from 1221 onwards, had a west gate called Gormund's. The Harbard's and Usher towers lay either side of the new NW corner, not far east of which was a gate facing the bridge which had replaced the original ford. The riverside wall ran past the Pitchet, Fyan and Case towers and the various new quays of the mid 13th century to Isolde's Tower at the NE corner. The base of this massively walled tower over 12m in diameter exposed in 1993, and thought to be of c1260, is on display below present ground level. From here the wall ran SE past a gateway called Buttevant Tower and the Birse Tower to meet the Dame Gate facing east and then went past St Mary's Church to the castle NE corner.

DUNDALK   Co Louth

Named after the nearby prehistoric fort of Dun Dealgan, Dundalk had a very exposed location at the northern extremity of Leinster and was very vulnerable to assault by the Ulster Irish, being burned by Edward Bruce in 1315 and Hugh O'Donnell in 1483. It was the focus of attacks by the O'Neills in 1233, 1444, 1596 and 1641. The town promptly surrendered to Cromwell after the massacre at Drogheda in 1649 but was held by the Jacobites in 1689. The town was developed by the de Verdons. They were succeeded by the Bellews, who built a new castle in the 1470s to replace John de Courcy's motte. The town walls seem to have been entirely removed by the early 18th century. The area they enclosed was up to 300m wide at the north end, where there was a bridge over the river, but was only 100m wide where the Warr Gate once lay 700m to the south. The church of St Nicholas lay in the middle of this enclosure and the Franciscan friary lay outside to the east. The Castletown Gate lay on the west and the Stafflane Gate to the east. Later on the walls extended almost as far again to the Ardee Gate facing SW and the Dublin Gate facing south, whilst the new enclosure also had a NE gate called Upper Seatown. This part seems to have been unwalled on the SE side, where the Rampart River and marshes beyond formed a sufficient defence. See map overleaf.

DUNGARVAN   Co Waterford

The walls were repaired in the 1460s and in 1537. They probably only enclosed the landward west and south sides of an area 260m square with the South Gate facing the church outside the walls and the West Gate facing inland. The south wall was just 1m thick. The 1.3m thick walls on the north and east sides and the Quay Gate facing the river were built in the 1620s when Richard Boyle, Earl of Cork controlled Dungarvan. In the 1990s excavations revealed traces of the north, east and south walls, with a D-shaped NE corner tower and a ditch near the SW corner. Still standing are the much-altered 13th century castle near the NE corner facing the harbour and two merchant's houses south of it. Dungarvan was captured by the Confederate Catholics in 1642, but soon recaptured by William St Leger. The Confederates took the town again in 1645, and held it until Cromwellian forces took Dungarvan in 1649.

Sheela-na-gig on the walls at Fethard

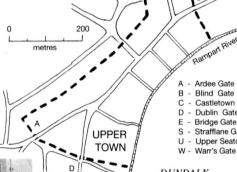

A - Ardee Gate
B - Blind Gate
C - Castletown Gate
D - Dublin Gate
E - Bridge Gate
S - Strafflane Gate
U - Upper Seatown
W - Warr's Gate

DUNDALK

The North Gate at Fethard

Corner tower and church tower at Fethard

The recently restored southern walls at Fethard

FETHARD   Co Tipperary

Fethard has the most complete circuit of medieval town walls in Ireland, the only substantial gap being on the SE. The enclosed area is quite small at about 410m east-west by 200m wide and is protected on the south and west by the River Clashawley. Murage for seven years was first granted in 1292 when the town was controlled by the Archbishop of Cashel. Another series of grants began in 1376 and ended with a twelve year grant from 1467 referring to the cost of repairing the walls "due to the efforts of the King's enemies and English rebels". The walls facing the river had their parapets restored to an external height of 6m in 1993. The wall-walk lies 2m above the level of the churchyard of Holy Trinity but twice that height above the ground outside. This section in the middle of the south side makes a fine grouping with a square three storey tower at the churchyard SW corner and behind it the larger and taller west tower of the church, both of them 15th century additions with restored parapets with corner turrets. There is a slight re-entrant angle of the wall to the west of the churchyard. See extra picture on page 222.

A round arch still survives of the North Gate, which had a D-shaped tower nearby to the east. There is a circular tower at the NE corner. Nothing survives of the East and West gates or of the Wickett Gate facing NE or the Water Gate on the south side. Beside the site of the latter there is a sheela-na-gig. East of the church lies a ruined tower house called Court Castle. South of it, forming part of the town wall, is the partly restored Edmond's Castle, another rectangular tower house belonging to the Everard family with a two-light window and a latrine projection overhanging the river-bank on two pyramidal corbels. It also has some original gunloops. North of the church is a later and more thinly walled building bearing a panel of the Crucifixion. An Augustinian friary lies 150m beyond the east corner of the town.

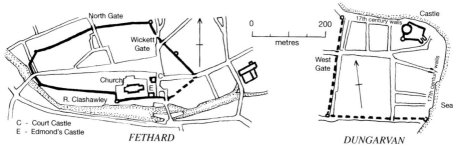

FETHARD

DUNGARVAN

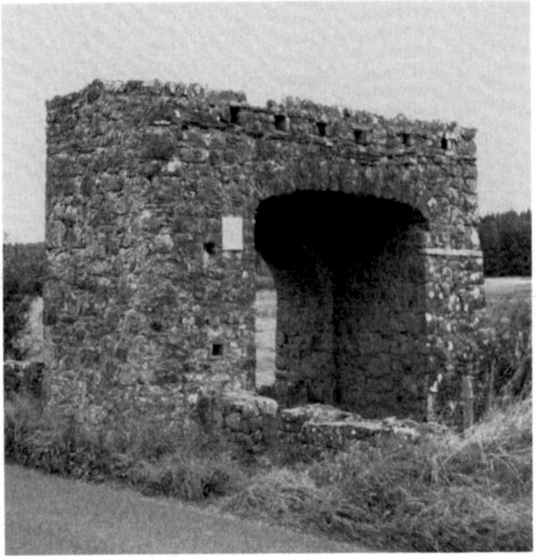

The West Gate at Fore

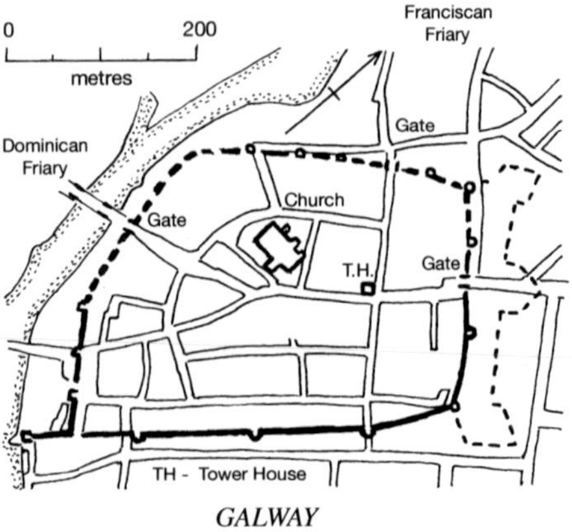

GALWAY

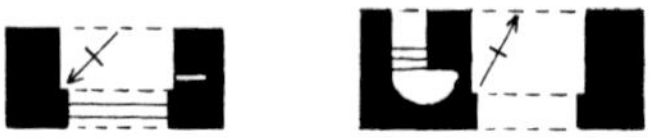

Plans of the gates at Fore

FORE Co Westmeath

Two round archways remain of the east and west gates, which lie about 450m apart at either end of the village main street. The west gate has a murder hole and the east gate has the base of a spiral staircase on the SW side to a lost upper room. Nothing remains of actual walls but a murage grant of Edward III's reign mentions a stone wall and another grant in 1436 refers to the construction of a ditch or stone wall. The early church of St Fechin lies just south of the West Gate and to the NE of the East Gate the defences are assumed to have bowed out round the churchyard of St Mary's church. A stream seems to have formed the NE boundary. Beyond it, 60m east of the northern corner, is a Benedictine abbey fortified with several towers in the late medieval period. A motte and bailey castle lies 300m beyond the eastern corner of the enclosed area.

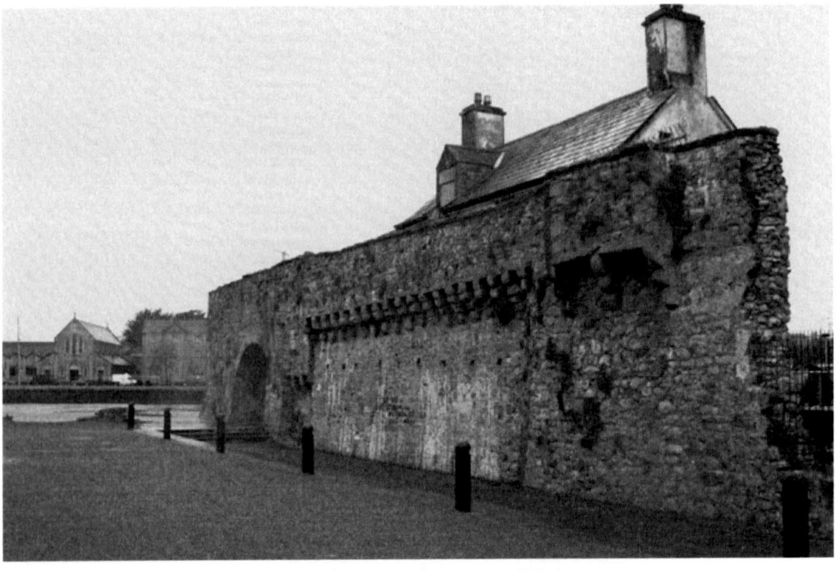

Walls at the southern corner of Galway

GALWAY   Co Galway

Nothing remains of the castle of the de Burghs begun in 1232, but of the town walls thought to have been begun in the 1270s there are considerable lengths on the NE and SE sides where there were quays beside the River Corrib. The Spanish Arch and the adjoining length of wall with a corbelled parapet may have formed part of new defences of the 1490s on this side. The West gate opened onto a bridge with a tower in the middle and another at the far end. One of the three towers (probably the outermost) bore the date 1549 and an inscription recording its construction as a protection against the "ferocious O'Flaherties", traditional enemies of the isolated English-speaking townsfolk loyal to the English Crown even after the Reformation when most of them remained Catholic. A postern gate to one of the quays is mentioned in 1557. The Little Gate lay on the NW side. The wall ran NE from here past the Colman Tower to the Lyon Tower at the north corner. The wall then ran SE past the Lynch Tower to the main landward facing gate, and then past the Pipe Tower to the Shoemaker Tower at the east corner. This section has recently been rebuilt as the focal point of a new shopping centre. There were three other towers along the SE side. The enclosed area was roughly a rectangle 410m long by 300m wide but with the west corner rounded off.

A new ditch was made on the landward eastern sides after the town was captured by the Burkes and O'Briens in 1504. Of about the same period is the ornate tower house of the Lynch family (now a bank) bearing the arms of Henry VII and the Earl of Kildare, then Lord Deputy. No less than 84 members of the Lynch family served as mayor of the town between 1485 and 1654. Just one other tower house now remains, but a map of 1651 suggests there were once a dozen or so. To the north of the centre of the town lies the large parish church of St Nicholas. West of the river lay the Dominican friary which was converted into an artillery battery in 1642 but destroyed ten years later to prevent Cromwellian forces occupying it. The Augustinian friary east of the town was also replaced by a fort. The Franciscan friary lay outside the NW walls.

In the 17th century the vulnerable NE side was strengthened by a new outer wall with arrow-head shaped corner bastions and a central bastion in front of the main gate. Excavations have revealed footings of the east bastion. Thus strengthened the town held out for nine months against the Cromwellian commander Sir Charles Coote's attempts to besiege it by land and sea until it finally surrendered in April 1652.

GOWRAN   Co Kilkenny

The large and fine collegiate church of St Mary seems to have occupied the SW corner of the original enclosure measuring about 400m long by 280m across at its widest, which is shown on an old map as having a stone wall on the south side and a rampart earth on the north side. There seems to have been a west gate just north of the church whilst the Magdalen Gate lay within a re-entrant angle at the NE end. A further enclosure of very irregular shape to the west was probably a later addition. The only record of murage is a document of 1414 allowing tolls for 40 years, specifying a stone wall, and mentioning a recent burning of the town by the Irish. Other documents of the mid 16th century suggest the town was then sometimes used as an English garrison post.

INISTIOGE   Co Kilkenny

Nothing remains of the town walls assumed to have existed around a modestly sized D-shaped enclosure 250m by 200m. A castle mound lies near the SW corner, and there was a tower house near the town centre and another at the east end, whilst the Augustinian priory with its two towers still surviving lay on the north side.

KELLS   Co Meath

Stone walls referred to in several documents once enclosed an area of irregular shape measuring about 500m from the Trim Gate on the south side to the Maudlin Gate on the north side and about 460m from the Cannon Gate facing west to the Dublin Gate facing east. In the middle of the NW side was also the Carrick Gate. Between the Cannon and Trim Gates the wall bowed inwards and on this section, but much closer to the site of the Cannon Gate, is a circular tower three storeys high and only missing its parapet. It is entered at second storey level and has a large corbelled projection on the inner side. The parish church lay just west of the centre of the walled town, which also contained at least one tower house towards the east side. An Augustinian abbey lay outside the Cannon Gate and a preceptory of the Knights Hospitaller lay beyond the Dublin Gate. Also in the town are a round tower and several fine crosses from the early monastery here, later the seat of a bishopric until the synod of 1152 abolished it.

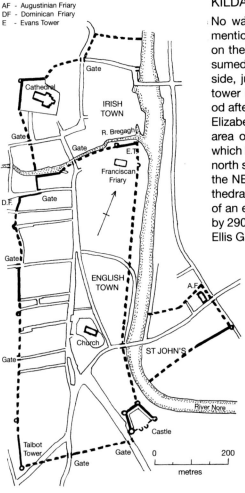

KILDARE   Co Kildare

No walls remain but a solitary murage grant mentions a ditch and the Black Ditch survives on the west side of the city, south of the presumed location of the Clare Gate. On the east side, just north of the site of White Gate is a tower house which may be mostly of the period after the destruction of the castle by Queen Elizabeth's officials in the 1580s. It adjoins the area of the castle bailey known as The Park which has 17th century artillery defences on the north side and one circular flanker. This formed the NE corner of the city. The close of the cathedral formed the central part of the north side of an enclosure about 320m from east to west by 290m wide. Between it and The Park lay the Ellis Gate. Another gate lay on the south side.

KILKENNY

The Talbot Tower at Kilkenny

KILKENNY   Co Kilkenny

Eleven murage grants are recorded for Kilkenny, from 1250 when the de Clares were its lords, to 1460. By then the castle built c1207-12 by William Marshal had become the chief seat of the Butler earls of Ormond following their purchase of it from the Staffords in 1391. The central part of the town known as Hightown, a roughly rectangular area 800m long from north to south by 300m wide, has the River Nore along the east side and the castle in the SE corner. This part was walled by the end of the 13th century. Irishtown at the north end with the cathedral on its west side was not walled until the mid to late 14th century and the walls of the suburb of St John's on the east bank of the river were probably built still later on. The town was besieged by James FitzMaurice in 1568 and in 1650 Cromwell battered down the SE side of the castle.

A gateway removed in 1769 stood close to the south corner tower of the castle. The next section of wall fell a victim to the building of the Castle Stables and Butler House in the 1780s and led to St Patrick's Gate. Ormond Road of the 1830s then cuts across the wall line and the first significant remnant of the wall is a rebuilt section 27m long and 2m high east of the circular Talbot Tower at the SW corner. Originally known as St Patrick's Tower this recently restored building is 8.8m in external diameter over walls 1.6m thick and rises 9.7m to the top of a plain corbelled parapet. It contains a single chamber rising 6.8m high to the apex of a dome vault with signs of wicker centering.

North of the tower part of the wall is 5m high and 1.7m thick. Behind the Ormond Hotel stood the former Myles Tower, beyond which is a rectangular internal projection seemingly a garden feature of fairly recent date. About 280m from the corner lay the Walkin's Gate first mentioned in 1305 and destroyed between 1758 and 1788. The next section and the Colliers Lane Tower disappeared in the early 19th century but beyond is a good section still 4.5m high with two cross-loops and a battered plinth. The arch of St James's Gate stood until 1860 although the upper storeys were removed in 1804.

The next section past the Tilbury Tower was lost in the early 19th century. A low and partly rebuilt section beside a car park then extends round to the surviving arch of the Abbey Gate, named after the Dominican friary just outside the walls. The River Bregagh flowed past the walls here, being bridged outside of the Water Gate, which was de-molished in 1759. Beyond the remains of the Franciscan friary is the Evans Tower, an irregular polygon set at the NE corner of the walls, where the Bregagh flowed into the Nore. Nothing remains of the east walls facing the Nore or of Bridge Gate.

Of the walls around the suburb named after the priory and hospital of St John's which stood in its northern corner there remains a rebuilt section of wall with two loops running SW from the eastern corner tower probably of the 1570s above Maud-lin Street. Irishtown had three gates, Deans Gate facing west between the Bretagh and the Cathe-dral, Troy's Gate facing NW in a slight re-entrant angle, and Green's facing east to where there was a second bridge over the Nore, remains of which were exposed in 2003. In this part the wall only survives in the form of retaining walls up to 3.5m high around the west and north sides of the Cathedral close. Projecting west from the corner is a square tower now containing just one lofty vaulted room. Here may have been the robing room of Bishop Ledrede, 1316 - 61.

The Evans Tower at Kilkenny

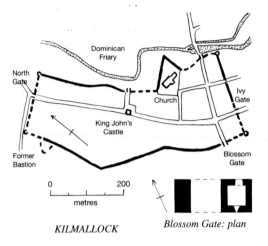

KILMALLOCK

Blossom Gate: plan

The eastern wall at Kilmallock

KILMALLOCK   Co Limerick

The FitzGeralds had the town fortified from the late 13th century onwards. In 1571 it was captured by a surprise night attack by the rebellious Sir James FitzMaurice in alliance with the Sweenys and Sheehys, who took three days to cart away the spoils. The area enclosed by the walls extended for 550m between the North Gate and the Ivy Gate facing SE and averaged about 200m wide. Three quarters of it still remains in some modest form. There seem to have been towers at the corners. Long sections up to 2m high survived amongst gardens and back yards on the SW side facing the former Ash Hill Lough, and the northern end of this side beyond the lough once had a triangular 17th century bastion. Near the south end there still stands the rectangular Blossom Gate with a small room flanking the east side of a passage 3.5m long and a small room above. Its counterpart on the NE side was the Water Gate facing a bridge over the River Loobagh. Much of the wall here too still remains with a very irregular line, projecting as a triangular flanker around the churchyard of the collegiate church of St Peter and St Paul. North of it, across the river lies the Dominican friary. The only survivor of several late medieval tower houses within the walls is King John's Castle.

The western walls at Kilmallock

Print of the former North Gate at Kilmallock

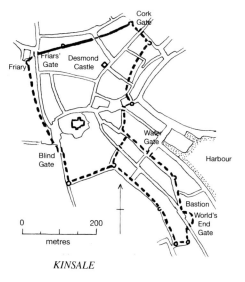

KINSALE

Blossom Gate at Kilmallock

LEIGHLINBRIDGE

Co Carlow

Murage for walling the town on the east bank of the Bannow was granted in 1310. One 10m long section of wall remains standing 3.5m high on the south side with a featureless circular turret. On the river-bank lies the tower and bawn of the Black Castle. There was also a White Castle built in 1408 by the Earl of Kildare.

KINSALE   Co Cork

The walls here are first mentioned in 1333 as being ruinous, having probably been begun in the mid 13th century. A grant for repairing them was made in 1348. The walls played a part in the battle of Kinsale in 1601 and were much damaged during a siege by Williamite forces in 1690. A substantial section of the 300m long northern wall still remains in use as field boundaries although somewhat reduced from its original height. A Carmelite friary lay outside the NW corner of the walls and the north facing gateway near that end was named Friars Gate. The Cork gate lay in the middle of an 80m long stretch of wall facing NE. On the east side the Water Gate opens towards the harbour and to the south of the parish church of St Multose was a SW-facing re-entrant angle within which lay Blind Gate. There were also fifteen flanking towers. In Cork Street lies a tower house called Desmond Castle or the French Prison. South of the Water Gate another gate opened into the suburb of Basetown which was given its own wall in the late 16th century with two gateways, the Lower Water gate facing NE and the World's End Gate facing SE, beside the north side of which was a semicircular bastion.

LIMERICK   Co Limerick

Originally founded by Norsemen in 922, Limerick was later the main seat of the O'Brien Kings of Thomond descended from Brian Boru until captured in 1175 by Raymond le Gros. The city was occupied by Edward Bruce in 1315 and was captured and sacked by the MacNamaras in 1369. From the mid 15th century onwards the citizens were forced to pay an annual tribute to the O'Briens of Thomond. King John's castle of c1210-16 was built on the site of a former royal seat lying on King's Island on the east bank of the Shannon. Englishtown containing the castle on its west side and the cathedral further south was walled by the end of the 13th century. North of the castle the Thomond gate opening onto a bridge over the river lay between it and a parish church. To the east are remains of a Dominican friary. Further south facing Island Road and beside Sheep Street are short sections of the walls. They enclosed an area 850m long by up to 250m wide and had a few circular flanking towers. Within the walls there were many tower houses and castellated houses, but just two fragmentary examples now remain.

In the early 14th century the surburb of Irishtown south of Ball's Bridge was given its own circuit of walls enclosing a pentagon about 330m across. It also had circular corner towers and the Mungret Gate faced SW whilst the St John Gate, named after a nearby parish church, faced SE. In Elizabethan times a small citadel was built beside this gateway, which was flanked by the largest of its three bastions. Limerick defied Cromwell for a year and a siege begun in 1650 only ended when traitors opened a gate in Irishtown. The city had been held by the Confederate Catholics since being captured in 1642. In 1690 William III arrived at Limerick but Patrick Sarsfield captured and destroyed his siege train at Ballynety and he was unable to start a full siege against the strongly fortified city until fresh artillery arrived. The wall of Irishtown was breached to the SW of St John's Gate but an attempt to storm the breach was driven back with heavy losses and after a month the siege was raised. The city only fell to the Williamites in 1691 and the castle only yielded after a heavy bombardment. The defences were dismantled after it was officially proclaimed in 1760 that Limerick would cease to be a walled city. In the grounds of St John's Hospital are some remains of the Irishtown citadel with a gateway and part of a bastion. A long section of the Irishtown NE wall with a postern remains between Old Charlotte Street and New Road, and other fragments lie beside West Watergate Street which is named after the gate at the northern end of this section. Another piece lies in Blackbull Lane to the south of the site of the SW-facing Mungret Gate.

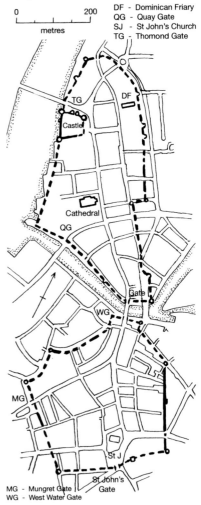

0   200

metres

DF - Dominican Friary
QG - Quay Gate
SJ - St John's Church
TG - Thomond Gate

MG - Mungret Gate
WG - West Water Gate

LIMERICK

LOUGHREA   Co Galway

Loughrea was a power base of the de Burghs in the 13th century but the town wall seems to be of later date and a reference to it in 1574 suggests at least part of it was newly built and still unfinished. At that time it was a seat of the MacWilliam Uachtair Burkes. No records of mural grants survive. The lough seems to have provided sufficient protection on the south side, where the castle lay. Reduced and fragmentary remains exist of the west and northern sections of a wall enclosing an area 600m long from east to west by an average width of 320m. There appears to have been one gate facing north and two facing west. Nothing remains of the east wall itself but one of the two gates there still remains. It is a three storey tower now used as a museum. The passage is narrow and may have been inserted through the base of a pre-existing tower house. (see picture on page 222). The parish church lay close to this end of the town and there are ruins of a Carmelite friary just outside the north wall, which would have been overlooked by the friary tower.

NAAS   Co Kildare

Parliament met at Naas eight times between 1461 and 1586, and there was a murage grant in the early 15th century, both of which make it likely that the town was walled (Ormond regarded it as fortifiable in 1641), although the documentary records mention only the six gates. These imply an enclosure 500m long from the south facing Green Gate to the North Gate and a width of up to 200m. Close to the Green Gate were the West Gate and the east-facing Corban Gate. The Jago Gate lay 80 NW of the North Gate and the Water Gate 90m to the SE of it. East of the parish church near the middle was St David's Castle and near the middle of the west side lay a motte called North Moat. The Augustinian, Dominican and Franciscan friaries all lay outside the assumed line of the walls. The last of several tower houses within the central area of the walls, Eustace Castle, was removed in 1973.

NAVAN   Co Meath

There is a record of murage in 1469, and the Provost was fined two years earlier for not producing an account of what a previous grant had been spent on. The walls seem to have been rebuilt after being badly damaged by an Irish attack in 1539, several merchants being bound over for £1,000 on condition of them building a wall of stone and lime within ten years. The walls enclosed a kite-shaped area about 400m long by 300m wide. The River Boyne may have formed the only defence on the east side, whilst the north wall lay somewhat back from the bank of the River Blackwater and contained the Water Gate facing a bridge over that river. The Trim Gate lay near the west corner and the Dublin Gate faced south towards where the parish church lay outside the walls. The Augustinian priory lay beyond the NW corner where a bastion remains with a 15m long section of thin walling probably of 16th century date.

NENAGH   Co Tipperary

The town was founded c1200-10 by Theobald Walter, ancestor of the Butler earls of Ormond, whose chief seat lay here until they acquired Kilkenny in 1392. Murage was granted in 1322 and 1344-45. Burning of the town by the O'Kennedys in 1348 probably hastened the building of stone walls around a triangular area with the castle at the north corner, the parish church in the SE corner and the Franciscan friary halfway between the two. The west-facing Thomond gate is mentioned in 1654-6. The castle and town at Nenagh suffered several attacks from the Irish during the 16th and 17th centuries and their defences were dismantled after capture by General Ginkell for William III in 1690.

NEW ROSS   Co Wexford

The walls enclosed quite a large D-shaped enclosure of over 100 acres measuring about 800m from north to south and 500m wide with the straight west side containing Bridge Gate and several posterns to quays beside the River Barrow. The north and south sides descended steeply down to other gates at each end of a long main street fairly close to the west side. The south gate survived until c1800. One side of the Fair or Maiden Gate remains at the NE corner and has a portcullis groove and traces of vaulting. This was once a fine show gateway with flanking towers and much more of it survived until the late 19th century. About 130m SE of it lay the Bunnion Gate, west of which is the very large parish church of St Mary remaining from the foundation of the town in the early 13th century by William Marshal and his wife Isabel de Clare. One D-shaped tower with two levels of slit windows survives in Nunnery Lane, about 60m NE of the site of where the Three Bullet Gate faced SE across Neville Street until removed in 1845. There is also a small surviving fragment of the south wall in William Street. At the SW corner lay what was originally a Trinitarian friary later taken over by the Franciscans. Here the town wall lay further back from the river than further north and the gap was later filled by a spur wall ending in a blockhouse. Murage was granted to the town in 1374. Other establishments within the walls included an Augustinian friary, the hospital of St Saviour and a church of St Michael. The unwalled suburb of Rosbercon on the west bank of the river had its own parish church and a Dominican friary.

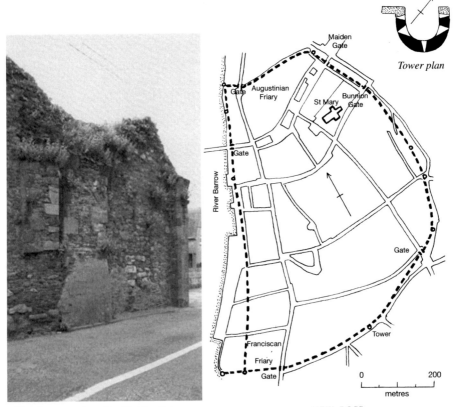

New Ross: remains of the Maiden Gate

NEW ROSS

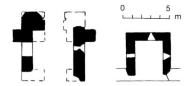

Plans of gateway and turret at Rinndown

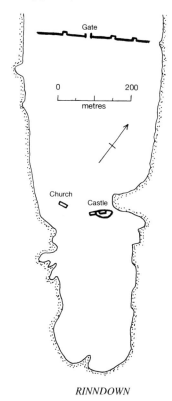

RINNDOWN

RINNDOWN   Co Roscommon

The town wall here is assumed to date from just after 1251, when Henry III allowed £80 towards walling the towns of Athlone and Rinndown and repair of their castles. Burgages are mentioned in the 1240s and leases were available in the 1270s to those that would dwell there. There was then also a mill "lately constructed". The site is a promontory beside Loch Ree which was here crossed by a ferry. It was provided with a Norman ringwork by Geoffrey de Marisco in 1227, soon replaced by a stone castle with a hall keep of which a considerable amount remains in a much overgrown condition. Near it a ditch closes off the tip of the promontory. The town lay further inland to the NW, and at a location about 700m from the castle and ditch its site is still closed off by a wall 500m long across the promontory. Much of the wall still remains although covered in ivy. Straddling the middle of the wall is the lower part of a gatehouse 7m square with a portcullis groove and there are three rectangular flanking turrets each about 4.8m wide and projecting 3.8m. They were solid below wall-walk level. After years of total neglect of the whole of this large and enigmatic site, which has been deserted for centuries, and is now just farmland, two of the turrets have recently been cleared of vegetation and repaired. Just outside the wall lay an Augustinian friary of St John and within the south corner of the town is a ruined 13th century parish church.

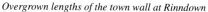

Overgrown lengths of the town wall at Rinndown

Tower at New Ross

Remains of the town wall at Thomastown

THOMASTOWN   Co Kilkenny

The town is named after Thomas FitzAnthony, who held it from William Marshal in the early 13th century. There are several references to murage, suggesting that the town was walled by 1300. Minor remains survive on the west side but there is no evidence from old maps or documents of the line of the wall on the north, nor is the number of gateways known. Gateways are assumed to have been across Marsh and Pipe streets and the enclosed area probably measured about 280m from SW to NE by 200m wide with the large parish church of St Mary on the NW side. Two tower houses lie on the SE side near the River Nore and there was a small harbour by the bridgehead but there is no evidence of a wall on that side.

THURLES   Co Tipperary

A motte in the SW corner of the as-sumed area of the walled town was destroyed c1800. On it stood a ma-norial complex once known as Durlas Castle later replaced by a 16th centu-ry bawn with flankers known as Croak Castle. The still surviving Black Cas-tle behind a house in Liberty Square on the walled town's west side super-seded the motte as the Butler seat here. The tower has traces of a bawn and has been used in more recent times as an abattoir. At the east end of the square is another tower called Bridge Castle, said to date from 1453, adjoining which is one surviving jamb of the East Gate of the town. A sheila-na-gig on the back wall of a tyre cen-tre in Slievenamon Road is said to be from the West Gate.

The Sheep Gate at Trim

TRIM   Co Meath

Trim was the centre of the lordship of Meath granted by Henry II to Henry de Lacy in 1172. By the early 13th century it had on the south bank of the River Boyne what has remained one of the largest and finest castles in Ireland, whilst a cathedral-priory was established on the north bank about 1km further downstream. The castle formed the SE corner of a walled town eventually extending across the river and measuring about 600m from north to south by 390m wide.

The original 13th century town wall may have enclosed a more modest area about 250m square between the north bank of the river and St Patrick's Church. Parts of its west wall still remain. The outer areas to the north and east with the Athboy Gate facing NW (marked on ground by granite setts) and the Navan Gate facing east were probably only walled later. The town never took up all the space thus enclosed, although despite this the Dominican friary remained outside the north side, which is the only part where the line is slightly uncertain. Otherwide boundaries mark the line of the missing parts. The lack of development has ensured the survival in open fields to the SE of the lower parts of several long sections of thin walling plus the Sheep Gate, a postern with a spiral staircase leading up to a lost upper room over a vaulted passage flanked by a guard-room on the south side. This quarter of the town also contains the lofty tower of an Augustinian abbey and two tower houses, one of which belonged to the Talbot family. In the 1540s it was suggested that the abbey precincts should be taken over by a new university specifically because of the security offered by the town walls.

The part of the town on the south bank, containing the Franciscan friary between the castle and the bridgehead, was probably only walled during the 14th century, by which time Trim had the Mortimers as absentee lords. This part had the Water Gate facing north to where there may have been a second bridge upstream of the first one, and the Dublin Gate facing south. Despite this area being more intensively developed, parts of the south wall survives beyond the road past the castle and railings mark out the line of a section at a new development.There is a long section on the west side with traces of a square turret, although it is mostly hidden at the back of properties and rather overgrown. There was once a tower at the SW corner.

Trim was captured by Silken Thomas during his rebellion of 1534 and was captured by Sir Charles Coote in 1647. The town is now growing quickly again, with consequent pressure on space, but a plan is in place for the preservation and presentation of the remains of the town walls.

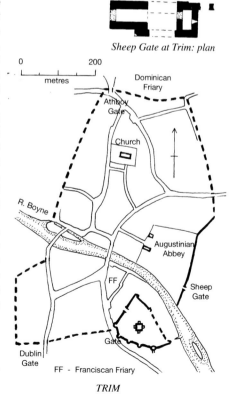

Sheep Gate at Trim: plan

TRIM

TULLOW   Co Carlow

A seven year murage grant made in 1343 is the only evidence of former walls here.

WATERFORD   Co Waterford

On the south bank of the River Suir a triangular area of 19 acres about 400m long east-west by 290m wide at the west end is thought to have been stone walled by Norsemen as early as the 10th century. This part of the city later contained the cathedral of Holy Trinity and the church of St Mary on the south side, a Dominican friary and the church of St Peter on the west side, a Franciscan friary towards the east end, and the church of St Olave in the middle, whilst the church of St Bridgid lay outside the east corner. As a result of early 18th century demolition to give better access to the quays nothing remains of the north wall, which ran from a circular tower called Turgesius's Tower at the NW corner past several later posterns leading out to quays and the north gate or Keyser's Castle out to Reginald's Tower at the eastern corner. Part of the SE wall survives near the tower with arches known as the Sallyports. Then after a 70m gap another section leads towards the site of the south facing Colbeck's Gate. Two thirds of the wall between there and the square tower of St Martin at the SW corner still remains up to about 4m high, although the one intermediate tower has been lost. Of the west wall of this part of the city a small fragment remains to the north of the gate of Our Lady, and another small fragment halfway between that and the side of the Arundel Gate.

Reginald's Tower played a crucial role in the successful defence of the city against the Yorkist pretender Perkin Warbeck in 1495. It is a circular donjon 13.4m in diameter over walls 3m thick in the two lower levels which are probably of c1200. The more thinly walled upper storeys and plain corbelled parapet around a conical roof are probably later. The tower is now a museum, having served at various times as a prison and a mint. It was originally entered at second storey level on the west side where there is a spiral staircase. This level has four embrasures for narrow loops. An inserted lower doorway on the east side led out to an adjoining oval platform or blockhouse with embrasures for eight guns added in the mid 16th century.

Waterford: Reginald's Tower

Waterford: Watch Tower

In the 13th century a western suburb including the churches of St Patrick and St Michael was additionally enclosed with a new wall 200m further west than the old one. By the early 14th century this part had been extended another 200m to the south. The re-entrant angle between the south side of the Norse city and the later extension was later filled with a bastioned outwork incorporating the former Augustinian priory. Quite long sections remain of the SE wall of the 13th and 14th century extension, except for a gap made by Parnell Street. The corner tower and the St John Gate facing south have gone but to the west of the gate is the lower part of a D-shaped tower forming part of a salient here. A section of surviving wall links it with the circular Watch Tower 7m in diameter remaining complete and having a stirrup-shaped loop for early firearms.

The Close Gate has gone but beyond it stands a rectangular tower and a section of wall which projected outwards. About 70m NW of there lies the D-shaped French Tower, still fairly complete. From here the new outer west wall ran almost due north past a square tower and the site of New Gate to the surviving semi-lunar tower. Beyond lay the St Patrick's Gate and the Square Tower where the wall bent round slightly to reach a circular corner tower. It passed another tower to reach the square Beach Tower at the end of Jenkins Lane and then turned through a re-entrant angle. A small fragment remains beyond Great George Street, between which and the corner of the older wall at Turgesius's Tower lay two more towers, one square and the other circular. A police station occupies the remains of a fort outside the St Patrick Gate commanding the whole city. It was begun by Captain Edmond York in the 1590s but not completed until 1625.

Despite the strength of its defences the Norman invaders led by Richard de Clare (Strongbow) and Raymond le Gros managed to take Waterford by storm in 1170. De Clare was then married in the cathedral to the heiress to the kingdom of Leinster. However in 1171 Henry II declared Waterford to be a royal city. It withstood a six week siege by supporters of Lambert Simnell in 1487 and a twelve day siege in 1495 by Perkin Warbeck. At the Reformation the citizens adhered to the Catholic faith and in the 1640s the city supported the Confederation of Kilkenny. In November 1649 Cromwell found the city well manned and fortified and lifted his siege after eight days, and it only surrendered to his forces after a ten week siege during the summer of 1650.

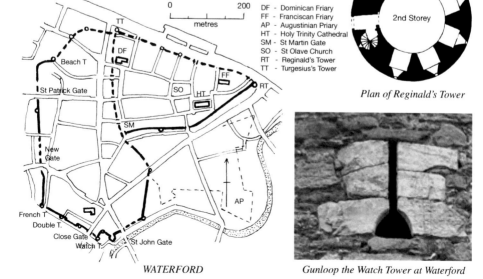

DF - Dominican Friary
FF - Franciscan Friary
AP - Augustinian Priory
HT - Holy Trinity Cathedral
SM - St Martin Gate
SO - St Olave Church
RT - Reginald's Tower
TT - Turgesius's Tower

Plan of Reginald's Tower

WATERFORD

Gunloop the Watch Tower at Waterford

WEXFORD Co Wexford

King John is said to have begun the now-vanished castle at the SE end of the town, which by the early 14th century seems to have been fully enclosed by stone walls mostly following the line of ramparts of the Norse period. There are no records of murage grants. The enclosed area was over 1000m long by 280m wide. There were six gates, of which the West Gate near the NW end still remains complete. It measures 8m by 7m and has three storeys of upper rooms with fireplaces and latrines over a vaulted passage with arcading on the SW side and with a straight staircase rising up over a small chamber on the NE side. The third storey has a doorway to the wall-walk of the main wall. The latrines are contained in a projecting turret on the north corner rising higher than the rest of the tower. East of here is the Augustinian priory of St Selskar.

West Gate at Wexford

A length of the wall up to 4m high extends 190m to the SW of the West Gate and has one circular tower only entered at wall-walk level, and traces of gunloops. Beyond the site of the St John's Gate is another 55m long section up to 6m high with a second round tower to the west of Abbey Street. Two shorter fragments of the long SW wall remain further south, one with a square tower not far from where a Franciscan friary stood outside the wall and the other near where St Patrick's church lay inside the wall and St Peter's lay outside it, the latter givng its name to a lost gateway in this area. The inner rampart here was probably added in Cromwellian times. Further south St Mary's lay within the walls but the lost gateway there was named after St Bride's Church outside the walls. A fragment of wall 4m high with traces of five gunloops remains at the SE corner. Beyond here were Rabby's Gate across Mary Street and Castle Gate. Two more ancient churches, St Iberion's and St Dulogue's lay along the seaward NE side of the town but have dissappeared.

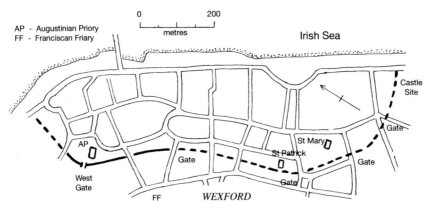

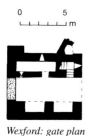

Wexford: gate plan

Youghal Town Wall

YOUGHAL   Co Cork

Maurice FitzGerald founded the town here by bringing over traders and craftsmen from Bristol in the early 13th century. Murage was granted in 1275 and on several subsequent occasions. Youghal was sacked by the Earl of Desmond in 1579 despite it having been under the influence of his family for centuries. The town was refortified in 1641-2 after it was reported ten years earlier that the walls were weak and ruinous and there was "no place to mount ordnance to defend the harbour". Most of the 500m long SW wall survives along a ridge high above the buildings of the town, with public access to part of the wall-walk from the churchyard of the large collegiate church of St Mary. There are three small towers along this section. The NW wall steeply sloping down from the churchyard also remains but the North Gate and its outworks have vanished. The 5m high wall facing NE towards the Blackwater is probably late medieval, being just 0.6m thick. At the SE end of the town is the Clock Gate, a four storey tower of 1776 on the site of a medieval gate. Beyond here is the suburb of Basetown, later given walls enclosing a square of about 100m. The NE-facing Water Gate lies here. No monastic houses lay within the walls but gables remain of a Benedictine priory of St John beyond the North Gate and of a Dominican friary on the north side, whilst a Franciscan friary lay beyond the SE walls. Near the NE side of the town stands Tynte's Castle, a tower house originally built by the Walshe family and later used as a grain store.

OTHER PLACES IN IRELAND POSSIBLY WITH MEDIEVAL DEFENCES:
Dunmore, Co Galway, Ferns, Co Wexford, Tipperary, Co Tipperary, Tralee, Co Kerry

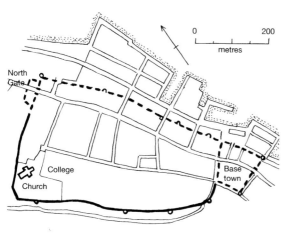

YOUGHAL

Youghal

Walls on the south side of Fethard, Co Tipperary   *Gateway at Loughrea, Co Galway*

WALLED TOWNS OF THE PLANTATION PERIODS IN IRELAND

BANDON, Co Cork - Fragmentary remains of walls of 1620-27 enclosing space 400m by 370m straddling the River Bandon, each part with its own church and two gates. The gates were demiliterised in 1690 by locals to prevent resistance to James II .

BELFAST, Co Antrim - No remains of enclosure 600m by 500m with ten bastions begun in 1642, equal trading rights with Carrickfergus having been obtained in 1637. Walls envisaged in foundation charter of 1612. Medieval castle also gone.

COLERAINE, Co Londonderry - Vanished bastioned trace of 1610-12 about 400m long by 370m wide. Neither the rampart faces or gates were of stone. The town survived an Irish attack in 1641 but was captured by General Monck in 1648.

DAINGEAN, Co Offaly - Once named Philipstown after Mary Tudor's husband but not walled until c1570. Ditches remain. Enclosure about 280m by 210m with central marketplace and church. Fort of c1550 in SE corner rebuilt in 18th century.

DINGLE, Co Kerry - Murage granted in medieval period and in 1585. "Not yet walled in 1599". Fragments remain on west side. Contained several tower houses.

DERRY, Co Londonderry - Most complete system in the British Isles of a bastioned trace with stone-faced earth ramparts (accessible to public) around an area 450m long by 260m wide. Grid layout of streets meeting at a central "diamond" and the contemporary cathedral in one corner. Four main gates plus several posterns. The north and NE corner bastions are now missing. Site previously fortified in 1566. Derry held out against the Confederate Irish in 1641, a Royalist attack in 1648, and a siege of 105 days by James II during the winter of 1688-9.

JAMESTOWN, Co Roscommon - NW corner with arrow-head shaped bastion and other fragments remain of walls costing £3000 built c1625 around rectangle 260m long north-south by 110m wide set close to west bank of River Shannon. Northern half only now occupied by houses. A fort lies to the west, and older friary to north.

NEWRY, Co Down - Walls proposed in 1580s and 90s. Shown existing on older map.

PORTARLINGTON, Co Laois - River Barrow protected the west, north and east sides of town founded in 1666. By 1678 about 20 acres were enclosed by ramparts with corner bastions and a wet moat on the south side, now all vanished.

PORTLAOISE, Co Laois - Fort of 1548 on west side still remains, but nothing of town walls shown on a map of Maryborough (as it was then called) of c1560.

ROSCOMMON - Lake once protected west side of enclosure of 1570s about 400m square. Murage granted as early as 1251 (ie earlier than castle in NW corner). Minor remains on east side and of north gate. Modern town now further south.

A GLOSSARY OF TERMS

Ashlar	- Masonry of square blocks with even faces and square edges.
Bailey	- Defensible castle enclosure with a ditch and wall or palisade.
Barbican	- A building or enclosure giving extra protection to a gateway.
Bartizan	- Turret corbelled out from near the top of a corner.
Bastion	- Flanking projection of about the same height as the main wall.
Berm	- Level space between the slope of a ditch and a wall or rampart.
Casemate	- Vaulted room with gunloops or gunports within a fortress wall.
Corbel	- Projecting bracket supporting other stonework or timber beams.
Crenel	- The cut-away part of a crenellated parapet, for looking out of.
Donjon	- A self-contained keep-like tower, especially one of circular plan.
Embattled	- Provided with crenels.
Glacis	- Long slope beyond a ditch where attackers are exposed to fire.
Gunloop	- Small opening suitable for firing pistols or muskets out of.
Gunport	- Externally splayed opening of some size for firing cannon out of.
Jamb	- Side of a window, doorway or other opening.
Light	- Compartment of a window.
Loop	- Small opening either for light or the discharge of missiles.
Machicolation	- Slot for dropping or shooting missiles down on assailants.
Merlons	- The upstanding portions of a crenellated parapet.
Murage	- Grant permitting taxation of goods to pay for town defences.
Moat	- Ditch, water filled or dry, around an enclosure.
Motte	- Steeply sided flat-topped castle-mound, usually man made.
Parapet	- Wall for protection at any sudden drop.
Pilaster	- Shallow buttress, common on 12th and early 13th century walls.
Plinth	- The projecting base of a wall, usually battered (sloped).
Portcullis	- Gate of iron and/or wood designed to rise and fall in vertical slots.
Postern	- A secondary or lesser gateway or doorway.
Ravelin	- Triangular shaped outwork used in artillery defence works.
Tower House	- Self-contained house with the rooms stacked vertically.
Turret	- Small tower, either solid, or containing tiny chambers.
Voussoir	- One of a series of wedge-shaped stones used to form an arch.
Wall-walk	- Walkway upon a wall, protected on at least one side by a parapet.

The East Gate of Totnes in Devon

The West Gate of St Andrews in Fife

INDEX OF TOWNS MENTIONED IN THIS BOOK

MEDIEVAL WALLED TOWNS IN IRELAND

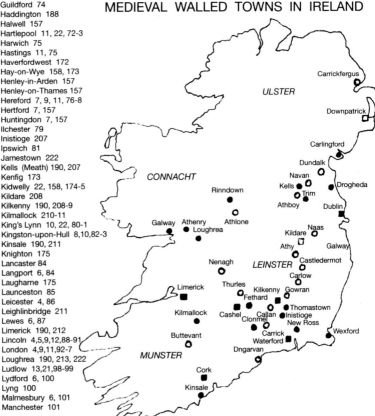